DESIGNBUILD EDUCATION

Designbuild Education adopts the intellectual framework of American Pragmatism, which is a theory of action, to investigate architects' compelling urge to build and how that manifests in collegiate designbuild programs. Organized into four themes—people, poetics, process, and practice—the book brings together new essays by some of today's most well-known designbuild educators, including Andrew Freear from Rural Studio and Dan Rockhill from Studio 804, to shed light on the theoretical dimensions of their practice and work. Illustrated with over 100 black and white images.

Chad Kraus is an Associate Professor of Architecture at the University of Kansas in Lawrence, Kansas, USA.

"Chad Kraus's *Designbuild Education* assembles professional and academic designbuild voices to engage the signal questions faced by educational designbuilders. With this analytical survey of successful designbuild pedagogy and practice, *Designbuild Education* is the next essential tool for the kitbag of each designbuild educator."

—Patrick Peters is an architect, professor, and director of the University of Houston Graduate Design/Build Studio, USA

"There has yet to be a definitive resource for the 'hands-on' architecture studio professor and historian despite more than eighty years of design-build education in the United States. *Designbuild Education* helps to fill that void as a much needed resource for those looking to frame the historical and theoretical underpinnings of this continually emergent mode of teaching."

—José Galarza, Director of DesignBuildBLUFF

"It is difficult to argue the value of learning by making. For designbuild projects to rely on that platitude, however, limits the potential for the student, faculty, and community. *Designbuild Education* understands the poetic value of making, but recognizes the expansive role that a designbuild project may play in the education of the architect as an agent for public good."

—Marc J. Neveu, PhD, Chair, School of Architecture, Los Angeles, Woodbury University, USA, Executive Editor of *Journal of Architectural Education*

DESIGNBUILD EDUCATION

Edited by Chad Kraus

NEW YORK AND LONDON

First published 2017
by Routledge
711 Third Avenue, New York, NY 10017

and by Routledge
2 Park Square, Milton Park, Abingdon, Oxon, OX14 4RN

Routledge is an imprint of the Taylor & Francis Group, an informa business

© 2017 Taylor & Francis

The right of Chad Kraus to be identified as the author of the editorial material, and
of the authors for their individual chapters, has been asserted in accordance with
sections 77 and 78 of the Copyright, Designs and Patents Act 1988.

All rights reserved. No part of this book may be reprinted or reproduced or utilized
in any form or by any electronic, mechanical, or other means, now known or hereafter
invented, including photocopying and recording, or in any information storage or
retrieval system, without permission in writing from the publishers.

Trademark notice: Product or corporate names may be trademarks or registered trademarks,
and are used only for identification and explanation without intent to infringe.

Library of Congress Cataloging-in-Publication Data
Names: Kraus, Chad, editor.
Title: Designbuild education / edited by Chad Kraus.
Description: New York : Routledge, 2017. | Includes bibliographical
    references and index.
Identifiers: LCCN 2016031539 | ISBN 9781138956285 (hardback) |
    ISBN 9781138956308 (pbk.) | ISBN 9781315665771 (ebk)
Subjects: LCSH: Architecture—Study and teaching. | Architects—Training of.
Classification: LCC NA2005 .D48 2017 | DDC 720.71—dc23
LC record available at https://lccn.loc.gov/2016031539

ISBN: 978-1-138-95628-5 (hbk)
ISBN: 978-1-138-95630-8 (pbk)
ISBN: 978-1-315-66577-1 (ebk)

Acquisition Editor: Wendy Fuller
Editorial Assistant: Norah Hatch
Production Editor: Elizabeth Spicer

Typeset in Bembo
by Apex CoVantage, LLC

To Oakley and Selma, and the rest of the future

CONTENTS

List of Authors	*x*
Foreword	*xiii*
by Alberto Pérez-Gómez	
Acknowledgements	*xvi*

Introduction: *Hands On, Minds On*: Motivations of the Designbuild Educator *Chad Kraus*	1

PART 1
People: Community Engagement and the Common Good

17

1 Backyard Architecture *Andrew Freear*	19
2 Design / Build / Evaluate: Connecting with Actual Humans *John Quale*	33
3 Embracing Uncertainty: Community Designbuild *Nils Gore and Shannon Criss*	48
4 Each One Teach One: Nested Associations in Designbuild Education *Larry Bowne*	62

viii Contents

PART 2
Poetics: Experience and the Human Condition

79

5 The Good of Doing Poetics, the Poetics of Doing Good
Coleman Coker

81

6 Architecture into Presence
Chad Kraus

93

7 The Action of Poetry
Lori Ryker

108

PART 3
Process: Methodology and the Tectonic Imagination

123

8 In Process
Marie Zawistowski and Keith Zawistowski

125

9 Embodied Making: Designing at Full Scale
Terry Boling

140

10 Practicing the Digital Vernacular: Raising a Barn and
Raising Questions
James Stevens, Ralph Nelson, and Natalie Haddad

154

PART 4
Practice: The Academic-Professional Bridge

169

11 Second Nature: Embedded Knowledge
through Designbuild Education
Tricia Stuth

171

12 Labor-Intensive: Innovation by Necessity
Erik Sommerfeld

187

13 From Scratch: How to Start a Designbuild Program
Eric Weber

201

Contents **ix**

14 Work Ethic, Ethical Work: A Conversation with
Designbuild Pioneer Dan Rockhill 214
Dan Rockhill and Chad Kraus

Bibliography *231*
Index *236*

AUTHORS

Terry Boling is an Associate Professor of Practice at the University of Cincinnati. He teaches design and construction, with a focus on questions of material research, technique, and fabrication. His award-winning designbuild practice has been widely published. He has been a recipient of the ACSA Design Build Award.

Larry Bowne is a licensed architect and principal of Larry Bowne Architects. He has previously taught designbuild studios at Kansas State University and Syracuse University. Both his professional and academic work have been widely published. He has been a recipient of the ACSA Design Build Award.

Coleman Coker is the Ruth Carter Stevenson Regents Chair in the Art of Architecture at the University of Texas at Austin and Director of the Gulf Coast DesignLab designbuild program. He is a registered architect, former principal at Mockbee/ Coker Architects, and now principal of buildingstudio. Coleman has taught at numerous schools of architecture and is past director of the Memphis Center of Architecture.

Shannon Criss is an Associate Professor of Architecture at the University of Kansas and a licensed architect. Prior to KU, she taught at Mississippi State University's School of Architecture where she directed the Small Town Center. At the University of Kansas, Shannon works with community partners to advocate for healthier communities.

Andrew Freear is the Wiatt Professor at Auburn University. Educated in London, he has practiced in England, Italy, and the United States, and has taught at the University of Illinois and the Architectural Association. For nearly fifteen years, following the untimely death of Samuel Mockbee, Andrew has served as the Director of Rural Studio.

Nils Gore is an Associate Professor of Architecture at the University of Kansas and a licensed architect. He has previously taught at Mississippi State University and the Boston Architectural Center. While Chair of the Architecture Department at KU, Nils helped establish the East Hills Designbuild Center, a 68,000 square foot designbuild classroom and shop facility.

Natalie Haddad is a graduate of Lawrence Technological University and a contributor to the university's makeLab through research and making. She has a focus in digital fabrication; exploiting digital tools and material processes to design and fabricate effectively.

Chad Kraus is an Associate Professor of Architecture at the University of Kansas and a licensed architect. He teaches architectural theory, advanced architectural design, and the designbuild Dirt Works Studio. Prior to teaching, Chad worked for Pritzker-prize laureate Shigeru Ban. He has been a recipient of the ACSA Design Build Award.

Ralph Nelson is an Associate Professor of Architecture at Lawrence Technological University. He is the founding principal of Loom, a collaborative practice of art and design recognized and awarded for work utilizing a minimum of means to maximum effect.

Alberto Pérez-Gómez is the Bronfman Professor of the History of Architecture at McGill University in Montreal. He has taught and lectured in numerous schools, was the Director of the Carleton School of Architecture (Ottawa), and founded the post-professional Master's and PhD History and Theory program at McGill. He is the author of several well-known books and multiple articles.

John Quale is Director and Professor of Architecture at the University of New Mexico. His expertise is in sustainable design, affordable housing, prefabrication, the environmental impact of construction, and collaborative and integrated design processes. Prior to UNM, John was on the faculty of the University of Virginia School of Architecture.

Dan Rockhill is an ACSA Distinguished Professor and the J. L. Constant Distinguished Professor of Architecture at the University of Kansas, Executive Director of Studio 804, and principal of Rockhill and Associates. To date, Studio 804 has completed nine LEED Platinum buildings, three Passive Institute Certifications, and has received numerous honors and awards for their work.

Lori Ryker is the Executive Director and Founder of Artemis Institute and principal of studioryker. She was previously a principal of the award-winning designbuild practice Ryker/Nave Design. She is the author of several books and has taught at Montana State University, Louisiana State University, Texas A&M University, and University of Texas, among others.

xii Authors

Erik "Rick" Sommerfeld is an Assistant Professor and Director of Colorado Building Workshop at the University of Colorado Denver. Since founding Colorado Building Workshop Rick has built nine community projects in Colorado and, in collaboration with DesignBuildBLUFF, five charitable homes in Southern Utah. He has been a recipient of multiple ACSA Design Build Awards.

James Stevens is an Associate Professor of Architecture and Chair of the Department of Architecture at Lawrence Technological University. He is also the Director of makeLab, a digital fabrication and design studio, and a licensed architect. Jim is coauthor of the book *Digital Vernacular: Architectural Principles, Tools, and Processes* (Routledge 2015).

Tricia Stuth is an Associate Professor of Architecture and the James R. Cox Professor at the University of Tennessee, and a co-founder and partner in the firm curb. Tricia is co-director of the award-winning A New Norris House—a designbuild/evaluate initiative. She has been a recipient of the ACSA Design Build Award.

Eric Weber is an Assistant Professor of Architecture, coordinator of the David G. Howryla Design-Build Studio and Building Technologies Laboratory, and a registered architect. He was the Principal Investigator for Team Las Vegas, UNLV's entry in Solar Decathlon 2013. In addition to designbuild, Eric has taught design studios and building technology courses.

Marie Zawistowski and Keith Zawistowski are principals of the designbuild architecture practice onSITE and the founders and directors of the designbuildLAB, located at Virginia Tech until 2015 and now at Les Grands Ateliers in France. They have been the recipients of multiple awards and honors for both their professional and academic work. They met as students of Samuel Mockbee, at Auburn University's Rural Studio.

FOREWORD

Designbuild pedagogies may be motivated by vastly different aims and methodologies, ranging from a practical desire to bring together academic design and architectural practices, to revealing to the student the possibility of the poetics of materiality. Regardless of such diverse intentions, designbuild pedagogies share a crucial belief in the importance of embodied knowledge for the design professional. Embodied skills are irreducible to theoretical knowledge: this is the fundamental common ground for contributors in this volume, yet one that seems easily contested in our culture of BIM software and robotic fabrication.

Techné is the Greek word for art, and the Ancient Greeks did not differentiate between "fine arts" and crafts. *Techné*, therefore, at the root of our words for technique and technology, is related to the poetic. For *poíein*, in Greek, also meant to make. Both Aristotle and much later Vitruvius, the first writer known to have spoken about such issues with regards to architecture, distinctly differentiate "theoretical knowledge" (the philosophy of architecture) from "technical knowledge." For Vitruvius (and still many centuries later for Leon Battista Alberti) these are two *autonomous* forms of knowledge that the architect must possess to produce good architecture. The nature of technical knowledge was well understood by all these authors: while some of its rules and stable principles (*mathémata*) may be learned from a master (and partially rendered in texts), technical knowledge is *ultimately* a bodily motor skill, dependent on practice (on habits), and on innate talents. For this reason, it is *irreducible* to theoretical (intellectual, representational) knowledge. It is only in more mature phases of modernity, starting with the writings of Claude Perrault (late 17th century) and crystallizing in those of Jean N.-L. Durand (early 19th century), that craft knowledge could be ignored or even derided as "getting in the way" of the perfect actualization of an architect's project, driven by some instrumental methodology (by then mistakenly identified with theory proper).

xiv Alberto Pérez-Gómez

This historical lesson is important. Clearly material, "techno-poetic" knowledge, and the acceptance and even celebration of the necessary interpretative translation (rather than mere transcription) between architectural idea (project) and built work contributed much to the rich emotive qualities of traditional architecture and urban fabrics. Yet today we have additional evidence of the crucial importance of embodied knowledge coming to us from cognitive science. Following insights from 20th century phenomenology, so-called third generation *enactive* cognitive science, articulated by neuroscientists and philosophers such as such Evan Thompson and Alva Noë, corroborate the belief that motor skills are *real knowledge*, and that our possession of them is in fact the foundation of consciousness.

Consciousness is not merely a passive event; it is always an *action*. In other words, consciousness is not like digestion, nor visual perception like the imprint of light on photographic material: it is something *we do*, and which in turn depends on our motor and intellectual skills. Consciousness is embedded in life, growing in complexity from the bacterium to the human; it is the sentience we share with animals. Just like each animal has its own world that emerges from their organic morphology, biology, and the way the environment appears through such conditions, the same is true for humans. The world of the fly and the world of the monkey, for example, have little in common, if anything at all: they co-emerge for each organism as it acts out its own life seeking its particular modes of homeostasis, the equilibrium that allows the organism to prevail in life and which is its own modality of meaning. Consciousness, furthermore, is not only in the brain: enactive cognitive scientists have demonstrated the absurdity of equating consciousness with information in a computer-like brain. Consciousness is embodied; it involves the whole nervous system and is always *in* the world. Alva Noë states this graphically: "we are not our brains," consciousness does not end in our skulls.

Human consciousness is in fact a continuum of pre-reflective bodily knowledge—better understood as motor skills, gestures, and habits and representational knowledge—the sort of knowledge that we acquire through attention and preserve through words and numbers. In this continuum, about eighty percent of consciousness is pre-reflective; it is NOT sub-consciousness or unconsciousness, but effectively pre-reflective emotive consciousness, so that theoretical knowledge is like the tip of an iceberg. Most importantly, because consciousness and perception are *action* and depend on our motor and intellectual skills, if we lack skills (or give them up—as an architect might, relying too much on algorithms, computers, or robots to execute his or her projects), we literally lose a dimension of knowledge. In other words, if we lack the motor knowledge associated with making, crafting of materials, or drawing, this *effectively* affects what we perceive and consequently, what we design.

Whatever we may think of our new digital modes of representation and fabrication, motor skills are still fundamental. This is what the important pedagogies featured in this volume contribute to architectural education. Depriving a future architect of this sort of knowledge, of these kinds of skills, effectively produces professionals that are less sensitive to the cultural and physical qualities of the lived world, to the expressive potential of materials; more liable to continue the nonsense of producing radically decontextualized buildings driven exclusively by the lure of geometric innovation and complexity.

Alberto Pérez-Gómez
Montreal, 2016

ACKNOWLEDGEMENTS

I had the fleeting thought: the time for a book on designbuild education is ripe. Thanks to the encouragement and guidance of my colleague, Kapila Silva, a fleeting thought became a labor of love. While I am hardly adequate to the task, I have benefited greatly over the years from my many mentors—Vladimir Krstic, who gave me my first encounter with designbuild education as a student; Shigeru Ban, who, more than anyone, shaped the architect I am becoming and inspired my love for "weak" materials; Alberto Pérez-Gómez, whose profound influence has sharpened for me a world of beauty and enigma; Dan Rockhill and Nils Gore, two designbuild educators who selflessly showed me the ropes; and my wife Regina Kraus, a beacon of light amidst the fog.

I would like to express my sincerest gratitude to all of the talented designbuild educators who have made this book possible. I would like to acknowledge my indebtedness to Marie-Alice L'Heureux for her countless hours poring over the manuscript, and to my many colleagues who reviewed one or more chapters; you have all been instrumental in improving our craft of verse. On behalf of the contributors to this book, I would like to acknowledge the support of the many academic institutions that have been willing to unleash the potential of designbuild education, often with some risk involved and against persistent bureaucratic and economic resistance—in particular those who have brilliantly and courageously championed these programs and projects through trials and tribulations. I would be remiss if I failed to acknowledge the more than twenty years of designbuild stewardship of John Gaunt, former Dean of the University of Kansas School of Architecture, Design, and Planning.

I would also like to recognize the critical role that our various clients, community partners, and professional collaborators have played. Were it not for you, these endeavors may very well have remained insulated in the siloes of last century's academia. Finally, I would like to acknowledge the dedication, tenacity, and talents of our many students, and in particular mine:

Ragan Allen, Rabia Bajwa, Damon Baltuska, Patrick Bayer, Melody Benyamen, Corey Boucher, Sean Brungardt, Michael Burch, Blaze Capper, Thomas Carmona, Katie Caufield, Xiaorui Chen, Nicholas Colbert, Anna Collins, Maria Comerford, John Coughlin, Connor Crist, Hannah Dale, Abigail Davis, Zachary Dawson, James DeFries, Michael DeFries, Kelli Dillion, Matthew Everest, Ryan Falk, Nick Faust, Pamela Gieseke, Justin Gomez, Vincent Graceffa, Patrick Griffin, Maria Guerrero, Chandler Hanna, Shelby Hartman, Emily Held, Christina Henning, Brittany Hodges, Chloe Hosid, Tanner Hyland, Benjamin Jensen, Lindsey Jones, Alexa Kaczor, Joseph Kaftan, Andrew Kloppenburg, Shira Kohn, Michael LaVanier, McKenzie Liebl, Mark Linenberger, Matt Livingston, Chloe Lockman, Stephen McEnery, Erin McFarland, Caitlin McKaughan, Jim McLarty, Jeshua Monarres, Scott Moran, Fatima Moufarrige Pacheco, Jarad Mundil, Abby Noelke, Dillon Park, Jared Pechauer, Ben Peek, Ariel Peisen, Taylor Pickman, Spencer Reed, Lauren Reinhart, Shummer Roddick, McKenzie Samp, John Schwarz, Theresa Signorino, Mitchell Starrs, Kevin Staten, Scott Stoops, Elayna Svigos, Tu Tran, Hannah Underwood, David Versteeg, Nicholas Weber, Jeremy Weiland, Yuejia Yang, and Zach Zielke.

Against seemingly insurmountable challenges, time and again you have risen to the occasion.

INTRODUCTION: *HANDS ON, MINDS ON*

Motivations of the Designbuild Educator

Chad Kraus

A Timely Meditation

Hands on, minds on.[1] This simple mantra expresses the basic aspiration of designbuild education: to think through making, to dream by sweating.

Since the 1990s, with the work of Dan Hoffman at Cranbrook Academy of Art, Steve Badanes at the University of Washington and Yestermorrow Design/Build School, and the founding of programs such as Auburn's Rural Studio and the University of Kansas's Studio 804, just to name a few, the influence of designbuild education on the academy as a whole has increased dramatically. Today, it is estimated that the majority of American architecture schools offer some kind of designbuild experience.[2] The significance of these designbuild pedagogies in shaping architectural education, and in turn influencing the profession, has yet to be comprehensively understood.

On the demand side, millennial students are increasingly calling for an education and career in which their talents are directly engaged with the communities they serve. Prioritizing meaningful social impact and possessing a desire to give back to their communities have consistently characterized this generation. A group of researchers recently observed that, "millennials are said to have a desire to 'save the world,' and are likely to have high expectations for social responsibility and ethical behavior on the part of their employers."[3] They tend to be results oriented and are drawn to opportunities that yield tangible benefits (i.e., that provide ample feedback and reinforcement). These prevailing conditions hold the promise for designbuild pedagogies to play an increasingly important role in the education of architects. In 2012, the Association of Collegiate Schools of Architecture (ACSA) added Design-Build to their Architectural Education Awards in recognition of its increased prominence.[4] Around this same time, a group of educators formed the Design Build Exchange with the expressed purpose of establishing a network of likeminded individuals.[5] In 2014, the ACSA Fall Conference, *WORKING*

OUT: *Thinking While Building* was focused entirely upon designbuild pedagogy.[6] In Europe, a similar storm has been brewing with the International Symposium, *Architecture 'Live Projects' Pedagogy,* taking place at Oxford Brookes University in 2012, the launching of the *Live Projects Network* website that same year, and the subsequent publication of the book *Architecture Live Projects* in 2014.[7]

At its most essential, *designbuild* is the synthesis of the action *design* and the action *build*. It is not meant, in the context of this book, to connote a process of designing followed by building, nor is it intended to refer to two distinct activities united under a common banner. Designbuild, as I use it here (a melded compound word), is a pedagogical model that must be distinguished from the professional services delivery method of design-build in which these two distinct activities and parties are brought into a more streamlined professional relationship to maximize economic efficiencies and conflict resolution. Superficially, designbuild pedagogy could be understood as a more radical manifestation of the basic intent of design-build delivery approaches. However, this reading is blind to the fundamental consequences of this synthesis. The true intent of designbuild pedagogy cannot be reduced to issues of economics and efficiencies. Instead, it addresses a knowledge gap within contemporary architectural pedagogy and contributes to building a better bridge between the academy and the profession.

While some observers have understood designbuild education and the *live projects* model that has emerged in British universities as two parallel and largely synonymous pedagogical models, one associated with US-based universities (although emerging globally) and the other associated with UK-based universities, this understanding is flawed. The live project, according to Jane Anderson and Colin Priest, consists of six factors "common to all Live Projects: external collaborator, educational organisation, brief, timescale, budget and product."[8] This product need not be a physical work of architecture. In other words, the architectural live project is a form of *experiential learning* in the architectural academy. When discussing live projects that engage construction or fabrication, UK educators will commonly append *design/build*—as in "a design/build live project." The term live project, then, is not a synonym for designbuild but rather an umbrella. The US context lacks a universally accepted term for architectural projects that engage constituencies beyond the architecture studio but that are not designbuild-based (which may explain why these two terms have been erroneously conflated). Therefore, it seems natural that *live projects* be adopted as the umbrella term that it is, in both UK and US contexts, as well as elsewhere.

Designbuild pedagogies are often associated with participatory design movements, such as *public interest design*, characterized by a renewed sense of social responsibility and community engagement in design and construction processes. According to Lisa Abendroth and Bryan Bell, "public interest design is a practice that first and foremost engages people in the design process."[9] They assert

> that it differentiates itself from other design practices because of its deep commitment to community engagement, public participation, and democratic

decision making. This practice informs the results of design because it is derived directly from the community or audience—individuals who share a common quality—for whom the designs are created.[10]

Public interest design (PID) represents an ideological shift in the way architects and allied professionals approach the design process. While PID and designbuild are two distinct frameworks, each with its own ideological underpinnings, there is a very real intersection between the two. Some designbuild activities fit within the domain of PID—and these are commonly referred to as *community designbuild* projects—while many remain focused elsewhere. Inversely, some PID activities can take the form of designbuild projects even if the majority of PID does not. In the context of academia, PID, as with designbuild, falls under the umbrella of live projects.

As forms of academic live projects, these types of activities are closely aligned to the profession and, indeed, have professional manifestations. The rise of contemporary designbuild education, in particular, mirrors potent trends in the profession, most closely identified with the nomadic and ad hoc Jersey Devil's Steve Badanes, John Ringel, and Jim Adamson; architect and builder Peter Gluck, who, as a student, provided the impetus for inaugurating the Yale Building Project; and the so-called "Resistance," a group of critical-regionalism-inspired architects including Brian MacKay-Lyons, Marlon Blackwell, Rick Joy, and Tom Kundig.[11] Designbuild education prepares future generations of architects not only to chart alternative paths in the profession but also to reinsert themselves at the heart of the whole culture of building. MacKay-Lyons frames this alternative approach as a "resistance to the unwholesome break between the academy and practice, between the head and the hand."[12] Yet, long before the Resistance, hands-on values were central to the pedagogy of the Walter Gropius-led Bauhaus. Gropius implored architects to mend the artificial divide that had opened up between the head and the hand. "Artists," he called, "let us at last break down the walls erected by our deforming academic training between the 'arts' *and all of us become builders again*! Let us together will, think out, create the new idea of architecture."[13]

Despite the influence of the Bauhaus curriculum, this artificial divide persisted in architectural education throughout the majority of the twentieth century, exacerbated by the disappearance of the architectural apprenticeship. The early twenty-first century return to hands-on attitudes opens possibilities to the discipline of architecture to reengage meaningfully with society at all levels—with our own communities, with the subtlety and nuance of local contexts and materials, and with innovative systems, processes, and tools formerly developed for architects by others outside of the discipline. Ironically, these marginalized architectural concerns live at the heart of the discipline, and designbuild educators, *en masse*, are just now beginning to readdress them. The myriad voices of the designbuild educators collected in this volume are reshaping architectural education in response to a contemporary world where the rationalist distance of the past century is rapidly collapsing. This book reflects a collective desire to answer Gropius's call to become builders again, to repair the "unwholesome break" that has occurred between the architect-designer and the architect-builder.

It Awakens in Things

> *That which sleeps in us awakes in things.*
>
> —Rainer Maria Rilke[14]

The hallmark of designbuilders is a deep-seated urge to build. From where does such an *urge to build* arise? Perhaps it is innate in all of us, evidenced by the formative tactile impressions received from wooden blocks held in the child's hand, or the gravitational resistance of a blocky tower of Babylon rising from the living room floor. Perhaps it arises from a curiosity that leads to constant tinkering with, poking, and prodding an unknown world. Or perhaps the *urge to build* is a means to another end, a privileging of learning at full scale and with full consequence; an embrace of haptic learning that arises from a show-me attitude. The urge to make and remake things often appears bred in the bone, akin to Picasso's argument that all children are born artists. Ironically, throughout the last few centuries, the architecture discipline appears to have possessed an uncanny lack of desire to build.

Long after the memory of the master builder and the craft guilds had faded, after the apprentice-master model of architectural education had almost completely disappeared, a rationalist streak gave rise to the *architect-designer* wielding design from a distance like a far-sighted prophecy. Disengaging from their master builder roots, architects had gradually lost their intense tactile engagement with material and tectonic concerns. Already by the time of Leon Battista Alberti, the architect was one who shaped matter through Platonic *lineaments*, operating at a conceptual distance.[15] The relatively recent advent of the architectural academy during the Enlightenment-inspired Industrial Revolution further trimmed architecture of its unwanted corporeal fat. The gentleman architect shed the persona of the *craftsman* in favor of the *philosopher*. Consequently, architecture of the early modern period, notwithstanding the influence of certain marginal forces, became largely aligned with the trending epistemes of the day, namely rationalism and positivism.

John Dewey, in *Art as Experience*, describes a pre-modernist engagement with the everyday: "the arts of the drama, music, painting, and architecture thus exemplified had no peculiar connection with theaters, galleries, museums. They were part of the significant life of an organized community."[16] By the mid-twentieth century, socio-cultural endeavors from the fine arts to architecture had largely disengaged from the quotidian social realm to the rarefied and exclusive realm of privilege, particularly in the North American context. The painter and the sculptor escaped the "banality" of the public square to showcase their work to potential patrons in art galleries and to an "enlightened" public in art museums. Musicians and actors reinforced the proscenium as an impermeable boundary in the halls of theaters filled with "elite" spectators. Architects, too, followed the path of disengagement as they transitioned the discipline into a quasi-profession.

The architectural profession began stratifying into increasingly discrete scales of practices, with large corporate firms growing in size by gobbling up their mid-sized, more designerly competition and small boutique studios holding out to form the requisite resistance. Yet, over the course of the last half-century, society has witnessed the potential ills of detachment resulting from the rationalist streak of modernism in nearly every human endeavor. Geographer Edward Relph grounds two fundamental critiques of contemporary placemaking—the standardization of hyperplanning and the excesses of commodification—in "relatively detached and abstract approaches that are insensitive to the specific attributes of places."[17] As architect and educator Stephen Ross astutely points out, "we convinced ourselves that . . . professionals could know what was best for others, that we could know this in advance and from a distance of any actual engagement with others."[18]

Our childish impulse to get our hands dirty has been suppressed by our enlightened rationalism and a culture of building that reinforces a separation of the architect from the builder. Following on the heels of the late twentieth century verve among architectural educators for postmodern theory—namely structuralism, poststructuralism, and critical theory—by the mid-1990s designbuild education as a movement arose as a reaction to the tendency of these schools of thought to obfuscate architectural discourse and exacerbate its disengagement from issues that "mattered." These architectural theorists reinforced the idea that architecture, as opposed to "mere" building, is exclusively an intellectual endeavor, a form of knowledge, autonomous from the realm of *builderly* concerns. Some went so far as to argue that the essence of architecture has little to do with building at all. Instead, building is just one of a variety of mediums, including drawings, texts, and events, through which architecture communicates or operates.[19] Architects, professionals as well as theorists, began to self-identify solely as designers, defined in the narrowest sense and in some instances quite conceptually oriented, leaving the execution of the building, and in extreme cases, most of the thinking about the execution of the building, to others.

In contrast, architects drawn to material, tectonic, and constructive concerns tended to eschew the trendiest -isms as being divorced from the concrete and tangible. Peter Zumthor, for instance, has expressed disinterest in architectural theory, instead favoring architectural *things* and the atmospheres that they engender.[20] Such architects have been described as returning to forgotten principles. In describing the integrative practice of Shop Architects, Philip Nobel writes, "It is a thrilling time when a putative avant-garde has so outstripped (or abandoned) the grand army it ostensibly serves that a countervailing, revisionist force can take a principled stand at the forgotten center of its field."[21]

Since the late twentieth century, "revisionist forces" in art and architecture have been turning toward reengagement, whether in the form of street theater, public and performance art, or designbuild and public interest architecture. While the forces that are shaping this reengagement are many and the proper subject of a

6 Chad Kraus

more extended examination, examples can be found in almost every aspect of contemporary entrepreneurial society. By the early twenty-first century, open-source knowledge, crowd source funding, and the maker movement had caught hold:

> The maker movement, as we know, is the umbrella term for independent inventors, designers and tinkerers . . . Makers tap into an American admiration for self-reliance and combine that with open-source learning, contemporary design and powerful personal technology like 3-D printers. The creations, born in cluttered local workshops and bedroom offices, stir the imaginations of consumers numbed by generic, mass-produced, made-in-China merchandise.[22]

The same can be said for architects and the general public reacting against equally generic, mass-produced, made-in-corporate-anywhere architecture.

Whatever the pressing cause behind these movements, whether as a reaction to the ills of disengagement, as a critique of specialization, standardization, consumerism, and/or globalization, or in the cause of social justice, these shared values are rooted in common ground. Those drawn to designbuild architecture tend to echo such sentiments. Unsurprisingly, some have resurrected the philosophy of *pragmatism* for its aim to realign theory with practice and to stress action. Tapping into the "American admiration for self-reliance," pragmatism is perhaps the only thoroughly American philosophical school of the twentieth century. It is probably not a coincidence that after a meteoric rise and subsequent post-war fall, pragmatism is currently experiencing a second, and sustained, wind.

The designbuild movement in architectural education appears to share much of the values inherent in these allied grassroots movements—direct engagement with people, places, and processes and a valorization of everyday experiences. Today, despite a general disdain for -isms among designbuilders, they tend to be closely allied with critical regionalism for its dedication to place, its anti-late capitalist position, and implicit sustainability.[23] Yet, it takes only a few small philosophical steps from critical regionalism to arrive at phenomenology, and by shared philosophical underpinnings, to its American parallel, pragmatism.[24] While pragmatism in architectural discourses has yet to receive the attention phenomenology has, one particularly fertile examination took place at Columbia University in 2000 and was captured in *The Pragmatist Imagination*, edited by Joan Ockman.[25]

Although it is not my intention here to expound in any great detail on the characteristics of pragmatism or to argue that pragmatism explicitly or consciously underpins all, or even most, of designbuild education, a few brief words regarding the relationship between architecture and pragmatism may serve as a useful guide. While it has been claimed that designbuild education resists theorizing,[26] it is clear that certain unifying motivations are discernable among its most influential protagonists, and what is more, I contend that these shared motivations are better understood by adopting the intellectual framework of pragmatism. Ockman points out that, "at the most general level, pragmatism defines itself as a theory of practice. It is also, more polemically, an anti-theoretical theory."[27] As such, pragmatism tends to resonate with designbuild educators and their professional counterparts, for no other reason than that it insists "that any theory of truth, meaning, or reality can only be verified in terms of the concrete differences it makes when implemented and tested in actual experience."[28]

Even prior to the renaissance of designbuild education in the mid-1990s, the influence of pragmatism could be observed in the first postmodern designbuild program of its kind. According to Richard Hayes, in his comprehensive account of the first forty years of the Yale Building Project, the program "is important from several perspectives: for its pedagogic role in the professional training of architects; as an expression of [Charles] Moore's own educational views; as a manifestation of the role of pragmatism in American culture; and as a reflection of a period of heightened social activism and dramatic institutional change."[29]

Framed through a pragmatist lens, the disparate intentions of designbuilders begin to cohere. Like the pragmatist, the designbuilder returns to the lived world of experience and to "things in the making."[30] In keeping with the original pragmatist philosophical intent to unite *theoria* and *praxis*, a way of thinking that might best be framed in the context of *phronesis* (practical wisdom), designbuilders are intertwining theory and practice in ways that, ironically, never materialized during the theoretical wellspring of the second half of the twentieth century. Contemporary American designbuild education appears to share pragmatism's concern with "connections of meanings determined by the world of practical realities and on the lived world as the foundation of all inquiry and meaning."[31] This book, through fourteen essays written by a representative sampling of contemporary American designbuild educators—expanding upon the legacy established by such works as *Learning by Building* by William J. Carpenter and other pioneering designbuild educators[32]—investigates the *urge to build* that does indeed appear to unite proponents of this emerging pedagogy and pries open its theoretical dimensions and logistical mechanics to better understand its opportunities, limitations, and future trajectories. It is, then, to the motivations of the designbuild educator that we now turn.

Four Themes Guided by the Head-Hand Synthesis

The synthesis of the acts of designing and making in the context of a live project is what fundamentally unites designbuild education; all other commonalities are extrinsic and, therefore, shed light on the perceived value of designbuild education. While I do not argue for a totalizing agenda in the absence of one, four essential themes appear to thread through the majority of designbuild initiatives in varying degrees of intensity. These motivations, well aligned with pragmatism, tend to stress a reengagement with *people*, *poetics*, *process*, and *practice*. Spreading out across the pages of this book are testaments to the pedagogical benefits of designbuild education—cultivations of tectonic imagination, exercises of multiple intelligences, the values of salutary failure, and the ingenuity to invent new systems and processes when the current ones inhibit creativity, to name a few.

8 Chad Kraus

For those who have benefited from a designbuild education, the experience can be truly transformative.

People: Community Engagement and the Common Good

In light of the type of pragmatism articulated by Dewey, with its treatment of moral principles in education, or the deep pragmatism of Joshua Greene that unabashedly argues for a philosophy that values whatever works best for the greatest number of people, it should come as no surprise that issues of social justice, democracy, and the public good were fundamental to designbuild education at its very conception.[33] According to Ockman, "the central pragmatist commitment to social amelioration and ethical praxis furnishes grounds for reclaiming a portion of that modernist heritage that many architects still refuse, in all conscience, to abandon."[34]

Samuel Mockbee, co-founder of the Rural Studio, held a profound and genuine desire to positively impact his local community, particularly the disenfranchised, through the influence of the built environment. Mockbee prodded the discipline, through hands-on education, to affect real change in society. To educate agents of change or subversive leaders, as Mockbee implored, the designbuild educator must abandon the relative safety and impotence of the isolated and hypothetical design studio to engage in sustained encounters with the public.[35] The four essays that comprise this first theme grow from the seeds Mockbee planted in the fertile ground of Hale County, Alabama, none more so than the essay by the studio's current director and successor to Mockbee, Andrew Freear. In "Backyard Architecture," Freear invites us to sit down with him on the proverbial front porch of the Rural Studio to glean some insight into how the studio has come to be one of the most respected in the country. In a refreshingly uncomplicated and accessible tone, Freear tells the tale of Rural Studio's genuine struggle to forge relationships with the local community and to chart a path of integrated engagement while acknowledging the precarious and ever-present risk of architectural imperialism.

Focusing on the complexities of working with students and underserved communities, John Quale, in "Design / Build / Evaluate: Connecting with Actual Humans," examines the benefits of designbuild education to students and to the communities they serve. Quale acknowledges, in response to an increased focus on community-engaged designbuild activities, that these projects are not always successful from the vantage point of the "beneficiaries" of the work. With an attitude toward meaningful assessment, Quale uses the model of *design/build/evaluate* for his ecoMOD prefabricated housing modules. He makes a strong case that our discipline needs to engage in a serious dialogue about appropriate methods of working with the non-profit organizations, community groups, and individual stakeholders impacted by our work.

In the essay "Embracing Uncertainty: Community Designbuild," the civic-engaged designbuild work of Nils Gore and Shannon Criss also finds its roots in the legacy of Samuel Mockbee. They make a compelling case that the tangible products of community designbuild validate the process. Their work knits together designbuild education with a growing public interest design movement. The situational character of their projects reflects their specific circumstances and results in refreshingly forthright approaches to the work.

Through three unexpected and delightful parables in his essay "Each One Teach One: Nested Associations in Designbuild Education," Larry Bowne explores the social and democratic dimensions of designbuild education, particularly in relation to times of crisis and need. He illustrates how an engaged pedagogy—through intentionally constructed communities of participants (students, faculty, and stakeholders)—facilitates deep and reciprocal teaching and learning for all involved.

Poetics: Experience and the Human Condition

While the essays in the first theme have a focus on engaging with *people* in the community, the next three can be characterized by their inward turn to explore the *poetics* of phenomena, place, and the human condition. Far from being escapist, these programs tend to explore the self in relation to the greater lived world, cultivating an increased sensitivity to the living being in its environment. In an era when aesthetics has been flattened to connote mere visual delight and stripped of its experiential dimension, Dewey's aesthetic experience reaffirms the aesthetic imperative of architecture.[36]

The Argentine poet Jorge Luis Borges once wrote that "the taste of the apple . . . lies in the contact of the fruit with the palate, not in the fruit itself." If I may be allowed to take liberties with the remainder of the passage by substituting a few keys words to suit my purposes here, we can observe a fundamental architectural truth. "In a similar way . . . *architecture* lies in the meeting of *building* and *dweller*, not in the *physical manifestation of architecture*. What is essential is the aesthetic act, the thrill, the almost physical emotion that comes with each *encounter*" [words in italics added].[37] Similarly, Tom Spector describes

> the aesthetic as something both intimately and commonly experienced by everyone in everyday experiences. The pragmatist aesthetic experience tracks the subject's engagement with the work of art; it is neither solely derived from the physical properties of the work nor from the imaginative experiences of the subject, but from something forged from the prolonged encounter.[38]

Designbuild educators tend to privilege the architect as a maker rather than as a disengaged designer. The design (idea) holds value only by virtue of its physical manifestation (execution). In true pragmatic fashion, the building itself, in turn, possesses value only in as much as it provides the opportunity to structure the encounter. Thus privileging the encounter naturally results in the architect's insistence on the work being materialized. The encounter and its attendant phenomena are not understood here as a means to an end but rather as ends themselves, just as Goethe reminds us, "one should not seek anything behind the phenomena; they are lessons themselves."[39] The designbuilder shares an appreciation for the fertility of *things* and their capacity to concretize the poetic dimension—its aesthetic and emotional significance.

The poetic, as Coleman Coker has described it elsewhere, is about uncovering and making explicit place and its phenomena.[40] Life on earth is central to the poetic. Similarly, Martin Heidegger writes, "poetry does not fly above and surmount the earth in order to escape it and hover over it. Poetry is what first brings man onto the earth, making him belong to it, and thus brings him into dwelling."[41] In "The Good of Doing Poetics, the Poetics of Doing Good," Coker traces the etymology of *poiesis* to reveal the fundamental "vehicles" through which designbuild education supports the cultivation of the poetic in architecture students—material, place, and time. To these, Coker adds a fourth, *geoality*, meaning that which is of the earth. The concept of geoality guides students in the unique environment that the designbuild studio offers to become better earth citizens. Coker's call for an enlivened theory-based discourse that approaches poetics anew reasserts the role of theory in architectural education.

In my essay, "Architecture into Presence," an explicit cultivation of phenomenal forces and their latent potential to act intersubjectively through biology, history, culture, and shared experience reinforces the experiential dimension of architecture. Designbuild education is a much-needed complement to traditional design studios. Designbuild activities open up design to be a poetic presence through building, and for building to be a poetic presence through design. The essay concentrates on the Dirt Works Studio, of which I am the director, as it relates to latent architecture, specifically through three interrelated, site-specific interventions in the ecotone prairie/woodland landscape of northeastern Kansas.

In "The Action of Poetry," Lori Ryker describes the immersion-based pedagogical model of her Remote Studio and its potential to engender a more poetic existence and relationship to the world. Ryker believes this unique way of teaching and learning encourages a wholesome integration of understanding and experience. She relates architecture to poetry—architecture constructed of materials and phenomena, when arranged with care, results in an intimate sense of belonging. In the explicit interplay between the human-made artifact and the natural world—in this particular instance, the sublime grace of the Northern Rocky Mountains—we experience ourselves and the world we live in through continually renewed ways.

Process: Methodology and the Tectonic Imagination

Philosophers Sandra Rosenthal and Patrick Bourgeois point out that the "concept of process is fundamental for pragmatism in understanding the nature of man's relation to the world in which he lives,"[42] yet it is equally fundamental to the designbuild educator who values process as an end in itself rather than as a means to an *a priori* end. The designbuilder appreciates the mutually beneficial relationship between ideation and execution. In opposing the tendency to conflate *design* with *ideation* and *making* with *execution*, the act of making is understood not only as productive but also equally as creative and intellectual. Making is imbued with equal capacity for ideation and execution. Thus a synthesis of designer and builder engenders a powerful feedback loop between the two. Further, ignorance of the maker's knowledge limits the designer's power of imagination, and similarly, dissatisfaction with existing modes of production that pose limits on ideation invites the designer to reimagine the process of making. In other words, the maker's knowledge emancipates the designer and, inversely, the designer's knowledge emancipates the maker. The intertwining of designer and maker results in a purposeful slowing down or, more accurately, an expansion of the ideation phase. In this way, design becomes more opportunistic, provisional and contingent, adapting and evolving to conditions unknowable prior to engagement with the real and the made. The design-builder honors the builder's tacit and tectonic knowledge as well as the designer's prophetic knowledge and powers of synthesis. The designer's capacity is no longer limited to architectural objects but can be applied to the actual process itself.

Keith and Marie Zawistowski's essay, "In Process," examines the potential of designbuild education to more holistically prepare architecture students for professional practice by balancing "theoretical underpinnings with technical aptitude." For their design/buildLAB, they insist on a pedagogical model that empowers students to engage in and, most importantly, lead complex architectural projects in the context of real-world situations. Akin to the guiding hand of Socrates, the Zawistowskis' role in the studio is as mentors and enablers to cultivate critical thinking skills. Through this interaction, their students gain an appreciation for the entirety of the process.

Rather than conceive of designbuild education as existing in the seam between designing and making, Terry Boling, in "Embodied Making: Designing at Full Scale," radically resituates designbuild education at the near total conflation of the two. Boling emphasizes the simultaneity of design and making; construction and fabrication are treated as design processes. Using full-scale tectonic "sketches" that are unbounded rather than prescriptive outcomes of a designed set of instructions, his students learn to understand full-scale material and assembly prototyping as primarily investigative and fundamentally creative.

In "Practicing the Digital Vernacular: Raising a Barn and Raising Questions," James Stevens, Ralph Nelson, and Natalie Haddad team up to heal the divide between designing and making in the most unexpected of places—the digital realm. Harnessing the computational advances of our information age, they bind contemporary technologies to the time-honored wisdom of vernacular architecture. The Digital Vernacular, as they have coined it, has the capacity to go beyond romanticized notions of both past and future by authentically engaging these new tools to perpetuate the evolution of architecture. Through a digital workflow, the team chronicles the raising of "the barn," a pre-fabricated plywood structure using friction-fit joinery.

Practice: The Academic-Professional Bridge

Designbuild educators tend to share a concern for the health and vitality of architectural practice itself. The "principled stand at the forgotten center" must be instilled in the next generation of architects.[43] A reengaged architecture is thus thrust back into the whole culture of building from whence it seems to have long ago retreated. Resisting the contemporary tendency to reduce architecture to superficial aesthetics or form making, designbuilders seek to reunite increasingly disparate realms of the allied disciplines of architecture. "When all is going wrong," says Zumthor, "a new movement emerges. Otherwise this profession will reduce itself to making forms and all the rest will be a task for others. It will be less important than drawing clothes. The architect who produces these kind of projects will be excluded by those who have to build the projects."[44] One of the central aims of designbuild education is to cultivate an alternative socialization of future architects such that they may earn greater authority through intimate constructive knowledge and thereby possess increased agency in the whole of the built environment. Through immersion in the construction process, the future architect develops an empathy with builders and craftspeople. Designbuild education begins to act as the bridge between academia and practice, between the designer and the maker, often adopting similar concerns to the profession at large. Today's designbuild programs, for instance, are becoming increasingly concerned with integrated building practices and, perhaps above all else, issues of sustainability.

In "Second Nature: Embedded Knowledge through Designbuild Education," Tricia Stuth observes that architectural education must adapt in the face of an increasingly complex architecture profession. Carefully situated between the academic design studio and the professional office, designbuild projects such as the New Norris House are uniquely suited to develop embedded knowledge and to act as an academic-professional bridge. With a strong commitment to environmental stewardship and applied research in architectural education, the New Norris House serves as a powerful pedagogical model. Despite its many virtues, Stuth acknowledges the significant challenges and drawbacks of such work.

In a similar vein, Erik Sommerfeld, in "Labor-Intensive: Innovation by Necessity," argues that due to scarce resources, lack of requisite skills, the potential of low-cost labor, and its essential experimental nature, designbuild programs tend to embrace labor-intensive building approaches, material reuse, prefabrication, lean project delivery methods, and passive design strategies. These constraints have led Sommerfeld to take advantage of interdisciplinary professional collaborations, in turn illustrating the importance of Integrated Project Delivery mechanisms. While these particular constraints may not translate directly to professional practice, they develop students' tectonic imagination, resourcefulness, and capacity for complex problem solving.

The creation of a designbuild program is not for the faint of heart. In "From Scratch: How to Start a Designbuild Program," Eric Weber graciously pulls back the curtain to reveal the details of the formation of UNLV's David G. Howryla Design+Build Studio. From initial start-up funding to the trials and tribulations of the US Department of Energy's Solar Decathlon project, the nascent studio must find its footing. Weber examines the sometimes-wicked logistics of liability, safety, and funding, while building the critical relationships necessary to establish a sustainable future for the program.

In my interview with Dan Rockhill, "Work Ethic, Ethical Work: A Conversation with Designbuild Pioneer Dan Rockhill," three primary themes emerge regarding designbuild education: its holistic nature, the virtues of hard work that are inherent to its practice, and the significant challenges that it faces. Rockhill makes a strong case for reengaging the whole culture of building. Central to this reengagement is his commitment to hard work as a necessary condition to do good work. Designbuild education, in this light, is positioned as an antidote to the "paucity of integrated tectonic experiences" that characterizes architecture students in the early decades of the twenty-first century.

For the sake of thematic clarity, these essays have been clustered according to the most explicit discourse each addresses; however, as will become evident, the work of these individual designbuild studios routinely embraces all or several of the themes of this book. The themes themselves are mutually compatible, coextensive, and synergistic. Put simply, designbuild education engages with the physical *live object* to better understand and potentially reinvent communities, places, phenomena, materials, construction methods, fabrication processes, client and consultant relations, and professional organizational structures, all in the name of better design.

A New Movement Emerges

The moment you make a design decision, you have already staked out an ethical position. I tell my students this when I catch them making indiscriminate decisions in the studio. But the same could be said for pedagogical decisions. What are the ethical implications of our current pedagogical models in architecture? How have they contributed to shaping the profession? What have we done well and where have we failed? If we gaze out upon our contemporary built environments, are we largely satisfied with what we see or are we left with misgivings?

This book is not an argument against design-studio-based models of architectural education. Nor is it a manifesto dedicated to designbuild education as a form of salvation. Designbuild education, as an emerging or even emerged pedagogical movement, is well positioned as a complement to the otherwise enviable design studio model—enviable in the sense that quite a lot of current education literature espouses the virtues of such models. In an era when architecture students—and young people in general—have largely been denied integrated tectonic experiences prior to their formal education, designbuild steps in to fill the void. Yet, the value of designbuild education cannot be constrained to issues of tectonics. It is not merely a robust substitute for more conventional technical instruction. The *hands-on* nature of designbuild invites us to physically reengage with the world, the world that we architects have a solemn responsibility to help positively shape. This includes its communities, its places, its material offerings, and its future. Yet the value of designbuild education cannot be constrained to physical engagement either. It is not merely vocational training, or outreach, or skill building. The *minds-on* nature of designbuild invites us to critically and intellectually reengage as well.

Designbuild education is the missing link between the generalist liberal arts education that has long served as the foundation of the architectural academy and the specialized professional education that appears indispensible in preparing students for the increasingly complex world that they will inherit. Designbuild studios, at their best, elegantly weave together the values of academia with those of the profession.

★★★

For the student of architecture, I trust that you will find inspiration in the quality and content of the work presented here, as well as discover a much-needed antidote to the ubiquitous hands-off attitudes that have steadily reshaped contemporary society for decades.

For the architectural educator, may this book not only shed light on the pedagogical and theoretical dimensions of designbuild education but also lay bare the inner workings of a few representative examples of designbuild education.

For the architectural practitioner, may this book contribute a modicum of hope for the future trajectory of our proud discipline and ignite in us the desire to reclaim its forgotten center.

Notes

1 Kent Spreckelmeyer and Bill Carswell, "Studio 804, Hands-On Thinking, and the Legacy of Harris Stone," unpublished manuscript, 2014. Harris Stone often repeated this mantra during his annual University of Kansas immersive summer Italian study abroad program in the early 1990s.
2 Geoff W. Gjertson, "House Divided: Challenges to Design/Build from Within," in proceedings of the Association of Collegiate Schools of Architecture Fall Conference 2011: Local Identities / Global Challenges.
3 Eddy S.W. Ng, Linda Schweitzer, and Sean T. Lyons, "New Generation, Great Expectations: A Field Study of the Millennial Generation," *Journal of Business and Psychology* 25, 2 (2010): 281–92.
4 Association of Collegiate Schools of Architecture, "ACSA Design Build Award," http://www.acsa-arch.org/programs-events/awards/design-build.
5 Design Build Exchange, "Design Build Exchange Network," http://dbx.squarespace.com.
6 Ted Cavanagh, Ursula Hartig, and Sergio Palleroni, "2014 Fall Conference, Working Out: Thinking While Building," Association of Collegiate Schools of Architecture, http://www.acsa-arch.org/programs-events/conferences/fall-conference/2014-fall-conference.
7 Oxford Brookes University School of Architecture, "Architecture 'Live Projects' Pedagogy," http://architecture.brookes.ac.uk/research/symposia/liveprojects2012/index.html. Jane Anderson and Colin Priest, "Live Projects Network," http://liveprojectsnetwork.org. Harriet Harriss and Lynnette Widder, *Architecture Live Projects* (New York: Routledge, 2014).
8 Jane Anderson and Colin Priest, "Developing an Inclusive Definition, Typological Analysis and Online Resource for Live Projects," in *Architecture Live Projects*, ed. Harriet Harriss and Lynette Widder (New York: Routledge, 2014).
9 Lisa M. Abendroth and Bryan Bell, *Public Interest Design Practice Guidebook* (New York: Routledge, 2016), 1.
10 Ibid.
11 Brian MacKay-Lyons, *Local Architecture: Building Place, Craft, and Community*, ed. Robert McCarter (New York: Princeton Architectural Press, 2015).

12 Brian MacKay-Lyons, Marie Zawistowski, and Keith Zawistowski, "Design Dialogue: Brian MacKay-Lyons," Inform, 26 September 2014, http://readinform.com/design-dialogue/design-dialogue-brian-mackay-lyons.

13 Walter Gropius, "New Ideas on Architecture," *Programmes and Manifestoes on 20th-century Architecture*, ed. Ulrich Conrads (London: Lund Humphries, 1970), 46–47.

14 Otto Friedrich Bollnow, *Rilke* (Stuttgart: W. Kohlhammer, 1951), 108; as cited in Christian Norberg-Schulz, *Nightlands: Nordic Building* (Cambridge, MA: MIT Press, 1996), 13–15.

15 Leon Battista Alberti, *On the Art of Building in Ten Books*, trans. Joseph Rykwert, Neil Leach, and Robert Tavernor (Cambridge, MA: MIT Press, 1991).

16 John Dewey, *Art as Experience* (New York: Capricorn, 1958), 5.

17 Edward Relph, "Modernity and the Reclamation of Place," in *Dwelling, Seeing, and Designing: Toward a Phenomenological Ecology*, ed. David Seamon (Albany: State University of New York Press, 1993), 34.

18 *Citizen Architect: Samuel Mockbee and the Spirit of the Rural Studio*, dir. Sam Wainwright Douglas (Big Beard Films, 2010); film quote from Professor Stephen Ross, University of Texas at Austin.

19 Bernard Tschumi, *Architecture and Disjunction* (Cambridge, MA: MIT Press, 1994).

20 Peter Zumthor, *Atmospheres: Architectural Environments, Surrounding Objects* (Basel: Birkhäuser, 2006).

21 Kimberly J. Holden and Philip Nobel, *SHoP Architects: Out of Practice* (London: Thames & Hudson, 2012), 36–37.

22 Joan Voight, "Which Big Brands Are Courting the Maker Movement, and Why," *Adweek*, 17 March 2014, http://www.adweek.com/news/advertising-branding/which-big-brands-are-courting-maker-movement-and-why-156315.

23 Kenneth Frampton, "Prospects for a Critical Regionalism," *Perspecta*, 20 (1983): 147.

24 Don Ihde, *Postphenomenology and Technoscience* (Albany: SUNY Press, 2009).

25 Joan Ockman, *The Pragmatist Imagination* (New York: Princeton Architectural Press, 2000).

26 Jori Erdman and Robert Weddle, "Designing / Building / Learning," *Journal of Architectural Education*, 55.3 (2002): 174–79.

27 Ockman, *The Pragmatist Imagination*, 17.

28 Ibid., 23.

29 Richard W. Hayes, *The Yale Building Project* (New Haven, CT: Yale School of Architecture, 2007), 12.

30 William James, *A Pluralistic Universe,* ed. Fredson Bowers, Ignas Skrupskelis, and Richard Bernstein (Cambridge, MA: Harvard University Press, 1977).

31 Sandra B. Rosenthal and Patrick L. Bourgeois, *Pragmatism and Phenomenology* (Amsterdam: Grüner, 1980), 17.

32 William J. Carpenter, *Learning by Building: Design and Construction in Architectural Education* (New York: Van Nostrand Reinhold, 1997).

33 John Dewey, *My Pedagogical Creed* (Washington, D.C.: Progressive Education Association, 1929). Joshua Greene, *Moral Tribes* (New York: Penguin, 2013).

34 Ockman, *The Pragmatist Imagination,* 17.

35 Andrea Oppenheimer Dean and Timothy Hursley, *Rural Studio* (New York: Princeton Architectural Press, 2002).

36 Dewey, *Art as Experience*.

37 Jorge Luis Borges, *Selected Poems 1923–1967* (New York: Delacorte, 1972), 272. The passage is originally from the Preface to *Obra poética*. The original passage reads as: "In a similar way . . . poetry lies in the meeting of poem and reader, not in the lines of symbols printed on the pages of a book. What is essential is the aesthetic act, the thrill, the almost physical emotion that comes with each reading."

38 Tom Spector, "Pragmatism for Architects," *Contemporary Pragmatism*, 1.1 (2004): 133–49.

39 Steven Holl, "Questions of Perception" in *Questions of Perception: Phenomenology of Architecture* by Steven Holl, Juhani Pallasmaa, and Alberto Pérez Gómez (San Francisco: William Stout, 2006), 41.

16 Chad Kraus

40 Coleman Coker, "The Good of Doing Poetics / The Poetics of Doing Good," ACSA Fall Conference 2014, Working Out: Thinking While Building, Nova Scotia, Halifax, 17 October 2014. Keynote.

41 Martin Heidegger, *Poetry, Language, Thought*, trans. Albert Hofstadter (New York: Harper & Row, 1975), 218.

42 Rosenthal and Bourgeois, *Pragmatism and Phenomenology*, 22.

43 Holden and Nobel, *SHoP Architects: Out of Practice*.

44 Peter Zumthor and Marco Masetti, "Multiplicity and Memory: Talking About Architecture with Peter Zumthor," *ArchDaily*. 2 November 2010, http://www.archdaily.com/85656/multiplicity-and-memory-talking-about-architecture-with-peter-zumthor.

PART 1

People

Community Engagement and the Common Good

1

BACKYARD ARCHITECTURE

Andrew Freear

Deep Local

Backyard architecture is about being deeply and inextricably immersed in a particular place at a particular time. It is about understanding the *ad hoc* circumstances of a community and its people. It is about building trust. *Backyard architecture* is resourceful, opportunistic, and inventive by necessity. For Rural Studio, establishing roots and growing alongside our community was never a conscious act or strategic decision; for Rural Studio founders Samuel Mockbee and D.K. Ruth, it was bred-in-the-bone. And it has remained with us, and a part of us, throughout these past twenty-two years. By working in your own backyard, you cultivate relationships. You become a neighbor. People in the community begin to understand what you have to offer, and you begin to understand what they offer in return. Folks know that they can come to us, not just for help, but also for advice. They respect what we have done and what we continue to do. That is a big deal to us. Our community trusts that we are not going anywhere, that we will not abandon them.

It seems that architects in the pursuit of doing good look far afield for problems to solve—housing shortages, impoverished communities, lack of access to healthy food, starving children, scarcity of water, and resource depletion—all in places they know little about. Yet often the most difficult problems are in our own backyards. Rural Studio has never been about *fly-off humanitarianism* or *architectural imperialism*. Here in Hale County, I have had the opportunity to forge relationships with people I trust. By listening, we learn how we might be able to help just a little bit (it is always just a little bit). Of course it was not always this way. When I came to Hale County, I was met with deep suspicion, in part because they assumed I was another professor coming out here to conduct my research, receive tenure, and disappear. It is easy to understand that kind of skepticism. Rural Studio has stayed.

Rural Studio students are immersed in their new community. They are thrust out of the ivory tower of academia (Newbern, Alabama, the home of Rural Studio, is 150 miles from Auburn University, to which it belongs). They tutor at the local middle school, they work local jobs, they go to local churches, they dine out locally, and they play on local sports teams. They do this as individuals, as fellow members of the community, even if only for two or three years. They build relationships that last a lifetime.

The act of designing and making a building is such an optimistic, provocative act that people are naturally curious. I think that for our community, seeing young people go to extraordinary lengths and seeing them labor so hard earns a lot of respect. Locals are very proud that Rural Studio is in their midst. Even so, students routinely have chance encounters with members of the community, where they may be asked: "What the hell are you doing?" "Why are you doing this?" "Why is it this color?" The students become accustomed to these interactions. Living and working in a small town can be trying, but it can also be uplifting and immensely gratifying, particularly when the community comes together with the Studio and, all of a sudden, there is this incredible barn raising. The ups and downs are all part of life in a small town, lessons that are collateral effects of the designbuild pedagogy.

Former Greensboro City Councilman Steve Gentry wished all small towns had a group of architects like Rural Studio. What he appreciated most was that he could "bend our ear," not necessarily to commission a project, but just to ask our advice or run an idea by us at a conceptual level. The mayor comes to us when he has questions of an architectural or engineering nature. Community leaders recognize that my students and I have good intentions for the town of Newbern. In some respects, Rural Studio has become the *town architect*. The real-life immersion of Rural Studio has set up the conditions in which the Studio has been able to assume this mantle. Our designbuild pedagogy, particularly in an impoverished community

FIGURE 1.1 Downtown Newbern, from left, storage barn, Red Barn (Rural Studio's design studio), post office, and Newbern Mercantile, Newbern, Alabama
Source: Tim Hursley

such as ours, empowers the Studio to create real and lasting change, and that has been key to developing our relationship with the community. The opportunistic and resourceful designs of Rural Studio often employ unorthodox materials and approaches, requiring the designbuilder's synthetic skills to pull them off.

The old adage about teaching a man to fish is really about the difference between enabling and empowering. A common criticism of designbuild programs is that they rely on donations, goodwill, and the free labor of students and—in the process of fulfilling their pedagogical mission—unfairly compete with professional architects and contractors. We at Rural Studio share this concern. I am diligent in making sure that none of these projects would happen without our collaboration. I am careful not to take food off the table of architects or contractors. Most of the time what we do contributes to the health of the local economy by creating opportunities where none previously existed. We hire local contractors to build parts of the projects that I deem are not academic. We collaborate with an architect of record. We work with our community partners to build skills that will empower them far beyond the fruits of our collaboration.

In the increasingly globalized world we live in today, where the creative nuclei of cultures are homogenizing at a sub-mediocre level and people are increasingly blinded by technology, place-based design is more important than ever.[1] Architecture is not just about making beautiful buildings; it is a dialogue with a place, its people, and a moment in time. The questions are essentially the same everywhere, but the answers must relate to place. It is a question of responsibility to the local culture and character. We build with what we have at hand. A house in Hale County ought to be different than a house in Chicago. Here the antebellum homes all have deep overhanging roofs. Tall ceilings and ample natural ventilation eases the discomfort of the hot, humid, stale air. The homes are raised off the ground, with generously shaded porches. These characteristics have survived for over 150 years, standing the test of time. A place-based design philosophy runs deep in the Studio; we believe people and place matter. When we work in our own backyards, we learn from the place. We learn from our mistakes. Since most of our projects are in a twenty-five mile radius, we naturally develop a healthy feedback loop with the community. If I design a building in Shanghai, how do I know whether the project was worth a damn?

Living with Your Mistakes

One of Rural Studio's strengths has been that design has always been a priority. We are a design school. While our dedication to serving our community is far from incidental, nurturing young designers and giving them an opportunity to prove themselves is central to our mission. We do not think of ourselves as do-gooders or humanitarians. We are not here to dig ditches. We strive to do the right thing, to figure out what it means to do the right thing in any given situation. It is never a question of what can we do, but rather what should we do. Our students get rebuked a lot about the vocabulary they use. They often say "our project," and when they do, my head immediately goes up. Nothing we do is possible without our community partners. There are, of course, programs that are more socially oriented than Rural Studio. There are programs that are more design-oriented as well. Rural Studio strives to balance these two values.

The academic year at Rural Studio is inaugurated with a rigorous and frank tour of completed Rural Studio projects. We discuss the aims and aspirations of each, and the gloves come off. Living with our mistakes means both acknowledging and accepting that we could do better and that the imbedded nature of the Studio allows us the opportunity to literally live with and learn from these mistakes when they occur. With somewhere between 150 and 200 projects in Hale County, we have great success stories as well as projects that have not lived up to their promise. Some of the latter have moved on from their intended purpose, as sometimes happens with buildings. With the community projects, their success is largely dependent on whether the doors are still open or not. And since we are here for the long haul, if we have made a mistake on a project, particularly one of our community projects, we hear about it. If there are maintenance issues, we are committed to chaperoning these projects into the future. It is important for our project teams to work closely with their community partners to ensure that there is a sufficient structure in place for the project to move forward and to sustain itself into the future. The Boys and Girls Club in Greensboro is a great example of the designbuild team guiding our community partners through the process. The team sat down with the nascent unit board, a group of folks interested in the idea of a Boys and Girls Club, and walked them through precedents from across the United States on how to go about establishing one.

Rural Studio Laid Bare

One of the greatest challenges of the designbuild approach, particularly with the socially motivated designbuild project, is honoring the fundamental pedagogical mission while fulfilling the promise to the community. There are moments when these two lofty goals can be at odds.

We, at Rural Studio, are disciplined in how we structure our projects to minimize future complications. Fifth-year students enrolled in Rural Studio spend nine months working with the community, developing their designs, and proving the concept through a series of *stress tests*, often including a full-scale mockup of the most challenging or structurally complex piece of the project. This stress test, in some respects, has become a rite of passage to proceed. Some students fail at that moment, others succeed. Still others get half way there and are given the opportunity to keep going because we trust they can pull through. Once they prove themselves, we give them the green light and at about this moment they formally graduate from architecture school. Then the building process begins, and this can take upwards of an additional two-and-half years. I have always been very proud of the fact that our students build these projects basically as volunteers; they do this because it is the right thing to do. Our students share the ethical convictions of Rural Studio. The bond between them, our community partners, and the Studio is stronger than the

FIGURE 1.2 Students testing eight-by-eight-inch cypress timbers comprising the entrance-door beam, *Newbern Town Hall*, Newbern, Alabama, 2011
Source: Andrew Freear

external pressures they face to move on. They are proof that, given an opportunity, twenty-two or twenty-three year olds are capable of extraordinary things.

Cultivating relationships with the community is essential to what we do in Hale County. We build trust, and we are careful not to betray that trust. So when a student joins Rural Studio, they understand the commitments the Studio/we have made on their behalf. The key to Rural Studio's success is that failure is always an option; only we do our best to isolate the tremors of failure before they impact the community. If we, as a studio, do not feel that a student has reciprocated that commitment, or if they have not proven themselves capable of moving forward, or if the students are capable but their proposal is ultimately not the right solution, we go no further. That is the deal. We are not afraid to determine that a project has not reached the right moment to move forward. To build is not a predetermined outcome. It is a privilege that is earned. If the project does not meet our internal expectations or those of the community, it does not go ahead. It is as simple as that.

The efficacy of this approach is owed to the fact that there is generally no hard and fast deadline for these projects. Our four-person student teams understand and our community partners understand that the projects may fail before they ever hit the ground, and that we may have to start over. Everyone involved understands that the process cannot unfold overnight; they understand that it can take two-and-half years for the students to acquire the necessary skills, knowledge, and experience to build a firehouse, a town hall, or a public library.

Healthy Eating, Healthy Living, Healthy Communities

The future trajectory of Rural Studio is a threefold initiative—to promote and advance the causes of healthy eating, healthy living, and healthy communities. The clearest manifestation of these three ideals are: the Rural Studio Farm (healthy eating), the so-called 20K Homes (healthy living), and community projects like the Newbern Library and Lions Park (healthy communities). While these initiatives each arose organically based on community need, without any overarching agenda, we have begun to formalize these investigations. Increasingly, we are beginning to understand these as *research* projects as well as *design* projects.

The Rural Studio Farm

Rural Studio has always striven to conserve resources, both in response to limited availability and as a principled position toward environmental stewardship. We have challenged ourselves to live more economically and more frugally. More recently, we realized how poorly we are all feeding ourselves. Why were we all driving ten miles to the nearest Piggly Wiggly grocery store to buy prepackaged, processed food when we live in a rural farming community? With the rise of real-food deserts and dependencies on unhealthy, fast food options, it is no wonder society is suffering through our current obesity epidemic. Although fundamental to our mission, it is not enough to provide all, rich or poor, with "shelters for the soul,"[2] we must also nourish our bodies.

We started to understand that the soil in Hale County is not particularly productive for farming. The over-cultivation of cotton had largely stripped the topsoil of its nutrients. In an effort to establish a sustainable model for local folks to learn from, the Studio created the Rural Studio Farm. Designed, built, and maintained by the third-year students living around the farm, the project is one of the most ambitious and exciting endeavors we have undertaken.

The project is truly interdisciplinary; we are collaborating with specialists including biologists, botanists, and horticulturalists. We quickly learned that we needed to grow our own soil to amend our unproductive native soils. We built raised beds and covered them with a large greenhouse, which serves as the farm's centerpiece.

In Hale County, the summers are too hot and the winters are too wet. The greenhouse, with its large protective glass roof, extends the growing season through both seasons. We are continually learning from local farmers, learning to better manage local resources and investigating methods to sustainably maintain healthy, local food production.

The 20K Home

Since the earliest days of Rural Studio, we have designed and built single-family homes for families in need of a better, more uplifting place to live. These homes were quite idiosyncratic. A little over ten years ago, frustrated with reinventing the wheel every year and only helping one family, we embarked with our fifth-year students on what became known as the 20K Home. The project was an evolution

FIGURE 1.3 An interior view of the solar greenhouse with a thermal wall of water-filled steel drums, *Rural Studio Farm*, Newbern, Alabama, 2010–present
Source: Tim Hursley

FIGURE 1.4 *Rural Studio Farm*, Newbern, Alabama, 2010–present
Source: Andrew Freear

26 Andrew Freear

in response to a significant need. You cannot just go out and decide that building small, affordable houses is going to be your main focus. These houses have become our main focus because the need for small homes that are affordable is locally the main issue. How are we as a community consuming, how are we wasting? How do we live within our means?

Folks in Hale County purchase trailer homes as they would a car. The interest rates on these homes are high, and after twenty years, just like an automobile, the value and condition of the home will have sharply declined. Our goal is to build homes for a similar amount of money that will last for 100 years and actually gain equity over time. We feel that, with our experience designing and building single-family homes, we are capable of developing a model that could help more than one family. The basic principle is to design and build a small, truly affordable beautiful house that is responsive to its region's climate and culture, while upholding the dignity that ought to be inherent to the idea of *home*.

Rural Studio feels both the responsibility and the opportunity to address the housing crisis in impoverished rural communities. We are in a situation where

FIGURE 1.5 Dave sitting on his screened porch, *Dave's Home (20K Home #8)*, Newbern, Alabama, 2009

Source: Tim Hursley

we have a steady population of motivated architecture students who provide their labor and talents for free and a largely elderly community in serious need of affordable housing. We have had the luxury of devoting more than 180,000 hours to these projects over the years. No architect or builder could afford to invest even a fraction of this amount of time on homes that have such small profit margins. Since we are deeply rooted in this community, we also have the privilege of watching how our clients live, and we learn how to improve our work.

The experimental nature of the single-family idiosyncratic homes we create help push the Studio in new, ever more inventive directions. These projects are essential to the future of Rural Studio. However, the iterative nature of the small, affordable-house model has become a rigorous research project with the potential of uncovering a different kind of knowledge. In the beginning, the design and construction of these houses were frustratingly reliant on rule-of-thumb decision-making. Over the last couple of years we have begun to approach this project with increasing scientific rigor.

In the early years of the 20K Homes, we focused on one-bedroom layouts. The increased square footage and more complex familial structure of the two-bedroom

FIGURE 1.6 MacArthur's recessed porch and broadside entry, *MacArthur's Home (20K Home #9)*, Faunsdale, Alabama, 2010

Source: Tim Hursley

homes demanded that we better understand the building science dimensions of the project to maintain the highest levels of efficiency and resourcefulness. We are currently forging relationships with Alabama Power, testing agencies, and others, who can help us design and build higher performing homes using the Home Energy Rating System (HERS) Index, blower-door testing, and other methods to quantify environmental performance. These additional measures are not typically employed on affordable housing models such as ours.

Each of the past ten years Rural Studio has designed and built a small affordable house, building upon previous iterations. We have steadily learned lessons from each, such as cantilevering a portion of the floor so that it counteracts the simple span elements, thereby maximizing the use of every piece of material in the floor. We apply this kind of resource-conscious logic throughout the house. We have built a body of research on making good homes that are affordable and are now beginning to transition into what we hope can become a cottage industry of building homes *in* a community *for* that community.

We feel we have a moral responsibility to propagate the knowledge acquired over a decade to impact greater numbers of families throughout Hale County and

FIGURE 1.7 Joanne's corner porch entry, *Joanne's Home (20K Home #10)*, Faunsdale, Alabama, 2011

Source: Tim Hursley

beyond. We have now developed three or four houses that could be considered models for others to build. We are trying to understand the real cost of building these houses, and working with builders to estimate the costs. It is an academic and a real-world challenge. We are in the process of working with not-for-profit community development organizations to implement the project on a larger scale. Our dream is to have quality site-built houses built by people in the local community, with materials purchased in local hardware stores, so that the greatest percentage of the costs feed the local economy. The dream is to empower the community to build better places to live.

The Newbern Library

Rural Studio's community projects have always been about the health, welfare, and education of the local community. The Newbern Library, a rare opportunity to reclaim a beautiful old 1906 bank building, was no exception. We had to be careful not to compromise the local icon as we transformed it into a library-as-community-center that bookended downtown Newbern. When you live in a community this small, you have to be sensitive and empathetic.

The former bank with its masonry exterior shell and prominent storefront once again contributes to the town's civic pride, serves as a place of social interaction, and inspires the community's thirst for knowledge. The four Rural Studio students

FIGURE 1.8 *Newbern Library*, Newbern, Alabama, 2013
Source: Tim Hursley

responsible for the design and construction of the Newbern Library developed a simple extruded addition behind the old bank in an attempt to preserve the iconic storefront while maintaining the adjacent empty lot along the main street. This open space was reimagined as a courtyard providing library patrons with an outdoor reading and activity space shaded by a canopy of nineteen Natchez Crape Myrtles. While the exterior of the former bank building is treated as a restoration, the simple cypress-clad box with thin galvanized steel-framed apertures complements rather than competes with the historic façade.

Within the library, the students sought to create cohesion with an open collaborative social space defined by bookshelves knitting the old and new together. An oversized table and a living room area provide places to browse for and read books or to gather in small groups. Complementing the larger social spaces, a series of alcoves within the bookshelves create opportunities for private study, access to computers, storage, window seats, bathrooms, and a second entrance.

The community is very pleased with their new library. The exterior preserves the qualities beloved by the community while pushing the envelope just enough to breathe new life into it. The calm, modest extension on the backside defers to the interior spaces while the courtyard reminds the community of its heritage by using elements built from reclaimed bricks from the old bank vault. As an example of the Studio's assimilation into this community, I was asked to be one of six members of the library board, otherwise comprised of former or part-time librarians. As an example of how the Studio has benefited the community beyond works of architecture, the student team for the Newbern Library worked hard to get 12,000 books donated, including an ongoing commitment with a book supplier to donate *New York Times* bestsellers every six months in perpetuity.

FIGURE 1.9 *Newbern Library*, Newbern, Alabama, 2013
Source: Tim Hursley

FIGURE 1.10 *Lions Park Scout Hut*, Greensboro, Alabama, 2012
Source: Tim Hursley

Lions Park

The remaking of Lions Park has been a multi-year, multi-phase, iterative effort that includes new baseball fields, restrooms, entrance gates, a skate park, concession stand, playground, scout hut, new park furniture and surfaces, and landscaping. Community engagement in the design process has been central to the success of the project.

Over a span of more than ten years, Rural Studio continues to redevelop this strategically important public space, bridging and integrating multiple surrounding communities. This timespan has allowed the design of the park to slowly evolve in relation to community feedback and to take advantage of unanticipated opportunities. Rural Studio has worked with the three stakeholder organizations—Hale County, the City of Greensboro, and the Lions Club—to restructure not only the physical space of the park but also to redefine its organization and management. Through our involvement with Lions Park, we helped the city establish a parks and recreation department to oversee it into the future.

Making Architecture

Rural Studio is, too often I think, dismissed as a bunch of folks messing around in rural Alabama, tinkering with unorthodox works of architecture. Or we are criticized for not living up to an ideal of how community engagement should be done, as if we ever claimed to have perfected our craft. It is a shame, because what Rural Studio succeeds in doing is questioning how young architects are educated, how the profession procures and makes architecture.

Designbuild education may not be appropriate for all places and all institutions, yet the opportunity for architecture students to wander into a workshop, to try their hand at making, to know that something significant is at stake is ultimately going to change these students. Students leaving Rural Studio are immediately capable of entering the profession and single-handedly managing small projects. They have no fear of the construction site. They understand the questions to ask and are empowered to discover who to ask.

The positive change Rural Studio has made in the lives of the community and the lives of the students who come here to learn how to be good architects is made possible by our designbuild pedagogy. As architects, professionally, we let the mantle of master builder fall away. We have grown more and more disconnected from what happens on the building site. Looking back, I wish I had had the types of experiences my students are afforded—to understand the importance of designing with material and assembly tolerances in mind; to understand the implications of a line on paper and then to hold the material in hand; to work collaboratively with communities, other architecture students, engineers, subcontractors, and building officials; to have something real at stake, to raise the bar, to go beyond the *game* of the design studio. It is a huge luxury and a wonderful opportunity. At Rural Studio, our students get taken to the very edge of their physical and emotional capabilities; for most it is a life-changing opportunity and probably the toughest thing they have ever/may ever undertake. Not wanting to fail and wanting to do the right thing makes them work harder, work smarter, and be more thoughtful and more rigorous.

Notes

1 Kenneth Frampton, "Prospects for a Critical Regionalism," *Perspecta: The Yale Architectural Journal* 20 (1983): 147–162.
2 Andrea Oppenheimer Dean and Timothy Hursley, *Proceed and Be Bold: Rural Studio after Samuel Mockbee* (New York: Princeton Architectural Press, 1998), 7.

2

DESIGN / BUILD / EVALUATE

Connecting with Actual Humans

John Quale

The last decade has seen a proliferation of design/build initiatives in architecture programs around the world. Many of these efforts fall into two categories: pavilions or installations (typically an educational investigation of formal, spatial, and technical ideas), or permanent projects that have a specific purpose or program (such as a house, playground, etc.), often sited in an underserved community. For the latter group, it is relatively common to see some form of community engagement integrated into the process. Among the projects in that category, some are considered exemplary in both process and design, while others are not perceived as successful by the "beneficiaries" of the work. Many architectural academics lack experience with community engagement processes, so it is no surprise that some of these efforts have dubious evidence of a legitimate positive impact on an underserved community.

In the 21st century, both the profession and the academy have seen a major resurgence in a commitment to what is now generally known as public interest design (PID). I have a few theories about why this has happened. One theory assumes that the evolution of sustainable design from a peripheral aspect of architecture in the 1990s to a fully integrated and respected aspect of architectural design in the 2000s has opened the door for PID to follow in those footsteps. In many cases architects and architecture students see sustainability and public-interest work as deeply connected. Just ten years ago it was still surprising to see respected design architects attempt to integrate rigorous sustainability into their work, and now we are starting to see the same trajectory with design in the public interest. The quality of design work by firms including Toshiko Mori, Perkins & Will, MASS Design Group, and Shigeru Ban is generally very high, and much of it is likely to benefit the community.

It is difficult to imagine today, but twenty-five years ago excellence in design was seldom connected to an interest in environmental impact or working directly with an underserved community. Many of the top architects were focusing on

FIGURE 2.1 A house designed and built by students for recent immigrants; partnership with Habitat for Humanity of Greater Charlottesville, *ecoMOD4*, Charlottesville, Virginia, 2010
Source: Sarah Oehl Greene

getting their work published. Professional pro bono work was nowhere near as common as it is today, and few architecture students were interested in pursuing this kind of work. Yet today quality architecture is no longer automatically perceived as less interesting when it addresses environmental and social sustainability.

My alternative theory is that the 2007–09 financial crisis and the ensuing Great Recession, which technically ended in June 2009, helped generate this interest in serving the public through architecture.[1] The recession was responsible for helping the public understand the substantial increase in income disparity in the United States.[2] Non-profit organizations experienced an increase in architectural volunteers in 2009–11, perhaps due to layoffs and out of concern for the widening gap between extremely wealthy Americans and everyone else. Income inequality, even though it had expanded considerably before the recession, finally emerged as an important topic of conversation in 2010. The Occupy movement took off in 2011, and suddenly many Americans were talking about the other ninety-nine percent.[3] In fact, according to the Pew Research Center, between 2009 and 2011, the number of Americans that say there are "very strong" or "strong" conflicts between rich and poor increased from forty-seven percent to sixty-six percent of the population.[4]

In recent years, PID has been the subject of several conferences, books, articles, and even major exhibits at the Museum of Modern Art and the Cooper Hewitt Design Museum. Regular training is held through the Public Interest Design Institute as well as the Structures for Inclusion conference, often organized with the Association for Community Design conference. A parallel training conference,

FIGURE 2.2 An accessory dwelling unit, certified as LEED Platinum; partnership with Piedmont Housing Alliance, *ecoMOD3*, Charlottesville, Virginia, 2010

Source: Scott Smith

36 John Quale

Design Futures, was established solely for architecture students. The Rose Architectural Fellowship, sponsored by the Enterprise Foundation, has helped launch the careers of several public interest designers. Participants of this well-funded fellowship for architecture graduates have had their salary paid by the Enterprise Foundation for three years as they work directly with a non-profit organization, often focusing on affordable housing.

Within academia, the term "community engaged scholarship" has become widespread, and offers faculty that participate in these efforts recognition for their work within the codified procedures for assessing faculty teaching and research loads. In other words, at most universities, this work can contribute to promotion and tenure packages. This marks a major transformation in academia over the past fifteen years. Some level of community engagement has long been common in architecture, but for faculty at universities where this is officially recognized, it means that they can intensify their efforts without negatively impacting their ability to be promoted. It also means that a broader range of grant funding can be found to support these efforts.

Listening Is Not Enough, It's about Creating a Dialogue

In late 2014, I received an email from a former colleague at the University of Virginia, asking if I had seen the OpEd in the *New York Times* that referenced a home designed and built by my students. ecoMOD is the design / build / evaluate initiative I founded and ran at that institution for ten years, and later brought with me to my current academic home at the University of New Mexico.[5] Since 2004, over 450 graduate and undergraduate students in architecture, engineering, planning, historic preservation, landscape architecture, business, construction management, and environmental science have participated in at least one phase of an ecoMOD project. Interdisciplinary teams have created nine new prefabricated housing units and eleven renovated units.

The essay begins with the story of one of the authors driving past a house in Charlottesville, Virginia, with his eighty-eight year old mother. She made disparaging remarks about the design of the home. While not named directly, it is clear from the mention of the street and city that they were referencing ecoMOD4, a house completed in 2010 by an interdisciplinary team of students for an immigrant couple through the local Habitat for Humanity affiliate.

Based on the aesthetics of this building, the authors imply that the students were out of touch with the clients and the community. They state, "The question is, at what point does architecture's potential to improve human life become lost because of its inability to connect with actual humans?" Additionally, they write: "We've taught generations of architects to speak out as artists, but we haven't taught them how to listen."[6]

I agree with many aspects of their broader critique, and that it could be applied to some university design/build efforts—especially programs that have little or no contact with the communities they aspire to support. While it was not an

FIGURE 2.3 *ecoMOD4*, Charlottesville, Virginia, 2010
Source: Scott Smith

accurate assessment of the team of students working on that particular house—or of the process we typically use for ecoMOD projects—their point is relevant in a broader sense. The authors made the incorrect assumption that anything in Thomas Jefferson's hometown that does not look like neo-colonial architecture is suspect when it comes to community engagement.

As for our profession's capacity to listen to *actual humans,* it seems to me that architects and architecture students are neither better nor worse at listening than anyone else. Careful listening is a skill that takes time to develop, but I believe it is commonly found among architects. I agree that listening is important; however, I do not see it as the only aspect of successful work in a community.

Our discipline needs to engage in a deeper dialogue about appropriate methods of working with non-profit organizations, community groups, and individual stakeholders that will be impacted by our work. These are serious questions that are seldom investigated fully. Often this is because the *community* is seldom clearly defined, and even when they are, they are perceived to have a potentially negative impact on the creativity of the design process. Yet a rigorous process of working with a community can often open up possibilities for designers, not narrow them. My students and I have experienced this—and found it rewarding. And just as importantly, understanding the needs of the client stakeholders and the potential impact the project will have on their lives is the best way to ensure the built work will have a truly meaningful and long-term impact on its community.

While there are many ways of working with underserved populations, the most common for architecture students (and increasingly practitioners) is to provide volunteer design and/or construction services. Models that assume designers are *serving* the community are now seen as passé. The current, and I believe more appropriate, focus is on *collaborating* with the community. The implication is that students and faculty coming into these communities from the outside are likely to be perceived (fairly or not) as patronizing, or simply using the community as a laboratory. The best way to build relationships is to spend time in the community and build trust with the stakeholders. But this does not mean that we should be passive listeners. We are creative individuals that have training and expertise in design.

Thoughtful design is an intensive process that responds to the inputs of the place and program, but it should always lead to an effective strategy or design unique to the situation. It is essential that we listen to the non-profit group or individuals that can explain the concerns of the community, but there is no point in simply accepting every aspect of what is said. In situations where these representatives do not have any background in design, it is often difficult for them to imagine anything other than what they have seen before. Everyone is taught math, science, English, and history in high school and college, but very few have ever been exposed to design. Our job is to listen very carefully to their words, and if possible, also to

FIGURE 2.4 Students building ecoMOD4 in a former airplane hangar serving as a fabrication facility at the University of Virginia, *ecoMOD4*, Charlottesville, Virginia, 2009

Source: John Quale

discern what is behind the words in an attempt to identify what they want to accomplish. Any non-profit organization that builds homes or community centers is capable of replicating a vernacular building if that will be the only acceptable solution, but academic design/build efforts should have higher aspirations. Architecture students should be future-oriented, and that future must include the ideas and aspirations of the stakeholders.

To begin that process, it is important to supplement the stated ideas from the community with questions that will tease out deeper ideas that are not easily described. Some of the questions will require clear answers at the outset, and others can be provisional answers until the partnership matures. These questions may also help the quieter participants in the community to express ideas that have not been voiced. Questions that should be addressed include:

1) *Who are the stakeholders?* It is essential to determine who are the most appropriate individuals to have around the table when decisions are made. At a minimum, they should include the people that will live or work in the building.
2) *What are the aspirations for the project?* The challenge for faculty and students leading community design/build projects is how to address aspirations that might be understood as conflicting. For example, what happens when the design is supported by an individual client but not by the non-profit?
3) *What are the most important specific goals?* Successful projects are those that limit the goals to one or two issues. How should the scope be defined? It is easy to attempt to take on more than what a single project can address and difficult to prioritize if that has not happened at the beginning.
4) *When and how does the design process get communicated to stakeholders?* When is input on the design appropriate? How is design input addressed?
5) *Who is liable if something goes wrong?* It might feel awkward to discuss this; but it is essential to determine the answer to this question before anything gets started.
6) *Who does what?* Are there scopes of work more appropriate for professionals than students? In ecoMOD, I always have professionals do the electrical hook-up, the plumbing hook-up, the mechanical systems, and anything that will have a warranty. This does not mean that students cannot participate in these scopes of work, it just means that the subcontractor has to agree to include students as volunteers. I like to sleep at night.
7) *How are the project goals assessed?* What is the result of these assessments? What was learned? Who benefited and how?

This is not an easy process, and in my experience it should never be done without the backing of a non-profit that is trusted in the community. I have worked with organizations with deep roots in the neighborhood, and I have also worked with organizations that are not considered trustworthy by members of that community based on perceived problems with previous projects.

For design/build projects, the participation of a non-profit partner is essential, especially if they are taking legal responsibility for the project. That is always the case in the ecoMOD working method—neither the University of New Mexico or the University of Virginia can purchase builder's insurance or accept liability when it comes to design/build efforts (although if there ever was a problem, the university would certainly be named in any lawsuit). The success of the project typically comes down to a solid working relationship with the non-profit and key members of the community (and for residential projects, the family that will occupy the home). This mimics the process of working with a commercial client, where a productive and open relationship with the owner and the contractor are essential for success.

All official meetings should happen with the participation of these representatives—and whenever possible, teams should divide up the locations of those meetings between the school's studio spaces (to eliminate the mystery of *design studio*), the non-profit organization's conference room, and if the project is a single-family home, the family's dining room table. All players need to be fully engaged in these efforts, feel comfortable expressing their opinion, and also feel comfortable hearing the opinions of others. This often means the students and faculty need to be listening more than speaking in the early stages. If this is done well, my experience is that the individual clients start to get excited about the possibilities and at times push for a more interesting design than the non-profit (and occasionally even the students) might imagine.

To get to that point in a successful process, students must be trained to clearly articulate the aspirations behind their design ideas. Clients without design training are not accustomed to talking about architecture in the way we do in architecture school or in a good architecture practice. We use narrative and analogies and make what may seem like huge leaps between an abstract idea and its physical manifestation.

FIGURE 2.5 Students seek feedback from a housing rehab client; partnership with Albemarle Housing Improvement Program, *ecoREMOD Block by Block*, Charlottesville, Virginia, 2013

Source: John Quale

When engaging in PID, I have always found that it is best to connect an important practical necessity with a spatial and/or conceptual idea, to open up more design possibilities. I often start my ecoMOD design studios with an exercise that requires students to analyze a common activity done at home or in the yard, and develop a fragment of a home or outdoor space that is optimized for that activity. I require that students address the ground and the sky, to ensure they build section models. Students must also create a scale figure that represents the client. This more easily allows clients into the dialogue because they can imagine themselves in the design. It also keeps everyone from getting fixated on the overall form of the building too early. I am a firm believer that, at least for affordable housing, design should begin on the interior—forcing students to form the spaces from the inside so they can understand scale immediately, while also bringing the client more directly into the process. It is not always possible to have these kinds of intensive interactions with a client, or even any interaction with an individual client if they are not identified until after the project is underway (or even built), but a couple of the strongest ecoMOD projects evolved from that interaction.

Design / Build / Evaluate

The "build" aspect of design/build is an important part of community engagement work for architecture students. Drawings and scaled models are not as important for their education as the process of creating an actual built structure. The act of construction allows the university and the community to come together around a specific effort that has the potential of fulfilling a community's aspirations. It is not uncommon to find low-income communities near universities that are tired of being treated like a lab rat when another university researcher or student comes around with a survey, or even worse, when they research a neighborhood, write an article about it, but never set foot in the place.

Implicit in question seven above (regarding assessment) is the strategy I have deployed since the beginning of ecoMOD: specifically that design/build efforts are meaningless without an assessment component. This is why I coined the phrase *design / build / evaluate* when I founded ecoMOD. I wanted to make it explicitly clear at the start that we need to focus on the impact of our work. A later team of students handles much of the evaluation phase, and some of these students go on to become designer/builders after the evaluation seminar.

In the very first year of the project, I developed a database and spider diagram model to help teams assess design strategies, equipment, and materials for the project. This assessment process has continued ever since, and during the evaluation phase, we often attempt to reassess those diagrams to see how our decisions played out. The primary categories for assessment are: aesthetics, energy, environmental, financial, social, and technical. Each team is responsible for defining the meaning of those words, and therefore they are required to determine the subcategories that fall within them and the ranking process. In 2011, we launched a digital tool to allow the research and ranking process for this activity to be accessible

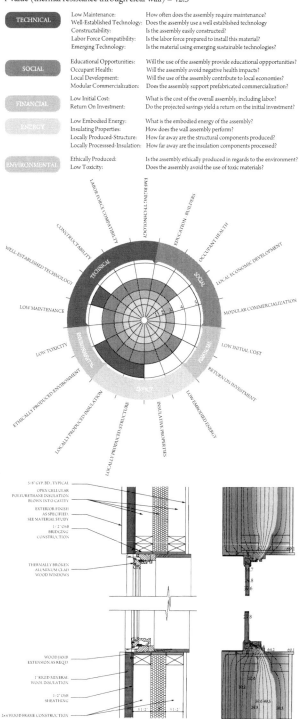

FIGURE 2.6 A sample of ecoMOD DAT used to assess one of several wood wall systems for ecoMOD South, *ecoMOD Decision Analysis Tool*

Source: Michael Britt

simultaneously by the entire team. In the digital form, the tool is called the ecoMOD Decision Analysis Tool, also known as ecoMOD DAT, and it allows the diagrams to be automated.

However, even with the concept of evaluation foregrounded from the very beginning of the project, the incredible complexities of organizing and managing an initiative like ecoMOD have made the assessment work the most challenging aspect of the projects to complete with any degree of rigor. This is largely due to the difficulty of finding legitimate comparisons when evaluating the success of a specific ecoMOD project. Rigorous science and social science depends on meaningful data from other projects for comparison.

Fortunately, the last ecoMOD project in Virginia, dubbed ecoMOD South, involves three homes that are exactly the same from the exterior.[7] Two homes were built to the Passive House Standard, while the third was built to the local building code. One of the Passive House homes is next door to the code-built house in south central/Southside Virginia. The area has a moderate/hot/humid climate. The other Passive House home is located in southwestern Virginia at a much higher elevation with more extreme winters and a solar orientation 170 degrees rotated from the others. This was the first time that we had been able to control some of the variables, and were able to make a much more rigorous assessment of the design of the homes. The project also marked the first time we commercialized one of our designs. The design of the ecoMOD South homes are based on ecoMOD4, the Habitat for Humanity home we completed in Charlottesville that was the subject of the *New York Times* essay. All the newly built ecoMOD homes use offsite construction techniques—mostly modular units built offsite and craned into place. This allows for better quality control and can lead to reduced environmental impact.[8] The ecoMOD South team partnered with modular home manufacturer Cardinal Homes to commercialize the design. Those three are the only ones not built by students.

When the occupants of an ecoMOD housing unit are agreeable, we install monitoring equipment to assess the energy use, thermal comfort, and occasionally indoor air quality. We use that data to adjust systems or help us figure out where we need to do a better job of working with the homeowners or renters in the first few months of their occupation of the home. Twice we have found we needed to train them further on how to maximize their comfort and minimize their energy use. We also try to compare this information with data from similar projects. In addition, we send surveys and/or interview the ecoMOD home occupants to perform post-occupancy evaluations.

We do all this because we want to know what we have done wrong. For example, based on the monitoring of a solar hot water panel on our very first ecoMOD project (a two-unit home), we identified that the system was not working as intended. Unfortunately, we did not have a warranty with the installer. From that situation, we learned that we should always get a warranty for a system, even from a subcontractor that is well known in the community. We found some funding to pay someone else to fix the system.

FIGURE 2.7 Late stage of on-site construction for two of the ecoMOD South homes, one Passive House Standard and one built to code, *ecoMOD South*, South Boston, Virginia, 2013

Source: Trent Bell

FIGURE 2.8 Modules being constructed off-site, *ecoMOD South*, Cardinal Homes facility, Wylliesburg, Virginia, 2013

Source: John Quale

Other than the "operation phase" of the Solar Decathlon competition, I am aware of only one other university design/build program in the country that has any form of an assessment phase. I came up with the term *design / build / evaluate* because I recognized this was an essential educational activity and will help prepare students for the professional world. Even more importantly, it is an ethical responsibility to the occupants of affordable housing. The ecoMOD evaluation phase involves asking hard questions—questions one might not want to know the answers to. We realize every project has some negative outcomes, but rather than hide that, we use it as fodder for educational opportunities.

In addition to learning about the mistakes that we make (both big and small) we have also discovered some positive outcomes. These include:

1) The homeowners/renters come to value good design. Specific design strategies that have been recognized by occupants include thoughtful and efficient floor plans; careful attention to views from important windows; a small detail that makes life a little more convenient; slightly taller ceilings in small homes; etc.
2) Across the board, owners have lower electrical and water bills than other homes in their neighborhoods.
3) Sometimes the students and the clients develop friendships—two groups that would seldom overlap outside this kind of project.

To help focus our design and build phases, we sometimes use guidelines or rating systems. In some ways, this helps simplify the evaluation phase—although we always try to come up with questions that these systems do not consider. We have used the LEED for Homes rating system, a very useful tool for tracking environmental impacts. Three ecoMOD projects have been certified as LEED

FIGURE 2.9 Interior of the main level, *ecoMOD4,* Charlottesville, Virginia, 2010
Source: Sarah Oehl Greene

Platinum. As mentioned previously, we have used the Passive House Standard, which exclusively targets energy used for heating and cooling. We are well aware of their limitations, but having a specific standard gives the team guidance. It is helpful knowing that experts on LEED and Passive House volunteer committees rigorously define what to prioritize.

However, a more recently developed standard has the most direct benefit to community engagement processes appropriate to university design/build projects. The Social Economic Environmental Design (SEED) Evaluator was initially developed as a social equity version of LEED.[9] A team of architects and community designers created it to address the lack of a standard to guide community-based projects for the built environment. So far, ecoMOD has used the SEED process for a group of home rehabs in Charlottesville working with the Albemarle Housing Improvement Program (AHIP). For these *ecoREMOD Block by Block* projects, students collaborated with low-income AHIP clients on home rehabs for two city blocks in order to help stabilize a neighborhood undergoing gentrification due to the adjacency of the university.

The strength of the SEED Evaluator is that it is highly adaptive to a variety of projects. The open-source platform allows the community and the designers working with them to identify primary objectives, and then frame questions and specific methods of assessment so that results will be tailored to the situation. The assessment process is phased. The first phase involves getting feedback from experts on the questions and assessment methods, and when the project is complete, it is expected that teams submit documentation showing the project was successful. We recently started a SEED Evaluation in collaboration with the Greater Albuquerque Habitat for Humanity for our first ecoMOD project in New Mexico. However, it is already clear that we need to revisit the effort before it gets fully underway.

FIGURE 2.10 Interior of a major rehab of a back porch into a weatherized in-home daycare facility, *ecoREMOD Block by Block*, Charlottesville, Virginia, 2013
Source: Dominique Attaway Photography

Conclusion

Architecture of this century should look like it was designed in this century. Building design in cities can and should be diverse—just like its residents. Design that represents a particular style or idiom is not inherently a better example of community engagement. Architecture is constantly evolving, and white middle-class visions of Jeffersonian style homes do not always translate across cultures (or across invisible boundaries in racially divided communities). Since 2004, we have consistently found that our ecoMOD clients want open interior spaces, durable materials, careful daylighting, large closets, low energy bills, and design that reimagines older methods of conceiving of space and composition. Most importantly, the clients love the ecoMOD homes. Inevitably that is what truly motivates students.

Notes

1 National Bureau of Economic Research, "Business Cycle Dating Committee, National Bureau of Economic Research," September 20, 2010, http://www.nber.org/cycles/sept2010.html.

2 Richard Fry and Rakesh Kochhar, "America's Wealth Gap between Middle-Income and Upper-Income Families Is Widest on Record," December 17, 2014, http://www.pewresearch.org/fact-tank/2014/12/17/wealth-gap-upper-middle-income.

3 "Occupy Movement (Occupy Wall Street): Chronology of Coverage," *New York Times*, http://topics.nytimes.com/top/reference/timestopics/organizations/o/occupy_wall_street/index.html.

4 Rich Morin, "Rising Share of Americans See Conflict between Rich and Poor," Pew Research Center, http://www.pewsocialtrends.org/2012/01/11/rising-share-of-americans-see-conflict-between-rich-and-poor.

5 John Quale, *Sustainable, Affordable, Prefab: The ecoMOD Project* (Charlottesville: University of Virginia Press, 2012).

6 Steven Bingler and Martin C. Pedersen, "How to Rebuild Architecture," *New York Times,* December 15, 2014, http://www.nytimes.com/2014/12/16/opinion/how-to-rebuild-architecture.html?_r=2.

7 Gideon Fink Shapiro, "2013 R+D Awards Winner: ecoMOD," *Architect Magazine,* August 2013, 108–111, http://www.architectmagazine.com/awards/r-d-awards/2013-r-d-awards-winner-ecomod_o. Wanda Lau, "The Path to Designing ecoMOD, an Affordable and Energy-Efficient Housing Module," *Architect Magazine* Online, March 27, 2015, http://www.architectmagazine.com/technology/the-path-to-designing-ecomod-an-affordable-and-energy-efficient-housing-module_o.

8 John Quale, Matthew J. Eckelman, Kyle W. Williams, Greg Sloditskie and Julie B. Zimmerman, "Construction Matters: Comparing Environmental Impacts of Building Modular and Conventional Homes in the United States," *Journal of Industrial Ecology*, 16, no. 2 (April 2012): 243–253. John Quale, Matthew J. Eckelman, Kyle W. Williams, Greg Sloditskie and Julie B. Zimmerman, "Two Recent Life Cycle Analysis (LCA) Studies for Buildings: On-Site versus Off-Site Construction and Building Material Reuse," *Green-Build Thought Leadership Proceedings,* U.S. Green Building Council Annual Conference, 2011.

9 The SEED Network, "SEED Evaluator 4.0," http://seednetwork.org/seed-evaluator-4-0.

3
EMBRACING UNCERTAINTY
Community Designbuild

Nils Gore and Shannon Criss

In 1993 Auburn University's Rural Studio brought the idea of students designing and building architecture in the public realm to national attention. Central to this activity was the idea that students would be exposed to many explicit lessons about design and construction and, more importantly, to perhaps less tangible lessons about other ways of being professional architects. Samuel Mockbee invited students of architecture to imagine a different kind of future for themselves and their profession thus: "It is my hope that the experience will help the student of architecture to be more sensitive to the power and promise of what they do, to be more concerned with the good effects of architecture than with 'good intentions.'"[1] Rural Studio, under Mockbee's direction, demonstrated that one can take into account social and community considerations as a way of tempering one's personal design pre-conceptions to make an architecture that reflects its roots in a particular place (ethics), while also still being a reflection of the architect's design impulses (aesthetics). In the stories that follow, we describe moments when the uncertainties of working in communities catalyzed a change in design direction toward a different kind of outcome rather than when we relied exclusively on our own pre-conceptions.

We first met Samuel "Sambo" Mockbee at a social gathering in rural Webster County, Mississippi in 1993, shortly after we relocated there to work at Mississippi State University (MSU). This meeting roughly coincided with the construction of the Bryant House in Mason's Bend, the project that put Rural Studio on the national map. His generous and gregarious manner was a revelation to us after moving to Mississippi directly from the distinctly different world of Cambridge, Massachusetts, where we were privileged to work for a variety of firms, both large and small, sincerely interested in doing good work with a high level of design quality. If we had stayed in Massachusetts, we might still be engaged, as most architects are, in that world of the luxury economy.

But our desire to try something different following graduate school took us south to a new place with a different culture of building and a different social dynamic. The complex social dynamics of race and class, entrenched tradition, and the vernacular do-it-yourself attitude caused us to rethink things we once believed to be true. As educators, inspired by Sambo's willingness to operate outside of traditional architectural pedagogy, we started engaging students with the real world, through community-based projects in Mississippi.

Around the same time (1996), Ernest Boyer and Lee Mitgang published *Building Community: A New Future for Architecture Education and Practice,* promoting the notion that

> schools of architecture should embrace, as their primary objectives, the education of future practitioners trained and dedicated to promoting the value of beauty in our society; the rebirth and preservation of our cities; the need to build for human needs and happiness; and the creation of a healthier, more environmentally sustainable architecture that respects precious resources.[2]

The Boyer report transformed our pedagogy in our work through MSU's Small Town Center, where we developed projects with communities that resulted in their eventual design and construction by students. It was tremendously challenging, rewarding, and fun. Here are some lessons learned while at MSU and later, at the University of Kansas.

Okolona Corner Park, Okolona, Mississippi (1999)

Okolona is a small town of approximately 3,000 people in northeast Mississippi. In the late 1990s the town was suffering from racial discord centered on the public school system. Seeking to do something about it, a bi-racial group of concerned citizens proposed the idea of building a small park straddling the dividing line between the white and black sides of town as a physical symbol of unified community cooperation. Patsy Gregory, the director of the Okolona Chamber of Commerce, was tasked with raising construction funds and coordinating the project with our help. To do the project, we decided to co-teach one large studio of 32 third-year undergraduate students. We began the work by having the students engage in a community-based photography project to understand the context. But an interesting thing happened as students wandered around town with cameras, generating discussion, suspicion, and interest.

Conversations with Okolona residents yielded a much deeper undercurrent of distrust and unrest than was visible on the surface. Race relations were a recurring theme: if the student was white and talking with a white person, the resident might complain about the black folk. If the student was black and talking to a black person, the resident might complain about the white folk. The one Taiwanese student in the class heard racist talk from both sides. These observations were discussed openly in class and began to negatively affect studio morale: "Why are we here?"

asked one student. "These people don't want us here." It was an alarming moment in the studio, and we could see the whole thing start to unravel before our eyes. When we shared this concern with Gregory, she did not seem surprised, and said she would work on it. So a few evenings later, she arranged a community meeting with some genuinely good-hearted people of both races, who acknowledged that their community, like all communities, had some issues that needed fixing, and that is why they were building the park as a gesture of reconciliation. It was amazing to sit across from the students and see the looks on their faces change from frowns to smiles as the evening progressed. This single evening of forthright and deeply personal sharing righted the ship and gave us all renewed enthusiasm to continue the work. It was a crucial moment in the life of the project that taught us the importance of honest speaking and honest listening.[3]

In another telling incident, we built a stage in the park for public performances. Literally five minutes after screwing the last piece of decking down, a pickup truck full of musicians pulled in and started unloading amps and instruments. They set up on the stage and began playing while work continued in the background. One fellow, Daddy I, a professional bluesman, was in town from Minneapolis for the first time in ten years to attend his grandmother's funeral. He found this chance to connect with old friends by playing in the uncompleted park.

Before the evening was over, some of our students had joined them on stage and helped create music for all to work by. It was the emotional high point of the project as we realized that the project might actually do what was intended.

The architecture and detailing of the project was born of its material circumstances, abstracted out of the initial set of context photos with which the students began the project. The wisteria arbor is constructed of #8 rebar, flexed into groin

FIGURE 3.1 Daddy I and friend playing on the newly completed stage, *Okolona Corner Park*, Okolona, Mississippi, 1999

Source: Nils Gore

FIGURE 3.2 Wisteria arbor, *Okolona Corner Park*, Okolona, Mississippi, 1999 (left) and 2015 (right)
Source: Nils Gore

vaults, and detailed in a way that does not depend on extreme precision. Its language of extreme overlaps fits the wild exuberance of the wisteria vines.

The retaining wall is made of ordinary parking bumper curbs, and the benches are made of red cedar 2x4s and concrete blocks. All of the elements are made of ordinary materials inventively and intelligently detailed that somehow evoke the nature of vernacular construction in this small, rural, Southern town.

In 2001 we moved to Lawrence, Kansas to teach at the University of Kansas (KU), a school with a well-established reputation for designbuild work through the pioneering efforts of Dan Rockhill and Studio 804. Since we came to Kansas, we have completed a number of community-based designbuild projects, with lessons learned that are relevant in this context.

The Porch Cultural Heritage Organization, New Orleans, Louisiana (2006–2007)

Like many people, we were riveted by the unfolding disaster in the aftermath of Hurricane Katrina. Shortly afterwards, our faculty agreed that we should participate in the rebuilding effort by engaging our students in ways that could also support their education. During the fall 2005 semester, Nils, in collaboration with our colleague Rob Corser, agreed to offer New Orleans-based studios. Without any real connection to affected people in New Orleans, we relied on what we could anticipate might be the needs of communities and people there. We imagined developing a community center that focused on citizen education about house maintenance and improvement, along with a tool lending library and classes that would help empower neighborhood residents. We started initial fundraising efforts along those lines with the hope of attracting partners in the building materials industry.

Rob Corser and Nils took their first post-Katrina trip to New Orleans in early January 2006 to meet potential community partners. At this time New Orleans was still pretty empty. Much of the city was still without water, gas, telephone, and electric services. Many stores operated on a cash-only basis. The worst-flooded areas of the city were still uninhabited, with small handfuls of people trickling back in. Dan Etheridge, of the Tulane City Center, and Rachel Breunlin, of the Neighborhood Story Project, hosted a dinner at their house with other local folks to help us make plans, and arranged a neighborhood walkabout in the Seventh Ward, which would be our focus area. We shared our ideas about a rebuilding-focused community center, which seemed to the others like a good idea, and we all agreed to proceed with that. We made plans to bring our students down in early February and offered to construct something to bring down with us—as a gift, a token of commitment—when we came back with our students. They suggested that some flat-pack notice boards would be useful, since the communications infrastructure was still largely non-existent.

When we returned, we showed up in the early evening at a church in the Seventh Ward and assembled the first notice board, then went inside for our first engagement meeting with the community. The meeting was facilitated by Rachel Breunlin and Helen Regis, a Seventh Ward resident and anthropology professor at Louisiana State University. They began the meeting by asking everyone to participate in a story circle, where you systematically work around the room and hear everyone's story about why they are there, where they came from, and where they hope the project goes.

It is an exercise based in African American church traditions, which "suggest that life is guided by songs and stories that unfold over generations within the African American culture."[4] The three-hour story circle was a transformative

FIGURE 3.3 Community engagement meeting, *Rebuilding the Seventh Ward*, New Orleans, Louisiana, 2006

Source: Rachel Breunlin

experience for all of us on the design team. People spoke of their relationship to the neighborhood; to the cultural traditions embedded there; and of their hopes, dreams, and fears moving forward. Two persistent themes emerged in this meeting: a focus on youth and children and a focus on cultural arts. It turns out they were not as preoccupied with rebuilding neighborhoods as they were in maintaining and strengthening their local culture as a way of resisting a potentially forthcoming tide of gentrification.[5] A third theme emerged as well, through a challenge from Willie Birch, a Seventh Ward community leader and visual artist, when he asked us to explore the "African roots of Creole architecture" in the things that we would design and build.

After this meeting, it was abundantly clear that our pre-conceptions were not particularly relevant, and our task became one of responding to the community in a gracious and respectful manner; of embracing their wants, needs, and aspirations.

FIGURE 3.4 Clockwise from upper left: Notice Boards, Tool Shed, Outdoor Classroom, and Mobile Stage, *Rebuilding the Seventh Ward*, New Orleans, Louisiana, 2006–2007
Source: Nils Gore

54 Nils Gore and Shannon Criss

This unexpected turn became the inspiration for our task ahead and led to far more meaningful and interesting work than if we had stuck with our original pre-conceptions.

We ended up building six projects in the Seventh Ward: a set of notice boards, a tool shed, two shade structures, a mobile stage, and an outdoor classroom. In all of these projects, promoting community participation and cultural life was a central emphasis in their design, execution, and, most importantly, their use after we left.

Dotte Agency, Kansas City, Kansas (2013–present)

Kansas City is a metropolitan region straddling the state line between Kansas and Missouri. It has two historically primary cities—Kansas City, Missouri (KCMO) and Kansas City, Kansas (KCK)—and a ring of suburban municipalities.

Today, the historic center of KCK is an ethnic stew of white descendants of Eastern European immigrants, African American descendants of transplanted southerners, native descendants of Hispanic immigrants from Mexico and Latin America, recent Hispanic immigrants, and a recent influx of immigrants from Nepal, Burma, and other East Asian countries. Our focus in KCK has to do with the intersection between the built environment and public health, to combat KCK's low rankings on indicators of public health, walkability, and access to healthy food.[6] We began working there on a hunch that our skillsets might be of use in that place when, in 2012, Shannon attended a gathering of academic researchers promoting trans-disciplinary collaboration. She saw a researcher from the KU Work Group for Community Health, Vickie Collie-Akers, present a project in KCK called the Latino Health for All Coalition, funded by the US Centers for Disease Control (CDC). As Collie-Akers presented, Shannon observed that the data driving the research was organized by zip code, rather than some other spatial or social subdivision (geographical, topographical, historic, ethnic), and she speculated that if they organized the data differently, they might be able to draw other understandings from their work. Shannon discussed the idea with Collie-Akers after the session and was invited, along with Nils and Matt Kleinmann, a PhD student, to further explore possible collaborations.

Through the aid of Collie-Akers and others in her work group, we were able to connect with some of the core civic and non-profit leaders that have long been immersed in this community. How we should proceed, as architects, was uncertain. There was no clear *program* given, only stories of experiences, feelings about how to best approach different groups, and general observations about needs and next steps. The best advice, from one of the community organizers, was to *put your boots on the ground and figure this out on your own terms*. By building relationships, showing up and listening, re-presenting what we heard in maps, images, and stories, we slowly gained the respect and interest of some. As we made our work public through events and engaging residents in the process, we found that more opportunities came our way: invitations to co-write grants; to help facilitate directions in alternative transportation and nutrition; to participate in events to share our findings; and to develop a vacant storefront, contributed by Community Housing of Wyandotte County, as a community design hub. We accepted.

We named ourselves Dotte Agency (from Wyan*dotte,* a nickname of the county)—anyone that wanted to serve the Dotte could join us. Since we are merely individual academics and not a sanctioned, funded research center of the university, we would need to secure volunteers, acquire recycled and creative low-cost materials, and barter time to keep the place active. We wanted to integrate ourselves into the community, careful not to be the big institutional element but rather creative partners. We developed a *20 keys* concept—whereby if someone had a compelling idea for how this space could be used, they would be given a key. Our partners are still emerging, but so far we have a partner that runs the Farmers' Market across the street (he opens it to provide a restroom for his customers and vendors); an artist next door wants to exhibit her ceramic lights in the space; the Free Wheels for Kids organization and other bicycle advocates who do not have a home base; and one of our leading community partners uses it regularly. The space displays drawings, models, mockups, and the leftovers of community organizing flyers and past conversations. Each person that uses the space leaves something behind, resulting in a rich compilation of stories and evidence of many simultaneous conversations. The process is unfolding with no clear, definable direction, but through the work, we are discovering what it is. It is about the making, the conversations, the intersections between different Dotte players and a trans-disciplinary set of students and faculty hungry to work outside of the siloes we traditionally dwell in. We believe we are all hungry for something unexpected and possible.

Parks improvement is an obvious place for us to be involved in the KCK landscape. Parks are spatial, they are environmental, and they have physical components.[7] Jersey Creek park is a large, 1.8 mile-long, linear park organized around a concrete-lined storm water drainage ditch installed by the US Army Corps of Engineers in the mid 1970s. Since then no significant investment has been made to maintain or revitalize the park. Today it shows its age; it feels disused. In talking to local residents, many feel unsafe in the park and see no good reason to go there, even though it is close to many residents, connects disparate neighborhoods, and has the potential to offer many recreational opportunities. Working with the coordinators of the Latino Health for All group, Nils's designbuild studio worked to develop physical prototypes of some to-be-determined park element. We discussed typical park elements, like benches, bike racks, and play equipment, as well as things like signs, water fountains, and lighting.

In early 2015 we held a series of community engagement events organized by KCK resident and activist Broderick Crawford in the New Bethel Church, a neighboring congregation. Crawford invited a broad cross-section of people to the meetings, and at each meeting we sat around large aerial photos, inviting people

FIGURE 3.5 Community engagement meeting, *Jersey Creek Fitness Stations*, Kansas City, Kansas, 2015

Source: Nils Gore

to share observations, fears, memories, and local knowledge about the park and its environs. We learned where both problems and opportunities lie, and we started to get a sense of what would make for a better park.

The funding for the park improvements was to come from the CDC through its awards program for Chronic Disease Prevention and Health Promotion.[8] It was necessary to filter what we learned from the residents through the funding criteria of the CDC, which is intended to "prevent obesity, diabetes, heart disease, and stroke and reduce health disparities through community and health system interventions."[9] We determined that we should focus on things that promoted direct physical activity. For instance, a light might make the park safer and promote park use, but is not something which *directly* affects physical activity. A bench, though desirable, is something that the funding rules disallow in favor of elements that promote activity, like a fitness station.

We learned from the neighbors that a small "spray park" (a park with active water play through fountains and misters) was one of the more popular spots, particularly for younger children. It sits next to a baseball field and directly across the street from a senior housing complex. It has the right mix of users and constituencies and seemed like a desirable place to test our prototypical element. But we still did not know exactly what to designbuild. We had a *mind-bending* exercise in the studio where each student was asked to develop a hybrid element that would do more than one thing: seating, messaging, biking, lighting, provide water, promote exercise. Students drew slips of paper out of a hat and were asked to mash them up in a singular design response.

Many, if not most, were unrealistic, because of budget, resources, physics, time, tooling, etc. In the end we developed a fitness station that was a hybrid bench/bike rack/exercise device.

Embracing Uncertainty 57

FIGURE 3.6 *Jersey Creek Fitness Stations*, Kansas City, Kansas, 2015
Source: Erik Stockler

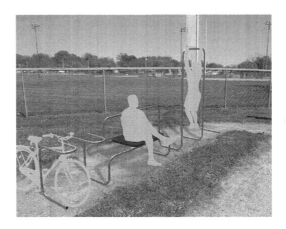

FIGURE 3.7 *Jersey Creek Fitness Stations*, Kansas City, Kansas, 2015
Source: Emily Davidson

The tectonic strategy was to use a continuous pipe that through a series of bends morphed its way from one end of the object to the other. We made a full-scale, proof-of-concept proto-prototype to share with the community, then followed up with a full prototype that was shared, to solicit feedback, at a community health fair organized by Broderick.

Since then, we have developed five variations on that first prototype and have installed them in the park for measured evaluation. If they are deemed successful by the evaluators, a plan to roll out more hybrid fitness stations, in other city parks, may be developed and funded over time.

FIGURE 3.8 Prototype at community health fair, *Jersey Creek Fitness Stations*, Kansas City, Kansas. 2015

Source: Nils Gore

Lessons Learned by Embracing Uncertainty

In each of these stories we have emphasized the start of each project to demonstrate the importance of establishing an open mind-set, as a way of overcoming the tendency to fall for one's own pre-conceptions. The beginning of a project is perhaps the most important place to find a productive alignment with a client/user and one's own skillset. By being open and flexible, one can find the wiggle room to realign for a good fit.

This work calls for a willingness to be *adaptive* to existing circumstances. Typically budgets are extremely limited, resources are tight, and the more willing we are to adapt ourselves to existing circumstances, the higher the likelihood of finding success. One needs to be willing to adaptively reuse materials, spaces, or buildings; adaptively accommodate programming on the fly; or adaptively embrace users that enter mid-stream. Generally citizen participation in these projects is voluntary and a designer must appreciate the motivations that may differ significantly from those of a professional participant in order to respect and dignify that volunteerism. Architects are accustomed to being hired for their expertise, leading them to be dismissive of those who do not share their expertise. But in many cases we do so at the projects' peril. For citizens are experts in their own right; they are experts about their own neighborhood dynamic, about their own habits and customs, about their own likes and dislikes. We need to cultivate the intelligence of citizen experts in our work.

Embracing Uncertainty 59

FIGURE 3.9 Community engagement at the Bethany Park Parade, Kansas City, Kansas, 2013
Source: Nils Gore

FIGURE 3.10 Barker neighborhood walkability event, *KU Mobile Collaboratory*, Lawrence, Kansas, 2014
Source: Nils Gore

We have developed tools for collaboration that may differ from those of conventional practice in order to secure full community participation and engagement and to collect quality intelligence from citizen experts. We go to community events with things that attract attention and invite participation:

- a tent at a parade where we hand out popsicles and create fun activities for children so that we can have a few moments with the parents;
- a shiny, renovated airstream trailer called the KU Mobile Collaboratory (moCOLAB) to attract interest and participation through exhibits and workshops;
- a mobile map cart that can be pushed around a neighborhood to aid in soliciting information from passersby;
- a mobile display system that can be deployed for information sharing in community meetings, churches, and outdoor events in conjunction with the moCOLAB.

The book *Spatial Agency: Other Ways of Doing Architecture* has encouraged us to believe that what we do and how we do it might be a needed educational experience for our students and a good service to our community partners and users. In that book, the authors state:

> Architectural Culture—expressed through reviews, awards and publications—tends to prioritise aspects associated with the static properties of objects: the visual, the technical, and the atemporal. Hence the dominance of aesthetics, style, form and technique in the usual discussion of architecture, and with this the suppression of the more volatile aspects of buildings: the processes of their production, their occupation, their temporality, and their relations to society and nature. The definition of architecture in terms of object-buildings thus excludes just those aspects of world that cause architects discomfort, because those often unpredictable and contingent aspects are those over which they have limited power. . . . [A] loss of control is seen not as a threat to professional credibility, but as an inevitable condition that must be worked with in a positive light. Buildings and spaces are treated as part of a dynamic context of networks. The standard tools of aesthetics and making are insufficient to negotiate these networks on their own.[10]

In our work we seek to draw from an expanded toolkit to deal with the contingencies of the world and strive to share these with our students and our users. The uncertainty that comes with that is something that we truly embrace in the work, and believe is an important lesson for students to draw from in these experiential learning projects. The designbuild aspect of the work further brings home the lessons learned in materially tangible ways as the built elements speak for themselves, and exist, in time, as physical evidence of the relationship between process and product.

Notes

1 Samuel Mockbee, "The Rural Studio," On Being. http://www.onbeing.org/program/architecture-decency/feature/rural-studio/1584

2 Ernest L. Boyer and Lee D. Mitgang, *Building Community: A New Future for Architecture Education and Practice* (Stanford, CA: Carnegie Foundation for the Advancement of Teaching, 1996), 27.
3 For a good explanation of the value of communities working through conflict publicly, see Richard Sennett, *The Uses of Disorder: Personal Identity and City Life* (New York: WW Norton & Company, 1992).
4 LaTasha K. Williams-Clay, Cirecie A. West-Olatunji, and Susan R. Cooley, "Keeping the Story Alive: Narrative in the African-American Church and Community," paper presented at the Annual meeting of the American Counseling Association, San Antonio, Texas, 2001.
5 Rachel Breunlin and Helen A. Regis, "Can There Be a Critical Collaborative Ethnography?: Creativity and Activism in the Seventh Ward, New Orleans," *Collaborative Anthropologies* 2, no. 1 (2009): 123.
6 *Community Dashboard | Kansas City Area Health Data | KCHealthMatters. kchealthmatters.org*, http://kchealthmatters.org/community-dashboard; Renee E. Walker, Christopher R. Kean, and Jessica G. Burke, "Disparities and Access to Healthy Food in the United States: A Review of Food Deserts Literature," *Health & Place* 16, no. 5 (2010): 876–884; Samina Raja, Ma Changxing, Pavan Yadav. "Beyond Food Deserts: Measuring and Mapping Racial Disparities in Neighborhood Food Environments," *Journal of Planning Education and Research* 27, no. 4 (2008): 469–482; *Agricultural Marketing Service— Creating Access to Healthy, Affordable Food*, http://apps.ams.usda.gov/fooddeserts/food deserts.aspx; *Sidewalk and Trail Master Plan for Unified Government/Kansas City, Kansas,* July 26, 2012; Latetia V. Moore, MSPH, and Ana V. Diez Roux, "Associations of Neighborhood Characteristics with the Location and Type of Food Stores," *Am J Public Health* 96, no. 2 (2006): 325–331.
7 See "Kansas City, Kan., Groups Work to Revive Deserted Jersey Creek Trail," *Kansas City Star*, http://www.kansascity.com/news/local/article29908723.html
8 "CDC Announces FY 2014 Funding Awards for Chronic Disease Prevention and Health Promotion," Centers for Disease Control and Prevention, http://www.cdc.gov/chronicdisease/about/foa/2014foa/index.htm
9 Ibid.
10 Nishat Awan, Tatjana Schneider, and Jeremy Till, *Spatial Agency: Other Ways of Doing Architecture* (New York: Routledge, 2013), 27–28.

4

EACH ONE TEACH ONE

Nested Associations in Designbuild Education

Larry Bowne

Introduction

In the antebellum South, a prescriptive saying urged a slave who had mastered a skill or trade to educate comrades and kin who lacked the same opportunity: "Each one teach one." When slaveholders denied Americans of African origin the gifts of literacy, divorced them from their heritage, and deprived them of their humanity, some resisted or were assisted; they became shepherds and stewards of literacy. More than merely describing a debt to be paid, the phrase resonates with a simple truth: each of us has knowledge; each of us can share it with others.

"Each one teach one" is a requisite component of the social capital developed and deployed in the contemporary university. In its egalitarian acknowledgement that we all give to and gain from each other, the aphorism embodies empathy, tolerance, and striving for self-improvement. Moreover, it describes aptly the learning dynamic in designbuild education. Given that so many divergent skills are required to imagine, visualize, document, and fabricate even the most modest building, students invested in public interest design, community engagement, and social practice must be willing to train each other in the skills needed to realize the work. How many nineteen-year-olds, for instance, can nimbly operate both an arc welder and Critical Path software?

In exploring how we assemble the expertise and experience required in order to prevail in designbuild education, I rely on a trio of authors who examine the role of team building, community, and social capital in the United States; further, I argue that designbuild is a unique instance of associationalism (the tendency to construct community around shared, even urgent, need). I look at the ways we house smaller communities within larger ones, rather like nested Russian *matryoshka* dolls of confederacy and alliance. Moreover, these nested associations help guide the tectonic direction and development of a project. Sometimes our collective collaborations are organized deliberately and sometimes *ad hoc*, but in all cases,

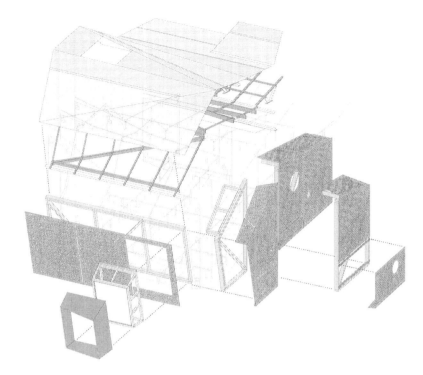

FIGURE 4.1 *Play Perch*, Syracuse, New York, 2013
Source: Larry Bowne

the communities formed by students and faculty are themselves a construction: we craft first a team, and then the characteristics of that team serve to determine form-making, material selection, constructional sequences, and detailing.

This essay recounts three projects, realized at two different universities both within and outside established curricular framework; together, they span a period of five years. In all three, I summarize the completed work, explicate the course structure and project organization we assembled to realize the work, and assess their formal, constructional, and tectonic realization in the studio and the field as outward manifestations of our nested associations.

Part I: Have We Built a Paradise in Hell? Catastrophe and Joy in Designbuild Education

> "The desires and possibilities awakened [in the aftermath of a disaster] are so powerful they shine even from wreckage, carnage, and ashes. What happens here is relevant elsewhere. And the point is not to welcome disasters. They do not create these gifts, but they are one avenue through which the gifts arrive. Disasters provide an extraordinary window into social desire and possibility, and what manifests there matters elsewhere, in ordinary times and in other extraordinary times."[1]
>
> —Rebecca Solnit, *A Paradise Built in Hell*

Greensburg Cubed (Greensburg, KS)

Kansas State University College of Architecture, Planning and Design
Fall 2007, Spring 2008, and Summer 2008

On May 4, 2007, a two-mile-wide F5 tornado destroyed ninety-five percent of Greensburg, Kansas, leaving two-thirds of the town's 1,500 inhabitants homeless. Though many thought the town would be finished, the townspeople opted to rebuild their locale using forward-thinking materials and construction methods.

Greensburg Cubed was undertaken as a temporary exhibition and installation by fifth-year architecture students enrolled in a professional degree program at Kansas

FIGURE 4.2 *Greensburg Cubed, The Quad*, Greensburg, Kansas, 2008
Source: Larry Bowne

State University in Manhattan, Kansas; an engineering undergraduate supplemented the team. *Greensburg Cubed* consisted of four 10'x10'x10' pavilions, sited in a garden linked by pathways lined with interpretative texts. The pavilions formed a mini-campus, *The Quad*, featuring environmentally sound technologies, including solar and wind power; solar water heaters; and recycled, salvaged, and reclaimed materials.

The project is an institutional response to the devastation wrought by disaster. Kansas State University has a long-standing agricultural extension office in town, and the College of Architecture, Planning and Design was called upon early to assist in its restoration and reconstruction, becoming one of what Rebecca Solnit describes as "the constellations of solidarity, altruism, and improvisation" that arise amidst a crisis.[2]

Solnit parses the origin of some words related to disaster:

> The word emergency comes from *emerge*, to rise out of, the opposite of merge, which comes from *mergere*, to be within or under a liquid, immersed, submerged. An emergency is a separation from the familiar, a sudden emergence into a new atmosphere, one that often demands we ourselves rise to the occasion. *Catastrophe* comes from the Greek *kata*, or down, and *streiphen*, or turning over. It means an upset of what is expected.[3]

We can understand not just *Greensburg Cube* but designbuild education itself in these terms: a separation from the familiar, a sudden emergence into a new atmosphere, an upset of what is expected. Designbuild and community engagement challenge the normative format of the architecture studio, in which "problem statements" prioritize abstract conjecture and ideation (or, worse, mere computational gesticulations) over location, performance, habitability, constructability, even gravity. In essence, designbuild education, particularly on a project like this one that aims to showcase systems that might prove useful in rebuilding a devastated town, demands that students exceed their prior understanding of their own potential. To do so, they must learn to share information, barter skills, and generate knowledge.

The organization of the *Greensburg Cubed* studio fostered this uncoupling from routine modes of learning and doing. In 2007/2008, I co-taught a fifth-year studio with colleague Todd Gabbard, tasked with completing Kansas State's inaugural entry into the Solar Decathlon competition, *Project Solar House*. In our year-long designbuild studio, *Greensburg Cubed* immediately followed the Solar Decathlon, which was initiated by Prof Gabbard and scheduled to be staged that fall on the Mall in Washington, D.C. Before the end of the Fall 2007 semester, faculty and students clarified project scope, identified potential funding sources, and initiated community collaborations.

Aspiring to pair project needs with students' skills and interests, we undertook interviews and portfolio reviews in order to establish interrelated job descriptions

66 Larry Bowne

for each of the fourteen students. These "administrative roles" assigned responsibilities for fundraising, budgeting, bookkeeping, file management, public relations, site management, and more. By harnessing students' inherent biases and predilections, these duties activated the technical expertise developed during the Solar Decathlon, particularly regarding solar and wind power, water collection and retention, and environmental stewardship.

Greensburg Cubed students elected to design and fabricate temporary demonstration pavilions, to be installed in town on the first anniversary of the catastrophe in May 2008. After winnowing down concepts and proposals, the group selected four viable modules: *The Greenhaus*, *The Ice Cube*, *The Watering Can*, and *The Recycling Bin*. As we proceeded, the studio was organized into design and fabrication teams for each cube, with the students' administrative roles spanning across these intense islands of activity. Each pavilion became increasingly distinct, as the skill sets of the three or four studio participants merged with the interests of townsfolk.

Designers had to consider numerous constraints: prior to *Project Solar House*, Kansas State University had no solid tradition of successful designbuild projects. Community engagement had no sustained place in the curriculum, but instead followed faculty whim or will. The woodshop lacked digital equipment and offered little more than a few table and band saws; there was no metal shop. We had nowhere to store materials, accept deliveries, or fabricate components. Perhaps most challenging, Greensburg is some 220 miles from campus. Whatever we built, we would need to first assemble it in a nearby warehouse, and then transport it overland to town. Nearly completed pavilions were therefore designed either to sit on the bed of a truck or, alternately, around purpose-built steel trailers which we could hitch to a pickup truck. We could allow only minimal site work.

The Greenhaus exemplified and exhibited innovative building materials that residents might deploy in the reconstruction of single-family homes. An austere, house-like form was alleviated externally by leaf-shaped photovoltaic panels and internally by vitrines displaying insulating materials as well as a pair of water storage tanks that fit between studs. The pavilion was designed and realized by students with the most field experience, with fabrication skills guiding details: consistent 3/8" reveals run between materials, planes, and volumes. Panels are flush, with little tolerance for error. The entire volume is comprised of two halves, transported separately, that latch together on site. Throughout, the level of fit and finish is exemplary.

The Ice Cube was a solar-powered drinking water and misting station, intended to serve public needs for fresh water, whether for immediate disaster relief, for community reconstruction, or within ongoing efforts to provide drinking water in public parks and gardens.

While this team perhaps lacked the shop expertise of their *Greenhaus* peers, they astutely deployed their *Project Solar House* experience and recruited professional

FIGURE 4.3 *Greensburg Cubed, The Ice Cube,* Greensburg, Kansas, 2008
Source: Larry Bowne

consultants and fabricators who could assist them in realizing a pavilion that channeled rainwater below solar panels to a filtration system that would supply a water fountain and mister.

The Watering Can was a low-maintenance, low-impact restroom, showcasing efficient water use.

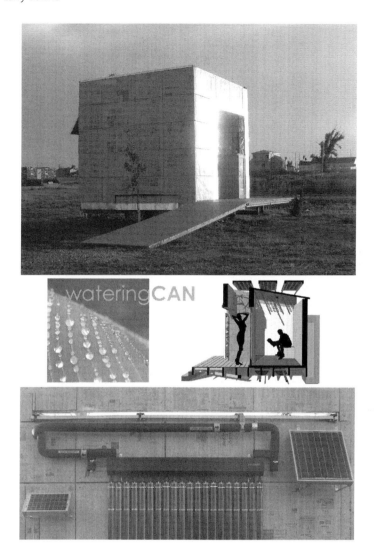

FIGURE 4.4 *Greensburg Cubed, The Watering Can,* Greensburg, Kansas, 2008
Source: Larry Bowne

It featured novel technologies such as a small cistern, a composting toilet, and evacuated-tube solar water heaters, a system the team first tested in the Solar Decathlon. The cladding is simple: students wrapped construction-grade cementitious panels with press plates from a local newspaper, whose two sides were alternately screen-printed or highly reflective. The combination of sophisticated systems and uncomplicated assembly allowed recent graduates, who had just completed their studies, to work with a new group of mostly second- and third-year students.

One of the new recruits was an experienced welder, who fabricated a bespoke steel chassis on which we mounted a deck and accessibility ramp. That steelwork proved essential when the hitch on the pickup truck failed during transport: the cantilevered chassis acted as a sort of rudder, preventing the gyrating structure from toppling over on the highway.

The Recycling Bin was a mobile shelter and ramp constructed over an out-sourced, shop-built steel undercarriage. Deploying dimensional wood framing and reclaimed cladding, *The Recycling Bin* was designed with high school students from "Green Club" in mind, as they would first participate in its construction and then use it as the central facility for Kiowa County's recycling efforts. This mobile cube had storage bins for glass, plastic, aluminum cans, and newsprint, each one graphically identified by suspended panels. The straightforward design included components (such as end-grain wood blocks for flooring) that had to be laboriously, even tediously, assembled and installed by hand. The high school students cooperated earnestly with their college-aged mentors, patiently sanding and inlaying small wood chunks onto the ramp, or carefully placing bottle caps into signage.

Solnit offers insight into the resourcefulness and resiliency of students engaged in this disaster-relief project. She writes of her own "intensely absorbing present" following the Loma Prieta earthquake of 1989, and speaks more broadly to "that sense of immersion in the moment and solidarity with others caused by the rupture in everyday life, an emotion graver than happiness but deeply positive."[4] She speculates whether "*enjoyment* is the right word" for emotions revealed after a disaster, in which "the wonderful comes wrapped in the terrible, joy in sorrow, courage in fear."[5]

The point here is not to equate the experiences of undergraduates to disaster victims, nor even to conflate the empathy and effort of volunteers to the heroic work of first responders to a tragedy. Rather, I wish to echo Solnit's assertion that disaster affords the opportunity to construct new social relations amidst the abeyance of normalcy and to find the resources to care for each other. Designbuild education offers a venue for what she calls "social desire and possibility," which we can manifest in times both ordinary and extraordinary.

Solnit suggests that when caregivers and aid-workers approach disaster sites, they

> demonstrate that the citizens any paradise would need—the people who are brave enough, resourceful enough, and generous enough—already exist. The possibility of paradise hovers on the cusp of coming into being, so much so that it takes powerful forces to keep such a paradise at bay. If paradise now arises in hell, it's because in the suspension of the usual . . . we are free to live and act another way.[6]

Compared with their peers in conventional architectural studios, designbuild students participate in just such a suspension of the usual; they are indeed free to live and act another way. What they build depends on it.

Part II: Are We Still Bowling Alone? Were We Ever? Bonding and Bridging in Designbuild Education

> [T]he core idea of social capital theory is that social networks have value. Just as a screwdriver (physical capital) or a college education (human capital) can increase productivity (both individual and collective), so too social contacts affect the productivity of individuals and groups.
>
> Whereas physical capital refers to physical objects and human capital refers to properties of individuals, social capital refers to connections among individuals—social networks and the norms of reciprocity and trustworthiness that arise from them.[7]
>
> —Robert D. Putnam, *Bowling Alone: The Collapse and Revival of American Community*

Park Studio (Syracuse, NY)
Syracuse University School of Architecture
Fall 2014

We turn now from catastrophe to crisis. *Park Studio* dealt not with natural calamity but with the social costs and consequences of poverty and despair, in particular the reimagining and restitution of a desultory field house in a public park in one of the most challenged neighborhoods in a depressed town. In the Spring 2014 semester, Syracuse University Professor Sinéad Mac Namara and I set up *Park Studio*, a collaborative design group between her seminar and my studio; the team received

FIGURE 4.5 *Park Studio, The Berg,* Syracuse, New York, 2014
Source: Larry Bowne

guidance and initial funding from Marc Norman, then director at UPSTATE: A Center for Design, Research and Real Estate. *Park Studio* approximated professional practice, pursuing a project that was supported by both the University and the City of Syracuse Department of Parks and Recreation.

In *Bowling Alone*, Robert Putnam discursively identifies a collapse of trustworthiness and reciprocity as Americans regress from civic association to individualistic anomie. He charts our social and communitarian divestment, which he asserts begins about 1965, citing our lax participation in politics, civics, and religion; our disconnections at work and at home; and our aversion to philanthropy and volunteering. In assessing social capital in the public realm, Putnam distinguishes between *bridging* and *bonding*: "[s]ome forms of social capital are, by choice or necessity, inward looking and tend to reinforce exclusive identities and homogeneous groups. . . . Other networks are outward looking and encompass people across diverse social cleavages."[8]

Uniquely, *Park Studio* fostered both bonding (or inclusive) and bridging (exclusive) social capital. Within the studio, bonding occurred around the same sort of organizational structure that characterized *Greensburg Cubed*: design students assumed administrative duties, including project management, fabrication, and marketing and public relations; seminar students surveyed facilities, prepared site documentation, and analyzed structural integrity. Bridging characterized the group's intensive relationships with community collaborators, as representatives from both classes formed outreach teams to work with civic users of the park, particularly schools and senior citizens. These teams could convey public concerns to the design team and respond with student interests and proposals.

Stakeholders in Syracuse's Near Westside helped to shape the project's programming, as students came to understand the neighborhood's desire to improve Skiddy Park by enhancing safety, security, durability, site-wide cross-programming, and aesthetic experiences, while also fostering environmental sustainability. *Park Studio* strove to treat their designs as exemplars for improvements throughout the parks system by creating environmentally responsive additions that incorporate public uses in keeping with twenty-first century needs and priorities. When the field house was first built, league athletics and organized group events were popular; we know from Putnam's *Bowling Alone* (and our own experience) that *ad hoc* cycling and pick-up basketball games are more apt these days to draw both participants and spectators.

The programming derived from this community outreach guided the students' design and detailing. Students enhanced the field house by opening up walls and roof to create *The Berg*, a universally accessible public classroom, meeting room, and community center. The proposal fills the interior with daylight and acts as an evening beacon, improving site lines from and through the space. A purpose-built storage and gathering pavilion, *The Little Berg*, when completed, will house the community cycling program and provide outdoor seating. For *The Little Berg*, students designed modular, abutting 8'x8'x8' cubes, clad in panels addressing siting, orientation, and formal aspirations.

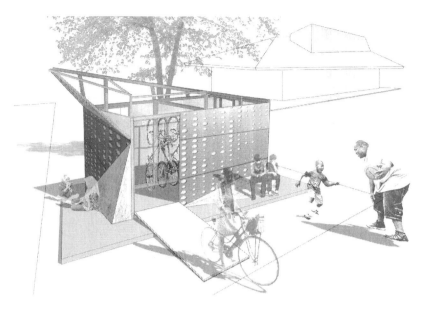

FIGURE 4.6 *Park Studio, The Little Berg,* Syracuse, New York, 2014
Source: Larry Bowne

Park Studio community engagement did not include the construction of habitable space, but instead produced artifacts from which to build (i.e., drawings, specifications, and prototypes at full scale). Discussions with the Parks Department Division of Skilled Trades, who would ultimately fabricate steel armatures and interior wall panels, influenced the detailing. Building geometries and constructional systems were uncomplicated and accessible, easing the burden on tradespersons working on city payroll. Students, however, possessed the computational expertise required to further articulate these simple systems: they designed exterior panels of layered translucent and opaque materials, as well as interior sheets of wooden laminates, that could be milled by local shops. Deliverables included a Construction Drawings set graphically depicting proposed construction (including the electronic files that would guide fabrication equipment); a Project Manual specifying materials, hardware, fittings, and the like; and large-format tectonic models and full-scale mock-ups of components to be realized by the Parks Department in the actual construction of the design.

Despite some difficulties (arising from clashes both of personality and professional perspective), the internal and external camaraderie of the designers and their community partners evinces a hopeful observation Robert Putnam made in 2000: "Against this bleak picture of social isolation and civic disengagement among recent generations must be set one important countervailing fact: Without any doubt the last ten years have seen a substantial *increase* in volunteering and community service by young people."[9]

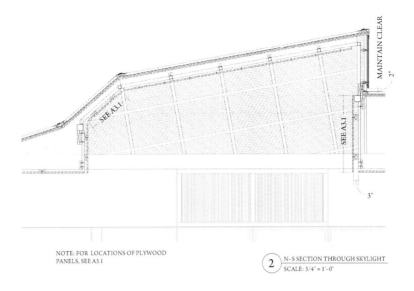

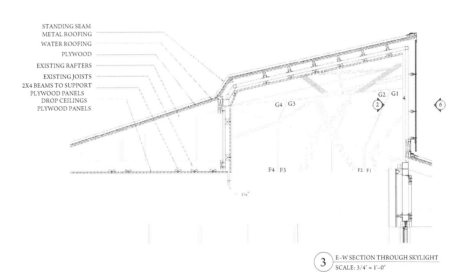

FIGURE 4.7 Construction section, *Park Studio, The Berg,* Syracuse, New York, 2014
Source: Larry Bowne

In the bonding and bridging of their nested associations, *The Berg* and *The Little Berg* proffer a renewed community engagement and bode well for civic relations, at least at the local level. Putnam provides plenty of evidence for the salubrious impacts of these efforts; in his chapter on "Democracy," he argues that "associations and less formal networks of civic engagement instill in their members habits

74 Larry Bowne

of cooperation and public-spiritedness, . . . [becoming] 'schools for democracy.' Members learn how to run meetings, speak in public, write letters, organize projects, and debate public issues with civility."[10]

As they realize their tectonic ambitions in community engagement projects, students involved in designbuild education learn valuable lessons in running meetings, speaking in public, organizing projects, and the like. In doing so, these students are not just designing within schools of architecture; they are building schools for democracy.

Part III: Are We Sending Missionaries to the Antipodes? Renewing Feelings and Ideas in Designbuild Education

> Americans of all ages, all conditions, and all minds are constantly joining together in groups. . . . Americans associate to give fêtes, to found seminaries, to build inns, to erect churches, to distribute books, and to send missionaries to the antipodes. This is how they create hospitals, prisons, and schools. If, finally, they wish to publicize a truth or foster a sentiment with the help of a great example, they associate.[11]
>
> —Alexis de Tocqueville, *Democracy in America*

Play Perch (Syracuse, NY)
Syracuse University School of Architecture
Fall 2012, Spring 2013

Writing in 1835, the French scholar Alexis de Tocqueville observed and analyzed the nascent United States. Saliently, he discerned the tendency of Americans to form associations, which is certainly among the most prescient of his observations (especially for those of us interested in fostering community engagement and developing social capital). *Play Perch*, a tree house and outdoor classroom for children who cannot climb trees, exemplifies this tendency at multiple moments in its trajectory from concept to construction.

Like many National Architectural Accrediting Boards (NAAB)-accredited programs, the School of Architecture at Syracuse University has a student chapter of American Institute of Architecture Students (AIAS) Freedom By Design, founded at Syracuse in 2010 by a group of students committed to activism and agency. Students shortly thereafter executed several capital improvement projects on private property, using work for clients with limited means to advance design intelligence, experiment formally, and innovate tectonically. *Play Perch* marked a significant shift towards student-involved institutional collaboration and architecture in the public realm, one that expresses civic, philanthropic, and curricular imperatives.

Play Perch began as an extracurricular undertaking for Jowonio School, a Syracuse institution for preschoolers that serves a population of special- and traditional-needs students. Though student volunteers had planned to realize the project as they had their earlier ramps (designing on evenings and weekends, building over academic breaks), budget and program compelled faculty to offer the equivalent of a studio as a three-credit-hour professional elective. The students on the

FIGURE 4.8 *Play Perch*, Syracuse, New York, 2013
Source: Susannah Sayler

team majored in architecture, industrial design, and sculpture; collectively, this group dedicated to serving the needs of the underserved instantiated Tocqueville's narrative:

> Suppose a person conceives of an idea for a project that has a direct bearing on the welfare of society. . . . [In America], he will publicize his plan, offer to carry it out, enlist other individuals to pool their forces with his own, and struggle with all his might to overcome every obstacle.[12]

Tocqueville could have been writing about the genesis of *Play Perch*; indeed he could have been writing about designbuild projects in general, which often have just this "direct bearing on the welfare of society." Revising the job descriptions from *Greensburg Cubed*, *Play Perch* students crafted their own individual project responsibilities. Here, however, students also formed clusters based on mutually overlapping tasks and duties, creating teams dedicated to Marketing and Public Relations, Project Management, and Fabrication and Construction. This tripartite organization dovetails with Tocqueville's list: the need to publicize the plan (i.e., marketing); carry it out (administration); and struggle to overcome obstacles (fabrication). Additionally, the three groups each selected a representative to a fourth, entrusted with developing the design. This project organization gave equal voice to students representing publicity, possibility, and practicality. Together, they vetted every formal proposition, critiqued every spatial exploration, and scrutinized every tectonic decision.

The marketing group designed a public relations and promotional campaign: they named the project, gave it a graphic identity, produced a short film that they distributed through social media, and launched a crowd-sourced fundraising effort. The administrative group set up informational sessions with campus experts in design for the disabled, brought together student designers and educational therapists, and engendered support with school and university officials. The fabrication team sourced products, fabricators, and suppliers who worked to optimize the building of *Play Perch*. The realization of the project deployed off-campus local artisans, on-campus modular panelization in the wood and metal shops, and on-site construction. Taking advantage of the deep knowledge of building and making in a rather depressed Rust Belt city, students specified laser-cut self-weathering steel sheeting, baked-on ceramic coatings for metal fittings, and digitally driven water-jet ceiling panels. A neighborhood artisan, who works with the city arborist, supplied the black locust timber framing, which is naturally weather- and termite-resistant. When a licensed welder joined the team, students

FIGURE 4.9 *Play Perch*, Syracuse, New York, 2013
Source: Susannah Sayler

began to incorporate bespoke steel fittings, including splines at the foundations and chamfered beams at the ceiling.

Play Perch embodies both the pragmatic and ethical values of association. From therapists at the school, students learned to incorporate enveloping spaces that encourage encounters with natural phenomena. Walls consist of timber frames with perforated weathering steel panels patterned after bird feathers; larger apertures are oriented towards views. The roof gutter cantilevers considerably so that children can observe water running off and falling on a splash rock below. Polycarbonate ceiling panels form an oculus around the tree so children might peer up into the branches. The large copper-clad cantilevered window, the beak, is a shatter-resistant acrylic sheet that tilts out to maximize the children's view. A custom climbing net stretches across the opening between the floor and the tree, both above and below the platform. In the interior, furniture invites children to crawl into cradle-like spaces lined with high-density, eco-friendly plastic panels inscribed with animal prints.

Play Perch students crafted more than just a building: they established unique and abiding relations with each other, their faculty advisors, and their young clients. They constructed a scenario that was, for all involved, not merely edifying but deeply satisfying emotionally. Whether with university administrators, Jowonio teachers, or regional suppliers, students constructed internal and external networks that echo Tocqueville's claims about community: "Feelings and ideas are renewed, the heart expands, and the human spirit develops only through the reciprocal action of human beings on one another."[13]

FIGURE 4.10 *Play Perch*, Syracuse, New York, 2013
Source: Larry Bowne

78 Larry Bowne

Play Perch, however, is not unique in this regard. We saw similar ties emerging in *Park Studio* and *Greensburg Cubed*. Broadly, these three projects demonstrate that we can critically locate designbuild education within the broader architectural curriculum; the project itself within a diverse gathering of students, makers, end-users, and stakeholders; the production team within a larger network of suppliers and fabricators; and its delivery or fabrication as an embodiment of the ethical mission of the university. All three projects encouraged students to deviate from normative ways of working and studying. Broadly, designbuild courses engender the social desire and possibility that Solnit argues is one of the gifts of disaster relief. For designbuild education to realize its potential, however, students working in this realm must develop the norms of reciprocity and trustworthiness that Putnam finds remiss in post-1965 America. Most significantly, these students might begin to see their work in terms of their audience: they can impact the social culture of not only architectural education, but also of the design professions more broadly. In that regard, they will evince Tocqueville's claim that associations publicize a truth or foster a sentiment: we all have something to teach, and we all have something to learn. We all have things to give, and we all have things to gain.

Notes

1 Rebecca Solnit, *A Paradise Built in Hell: The Extraordinary Communities that Arise in Disaster* (New York: Penguin Books, 2009), 6.
2 Ibid., 10.
3 Ibid., 10.
4 Ibid., 5.
5 Ibid., 5.
6 Ibid., 7.
7 Robert D. Putnam, *Bowling Alone: The Collapse and Revival of American Community* (New York: Simon & Schuster, 2000), 18–19.
8 Ibid., 22.
9 Ibid., 265.
10 Ibid., 338–339.
11 Alexis de Tocqueville, *Democracy in America*, trans by Arthur Goldhammer (New York: The Library of America, 2004), 595.
12 Ibid., 107.
13 Ibid., 598.

PART 2

Poetics

Experience and the Human Condition

5

THE GOOD OF DOING POETICS, THE POETICS OF DOING GOOD

Coleman Coker

Gulf Coast DesignLab, a field-based program at the University of Texas at Austin, merges *theoria* and *praxis* to act as one. Critically guided, this fusion tests a student's theoretical design investigations by building what they design. Gulf Coast Design-Lab is not focused on the product of the built work itself but rather on the *process* in such a way as to bring the students closer to the world. Designing through a field-based approach like this allows the designer to "feel" the dimensionality of their work through tangibly occupying the livingness of their design as they immerse themselves in its materiality and context. Testing their designs in this way, students experience the veracity of gravity firsthand, they find relationship with the elemental—earth, air, fire, water—and they find the fullness of *poiesis* only imagined otherwise through two-dimensional computer screens and scaled models.

Gulf Coast DesignLab asks students to develop *poiesis* through social engagement by working closely with those for whom their work is intended. Equally, they are also asked to develop a deep sense of the ecology of the place in which their work will become a part. This is taught through the applied research workshop (studio) and an associated investigative laboratory (seminar). In most schools of design the studio is supreme, but there is rarely the time needed in studio for extended reflective thought necessary for poetic design. In many ways the Gulf Coast DesignLab seminar / studio relationship is inverted in that the thinking that goes on in seminar is meant to drive the design approach of the studio so that time for reflection is provided. This underscores the process of designing / making as a means to "see" just a little deeper, nurturing a more profound relationship through which students recognize their work as one tiny part of a much greater whole. What better way for designers of palpable and substantial things—buildings, landscapes, cities—to hone their craft?

The work that students do is centered on environmental education and on understanding the dynamic changes taking place in our world today. An excellent

FIGURE 5.1 UTSOA students studying early sand dune development on the Gulf of Mexico Coastline, Port Aransas, Texas, 2014

Source: Barron Peper

laboratory for this is found on coastal edges. Here, dynamic change—sea-level rise, warming ocean temperatures, increased population, agricultural runoff, overharvesting of the ocean—is magnified and brought to bear on coastal communities that are most impacted by this environmental change. Rather than reducing this to statistical facts and figures in the way this is often framed, students are asked to try and reveal what is otherwise not seen by getting close to the place where they will design and build. Calculation and engineering will not solve all of today's issues. It will also require reflective thinking and poetic making if we—and all other beings we share the planet with—are to thrive. This is the foundation of Gulf Coast DesignLab where students come to develop a deeper relationship with their world and through that, develop their potential of poetic thinking and doing.

Yet making something poetic in this world that increasingly reduces everything to image for instrumental use can be a challenging and elusive end. One "knows" *poiesis* when one experiences it, but there are no formulas by which it is achieved. In the best of circumstances, the slippery slope of poetics is fraught with dead-end trails, jagged boulders, and precarious abysses. To use the words *poetics* and design side by side in some academic circles is even tantamount to labeling oneself as a starry-eyed daydreamer, one who longs for that never-having-existed gentler past.

And that is for good reason. As an antidote to the sterility of late modernism in the mid-twentieth century, much of the *poiesis* promoted at that time was based on naïve historicism—reconstituted romanticism—rendered picturesque by non-critical thinkers. The pursuit of poetics seemed little more than teasing out the pictorial.

However, if we might rescue poetics from the trash bin of irrelevant contemporary pedagogical method for a while and redirect its inherent potential, poetics might not only be resuscitated, but also reenergized. We can do this by thinking back to the ancient Greek verb *poiein,* which meant "making," from where we get our word *poiesis*. For the Greeks *poiesis* did not veer off into some imaginary realm, taking flight from the reality of their harsh world. Instead, making—*poiesis*—offered its own kind of *self-showing*. More than mere craft and certainly more than aesthetics or high fashion, making transformed the world. *Poiesis* brought forth. *Poiesis* renewed and revealed something about the already-here world. In other words, *poiesis* was—and *is*—the unfolding of a thing out of itself. From this perspective, we do not create anything. Instead, we *rearrange* the world. If we set aside our hubris for a moment and see ourselves as a part of this world that is integral in how it shapes itself, we might begin to realize just how we cultivate and reshape that which is already here into likenesses we recognize as humanmade. We do not make the world happen, we do not create it. Instead, through expressing what is already here, that which is otherwise unseen unfolds in its own self-showing.

This is its potential, anyway. But in our modern world, making—*poiein*—has taken a turn toward *techne,* where invention and originality are now caught up in production, in a way meant to produce all that is. This sort of making has little place for self-reflection and the poetic. For here in this drive for the novel,

FIGURE 5.2 UTSOA students on a boat trip to the early eighteenth-century Spanish settlement of El Copano to study shellcrete construction that was comprised primarily of oyster shells, Copano Bay, Texas, 2014

Source: Coleman Coker

nothing is revealed except production itself. For those who choose to reflect a little more on this modern dilemma, *poiesis* offers a counter to this by allowing a more thoughtful sense of what it means to be in the world. To understand its potential, Gulf Coast DesignLab students are challenged to reveal that which is already present but not otherwise seen in what they design and build, so that they experience a deeper relationship with their world. Not just for themselves, though, but through engendering that in their work, so that those who will use what they have designed find a similar relationship, one that opens them onto the beauty and integrity of their world just a little more.

Doing this becomes an *ethical* endeavor for the students. The question asked each semester in our investigative seminar is *just what is the ethical dimension in the gift that poetics offers? And how might it be brought out from under the long shadow of form-driven aesthetics and into a social / ecological realm of giving?* Through their reflective thinking and designbuild explorations, students might better see the potential in making transformative and inspiring places for others. So, if the poetic brings to light that which is already there but not otherwise seen, then *poiesis* offers others a better sense of being in harmony with their world. In other words, poetic works have the potential to reconcile another with their world. Reconciliation means that a work has the potential to restore one to their world, to bring them closer to it, and to allow them to exist in greater harmony with that world. Bringing that other person—who the student's gift of poetic making is intended for—closer to the world, to experience its fullness, to be more fully awakened to it in ways they might not have experienced otherwise, is by most everyone considered a good thing. And since goodness towards others is the goal of the ethical, then doing *poiesis* is doing the ethical. To achieve that through the students' designbuild work, considering the good of others—the individual, the community, and the

FIGURE 5.3 UTSOA students framing the pavilion roof on the Marine Science Institute campus, *Dune Ecology Pavilion at Marine Science Institute*, Port Aransas, Texas, 2014
Source: Coleman Coker

FIGURE 5.4 UTSOA students constructing the northwest screen wall, *Dune Ecology Pavilion at Marine Science Institute*, Port Aransas, Texas, 2014
Source: Coleman Coker

environment of which they are a part—is an ethical undertaking. So, if the work of the students is to be poetic, it somehow must bring others closer to their world. In this, doing *poiesis* is doing good.

So, this relationship between the poetic and the ethical is critical to understanding how we are to be in the world. *Poiesis* requires a deep mindfulness of this interdependence with all that is. All that is the world, connected and intertwined, all the earth and everything in it—any act of making, any act of bringing something new into the world, no matter how small or grand—impacts everything else in some way. Only through understanding this with their hearts can students then build responsibly. Today, as we become ever more aware of the fragility of our home—earth—one has no business building otherwise. This is the deepest sort of ethical responsibility where building poetically means more than just offering aesthetic experience. Another, perhaps more familiar, word to describe this is *beauty*—uncovering the beautiful through discerning a kind of truth about our relationship of being in the world. Poetic beauty opens us anew to something about how we might be on the earth, in greater harmony with it, and in this better express our humanness—our humanity. Seeing their relationship with others like this is a particular way for the student to live in the world reflectively, with eyes wide open, with care and compassion—with a full heart.

Each semester four means—four *vehicles*—are presented to students through which the poetic might be rendered. These are: *materiality, context, temporality,* and *geoality*. Each is tied to the physicality of the world in elemental ways; each springs from the sustenance of the earth just as the acorn grows to become the majestic oak. Or seen in the light of architectural design, when a building, landscape, or any work of artifice is made, it too in a real way arises from the elemental earth.

This is literal, in the fact that first of all buildings are *tangible* things. Designbuild students of course experience this physical embodiment in a real way when they strain their muscles to the limit raising a beam or run their hands across a cool concrete surface they just made. As students doing designbuild, they work with the hard, heavy, tangible things that go into making buildings what they are. They feel the weight of a brick as they are mortaring it into place; they smell the cedar plank that has just been cut; they hear their footfall on a loose granite walkway and taste the sweat from their brow as they build. The work of their hands and minds inform them about this physical world in genuine ways. By designing through the

FIGURE 5.5 UTSOA students applying preformed metal sheathing, *Dune Ecology Pavilion at Marine Science Institute*, Port Aransas, Texas, 2014
Source: Coleman Coker

real this way, they begin to intuit that every made thing around them is in one way or another made from the elemental earth. This leads to a deeper understanding of what they are doing as designers as they reshape the earth into chairs, rooms, buildings, and cities. The best poetic works articulate this—the earth's substantiality, its solid bearing, its bluntness and integrity, so that the whole is greater than the sum of its parts.

For one of the vehicles for Gulf Coast DesignLab, I coined the word *geoality*. That word might help describe this relationship with the elemental further. "Geo" comes from the ancient Greek goddess *Ge*—later *Gaia*—meaning earth. It can be found in words such as geology, geography, and geomorphology. Add to that the suffix "ality," which refers to the property of something, and you have geoality— that which is of the earth, or, that which is earth. A poetic designer works with this degree of connectedness to the earth and thinks about their design as literally rising out of the ground on which it would sit. But they also give thought to how our relationship with the earth has radically changed since the time *Gaia* was revered as the great mother of all. In our two million plus years of evolution, we have spent most of our time developing as a species driven to overcome nature. What it gave us seemed limitless—inexhaustible. More of late, though, we have become so efficient at reaping this harvest that nature now hardly seems an obstacle at all. Just recently we have come to understand that earth's gifts have reached their limits. Our modern way of living has over-burdened earth's bounty. We gamble in this high-stakes, loser-takes-nothing game pushing us toward a greatly diminished world in which we all lose. We will not politicize our way out of this by continuing to ignore the impact we are having. And we will not succeed through ever more sophisticated technology.

FIGURE 5.6 UTSOA students constructing a bird blind viewing area for middle and high school students who frequently visit the Wetland Education Center, *Bird Blind at the National Estuarine Research Reserve Wetland Education Center*, Port Aransas, Texas, 2013

Source: Coleman Coker

FIGURE 5.7 UTSOA students constructing a bird blind using recycled oilfield drill pipe, which will be used as a teaching tool for students visiting the Wetland Education Center, *Bird Blind at the National Estuarine Research Reserve Wetland Education Center*, Port Aransas, Texas, 2013

Source: Coleman Coker

Yet, in spite of our disembodied thinking, we are beginning to once again understand that it takes the distinctiveness of the discerning hand (and its body) to find relationship with the world. Students thinking about the poetic within this framework discover that they need not only their vision, but their touch, smell, hearing, and taste—their mouths, hands, nose, and ears—if they are to make poetically. If we take our current predicament to heart, embrace what is at stake, and poetically reflect on what is already here but otherwise unseen, a response will then arise that resists the mere instrumentality we have grown so accustomed to. For any sort of lasting response that embraces the whole will take not only our cunning as technological beings, it will need our reflection in how we might live in the world poetically. Affirming its beauty, its wonder, and the whole, we need only remember that the relationships we build—every condition we shape, whether light, shadow, texture, sound—are in some way re-formed from a combination of the elemental earth.

Geoality finds its foundation in the elemental—*earth, air, fire,* and *water*. As long as humans have existed, we have evolved with and through the mystery that earth, air, fire, and water offer. In fact, *we are these elements*. The awe, fascination, and power that fire once held still lies deep within our evolutionary makeup. The very structure of our jaws was reshaped once we learned to eat meat by cooking over a fire. Each time we breathe in, our bodies are filled with and partly become air. Our bodies are mostly made of water so we are never far from that essential element, which makes up the oceans—our primordial womb. What we eat—the daily sustenance that fuels us—comes from the earth. And when we die we return to the bosom of this earth. Earth, air, fire, and water are at the core of geoality because the elemental fourfold is deep in our collective imagination and being. And every other physical thing that we daily use and design with is encompassed by the very same elements. Wood, stone, concrete, steel, aluminum, and glass all are of the elements. By seeing our relationship as designers to the world through the elemental we have the opportunity to express this deep connection through what we make. Students have an opportunity to sense the richness that is this elemental earth—the elements at their most raw being what a poetic design answers to. Sheltering us from the rain, temperature extremes, the harsh sun and so forth, these fourfold elements come together in thoughtfully designed works in ways which can bring us closer to the world. All we need to do is reframe our relationship with the elemental a bit, to see and shape it as revealing that which is already here. In doing so we may again become reenchanted by it, so that a poetic work might open onto the mystery of being, bringing it into presence, giving it shape and form.

Thinking about the elemental in this way, instead of imagining form as the driver of design, encourages students to envision for a moment that the *materiality* of the design itself determines the building's expression. Earth, air, fire, and water themselves inform the designer's decisions in shaping space into place, instead of being at the beck and call of the unbridled will of the designer. The elemental grounds us and shows us *how* buildings, in order for them to be, overcome gravity, how they endure wind and rain, how they celebrate the people who use them.

FIGURE 5.8 Detail showing oyster shell gabion wall and bench, *Goose Island State Park*, Lamar Peninsula, Texas, 2014

Source: Luke Stevenson

As an example, the elemental earth shaped by fire and expressed as steel provides us with material we call beams, columns, and trusses, and these afford extraordinary breadth for enclosure and form. The poetic can be found when looking at the materiality of steel as not mere steel, but as earth reshaped by fire. Concrete offers beauty, strength, stability, and pliability of form, but it can also be seen as the elemental when recalled as earth (sand, limestone) and water reformed through air and fire. A similar beauty is offered by glass, made from earth (sand), air, and fire, and rendered in such a way that remembers this relationship. Through these materials, today's buildings are given their form. But only through recalling the elemental of the materials that make up built works can *poiesis* be expressed. This can be thought of as the elements *structuring* form. So, seeing the relationship of the elemental to form in a slightly different light, one in which the elemental provides this expression, this is another way of celebrating the materiality of a poetic work.

From this grounding of structuring form comes a realization that buildings are necessarily of a specific place, of a particular *context*. *Genius loci,* the ancient Romans used to call it. For them it was the spirit of place, protecting its inhabitants with its own particular sort of character, distinctive and caring in an animate way.

FIGURE 5.9 Nature Interpretative Center showing oyster gabion wall, seating, and fire circle for Texas Parks and Wildlife Division, *Goose Island State Park*, Lamar Peninsula, Texas, 2014

Source: Thomas Johnston

Contextuality, seen through the lens of the elemental, builds on this very relationship for a work's locale, its place. For a building to be poetic through its context, it necessarily expresses its locale in straightforward ways. Grounding the work in locally recognized material, expressing the local quality of light, acknowledging the place's weather conditions, using materials that offer relationship to the place they come from, recognizing and respecting its ecological limits, all point toward developing a poetics based on context. *Poiesis* built around the elemental seeks out this familiarity through teaching us how to be at home in the world.

An elemental way of bringing earth, air, fire, and water to the forefront in the design ensures that a built work expresses *temporal* quality. A poetic building genuinely expresses change over time through the rusting of a steel surface, handprints left on a corner at the hallway's turn, rain runoff that stains a concrete surface, the curl and soft silvering of cedar shakes, the patina of an oak floor caused by generations of people walking on it. Temporality shows us the beauty of the material unfolding in ever-new ways as it responds to its environment. How these—materiality, contextuality, and temporality—are expressed is the heart of *poiesis*. And all are folded within the embrace of geoality. Connecting with the elemental this way brings a built work into rhythm with the world, embracing all things that

FIGURE 5.10 Nature Interpretative Center at night with fire, for Texas Parks and Wildlife Division, *Goose Island State Park*, Lamar Peninsula, Texas, 2014

Source: Luke Stevenson

are earth. Through this we might begin to recognize that we do not so much build a relationship with a building as it builds a relationship with us.

Through the elemental, geo-centricity affords design students a different way to see their relationship to their world, a way to become better citizens of the earth—better earthlings. Asking them to think about geo-centricity this way and then designing with the elemental in mind, they can reflect on their work as building relationships, rather than making objects. Through an enlivened theory-based discourse that approaches poetics by growing out of geo-centricity, Gulf Coast DesignLab students might begin to see their role on the earth reframed through reflection. As poetic designers and makers, this sort of reflection becomes vital if they are to become better equipped at finding relationship with all that is. And through that unfolding, students may expand the much-needed, life-affirming conditions that help cultivate a beneficial environment where all can prosper. In taking this to heart, something otherwise unimagined comes forward and reveals itself through its own self-showing. From this viewpoint, the highest sort of poetry that might be had in design today is the kind that refocuses the young designer's perspective, so that they begin to see their relationship of being in the world made whole through embracing its interrelatedness, through taking to heart its elemental beauty. As reshapers of the world in this way, applying this relationship is what the good of doing poetics is for, what the poetics of doing good is for.

6

ARCHITECTURE INTO PRESENCE

Chad Kraus

Deep Marks

Viscerally and experientially, architecture makes its deepest marks on people. Yet, in the architectural design studio—the unique, insatiable incubator of ideas—students are predominantly educated to design buildings cerebrally and analytically. On paper or in a digital environment, indistinct concepts grow into detailed, clearly formed designs without ever needing to engage the experiential dimension. Students exercise their knowledge and skills in the creation of primarily hypothetical works of architecture for hypothetical clients and a hypothetical public. Necessity requires that educators bracket out certain aspects of their students' future professional lives, such as economic value-based decision-making, a myriad of real-world concerns, and, perhaps most damning, a phenomenological understanding of the consequences of their design decisions.

Designbuild programs, on the other hand, provide opportunities for educators to shift the brackets to include these additional aspects of the discipline, such as directly engaged collaboration with communities, clients, and consultants; cost estimating, budgeting, and construction costs; product and material research and testing; detailing, craftsmanship, and fabrication processes; and the means and methods of construction—issues that are understandably excluded or marginalized in the conventional design studio. Even design principles, caught in the overlap of these two purposefully misaligned brackets, are given a new perspective.

The emergence of designbuild programs throughout North America should be understood as a clarion call; a call to fill the vacuum left by the absence of integrated tectonic experiences in the young lives of the millennial generation. The dissolution of haptic experiences has come, in part, due to our increasingly technological society. These real experiences, largely unmediated by a digital environment, are very attractive to aspiring architects. In the words of a former student,

94 Chad Kraus

"[designbuild education] puts the architect in a position to discover opportunities—leading to innovations—which are otherwise obscured by the fractured nature of today's design and construction environment. . . . This gives students a much more rounded background and, to my knowledge, cannot be taught in any other way."[1] Consequently, designbuild studios and hands-on course offerings have expanded rapidly to address this demand.

While these developments are propitious, many designbuild offerings are only available to a small percentage of students as electives or options. According to one study, only 14% of the designbuild programs surveyed were tied to the required professional curriculum.[2] At the University of Kansas, where I teach, designbuild education dates back more than twenty years with the formation of Studio 804. Widely considered one of the preeminent designbuild programs in the county, Studio 804 is limited to approximately twenty graduate students each year. In 2006, the architecture faculty at the University of Kansas, having witnessed the transformative potential of Studio 804, reiterated the school's commitment to hands-on education when it transformed Arch 509 into a one-semester, third-year, undergraduate designbuild studio situated at the heart of the required core curriculum of the accredited professional degree program. The requisite nature of the studio reflects a belief that the intertwining of the action *design* and the action *build* in the context of architecture is 1) greater than the sum of its parts and 2) essential to the education of the twenty-first century architect. Students tend to agree: "Designbuild should be required in all universities in the same way that basic structures courses are."[3]

Beyond pragmatic professional concerns, designbuild education has the potential to make explicit the work of architecture as an act of "making present" or presencing—that is, to paraphrase Martin Heidegger, the work of architecture actualizes its particular place and circumstance.[4] Through architecture, spatiotemporal place *comes to presence*. Humankind experiences a locale as a *place*—with specific characteristics and qualities—by virtue of the intervention that has brought humankind into relationship with the place. Through designbuild experiences, the *act* of making architecture, not just the resultant architecture, invites the student into a more sustained encounter with its presencing. The thickened immediacy of the act privileges the opportunities and constraints of real materials, budgets, schedules, and people over simulation or projection. The real-time experience of phenomena during on-site reflections and throughout the process of making reshapes and redirects the original design, creating a potent feedback loop that is not possible in the conventional conceive-execute model.

The Phenomenological Dimensions of Designbuild

Designbuild pedagogy is not philosophically innocent, that is, it is not simply another method of delivering the same basic content. The Dirt Works Studio, my particular variant of the KU Studio 509, tends to eschew formalist concerns in favor of a heightened sensitivity to the cultural and natural forces latent to the specific conditions of the project. Through direct engagement with place, community partners, materials (such as rammed earth and reclaimed timber), and a theory-laden tectonics, students find themselves in a confrontation with a material reality. The shield of the hypothetical is no longer a refuge. Early prototyping, testing, and mockups often lead to discoveries about the materials' characteristics, which in turn create a feedback loop in the design process.

Form is almost always incidental, a resultant of other intentions and discoveries. The studio, as a collective, continually seeks to impart to the projects an air of inevitability. John Dewey expresses this idea in *Art as Experience* when he writes, "Form is arrived at whenever a stable, even though moving, equilibrium is reached. . . . Order is not imposed from without but is made out of the relations of harmonious interactions that energies bear to one another."[5] In *Architecture's Desire*, K. Michael Hays expresses this idea with a sense of urgency: "Architecture's imperative is to grasp something absent, to trace or demarcate a condition that is there only latently."[6] Fumihiko Maki is most succinct when he writes, "Architectural creation is not invention but discovery."[7]

Design principles are often, in potential and raw form, already present within the complex and disparate forces coming to bear on a project. In the creation of meaningful places, geographer Edward Relph advises designers to "adopt the gentle and patient manner of an environmental midwife, while rejecting utterly

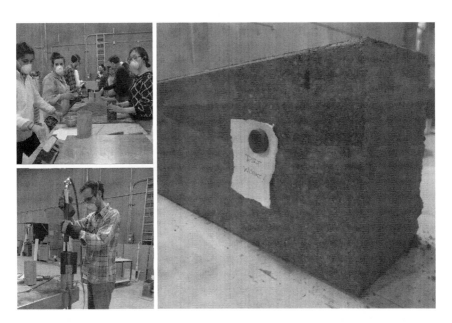

FIGURE 6.1 Students researched and built a successful mockup of iron-stabilized rammed earth, resulting in the first known magnetic rammed earth wall, *Ferrimagnetic Rammed Earth Research and Prototyping*, Lawrence, Kansas, 2015

Source: Chad Kraus

96 Chad Kraus

the machine-driven arrogance of some environmental equivalent to a genetic engineer."[8] Similarly, architect Bjarke Ingels astutely draws parallels between the architect and the midwife in identifying the former's responsibility to assist society in delivering or making manifest works of architecture that concretize culturally significant aspects of the world.[9]

While this architectural imperative does not necessitate a designbuild pedagogy, this experiential learning model opens up the potential for design intentions to be brought into a visceral presence—that is an intentionality-laden existence— through building. Yet, here we have merely scratched the surface. Chiastically, designbuild activities equally offer the potential for builderly intentions to be brought into presence through design, that is to say the fact of the work having been made in a particular way is rendered explicit through design decisions. Making leaves its marks.

The Dutch psychiatrist J. H. van den Berg, in his book *Things: Four Metabletic Reflections*, divided reality into two fundamental structures—the first (subjective) and the second (objective).[10] The second structure of reality, which is given through measurement and analysis, includes all that we do not naturally perceive yet that organizes our world. It consists of absolute dimensions and absolute time. It is the numbers and the chemicals, the underlying mathematical and biological structures of all things. Since the Enlightenment, this has become the dominant and nearly exclusive structure of the world that we understand to be real and true. Our positivistic modern mentalities have all but forgotten or marginalized the first structure, the structure of reality given in experience. This first structure includes all that we perceive: contingent dimensions, contingent time, contingent color and texture. Christian Norberg-Schulz observes that "everything else, such as atoms and molecules, numbers, and all kinds of 'data', are abstractions or tools which are constructed to serve other purposes than those of everyday life. Today it is common to mistake the tools for reality."[11]

For van den Berg, both structures are critical in understanding reality; however, he insists on placing the subjective structure on equal terms with the objective. Van den Berg observed that the human condition cannot be removed or isolated from the first structure, else it ceases to belong to this first structure at all. Therefore, within the first structure nothing is absolute, constant, or stable: distance is relative, colors are relative, time is relative. Phenomena are relative to the experience of the subject, and the central structure of experience is intentionality, that is, we direct ourselves toward the world in order to perceive it. Sandra Rosenthal and Patrick Bourgeois state this in another way: "perceptual objects are 'theory laden' in the sense that they are constituted via the meanings through which man perceives his world and which he has brought to his world."[12] This way of thinking about design shapes the philosophical approach of the Dirt Works Studio. We understand our work to be a series of experiential events bound to situation.

The heightened subjectivity guiding the studio, however, is not doomed to lead to pure relativity. As Edmund Husserl wrote, "all subjectivity is intersubjectivity."[13] Through our pre-reflective subconscious bodies, certain primal readings of the world emerge. According to Gianni Vattimo, "every act of knowledge is nothing other than an articulation or an interpretation of this preliminary familiarity with the world."[14] The quality of a work of architecture is not something strictly attributed to it, as is often implied by the phrase *beauty is in the eye of the beholder*. The work itself is responsible for opening up and allowing it to appear in a particular way. "Variation in interpretation," writes Vattimo, "depends on the richness of the 'object' to which it is applied and not just on the mutable subjectivity of interpreters."[15] It is no coincidence, then, that the Dirt Works Studio tends to concentrate on basic gestalt relationships.

In building consensus among a dozen or more aspiring designers, I frequently make use of a structured, yet necessarily messy, democratic process to advance the design from broad strokes to the resolution of design principles at the intimate scale of the detail. During this process I am acutely aware of the risk of recreating Frankenstein's monster—a compromised vision pieced together with disparate fragments. By redirecting my students' usual focus on form making to experiential/gestalt qualities, we are better able to avoid this fate. I recall during one design session discussing at length the respective merits of a series of inline rammed earth masses versus two parallel groups of rammed earth masses—what we referred to, in shorthand, as the one-wall and two-wall schemes. The basic lines of discourse revolved around directionality versus centrality, expansion versus enclosure, and boundary versus threshold. The resulting design resolution subtly infused qualities relating to both schemes, for example, maintaining a strong sense of directionality overall while, through a slight misalignment of the one-wall scheme, creating a thickened center.

FIGURE 6.2 A rammed earth trailhead with a charred timber sunshade cantilevering over a tallgrass prairie, *Roth Trailhead*, Lawrence, Kansas, 2012

Source: David Versteeg

Although designbuild education provides students with the opportunity to make things in the world, it occurs to me that it is not the thing (architecture as a product) itself that is of primary value. Rather, it is the *encounter* with the work of architecture that matters most. The true potential of architecture lies somewhere between the consciousness of the person experiencing it and the physical work itself. The architectural encounter is arguably understood most viscerally though designbuild activities, which anticipate future encounters *while the design is still mutable*.

Prairie Earth

Over the course of three springs, three groups of architecture students designed and built a series of architectural interventions in the ecotone landscape of the University of Kansas Field Station in northeastern Kansas. These interventions—a trailhead, a gateway, and a pavilion, collectively *Prairie Earth*—were constructed primarily of reclaimed timber and rammed earth. Each of the structures takes its form from essential characteristics of the place. Each was conceived of and built over the course of approximately fourteen weeks. Each group of students was responsible, from conception to fruition, for one of the three interventions. The second and third interventions built upon the work that came before, resulting in a dialogue between projects across space and time.

Visitors to the Field Station approach along a typical gravel county road. Negotiating a few bends in the road, they see a tallgrass prairie open to the west, framed

FIGURE 6.3 A 122-foot long punctuated rammed earth wall registers the gentle topography of the landscape, *Roth Trailhead*, Lawrence, Kansas, 2012
Source: David Versteeg

by dense woods to the north and east. The Roth Trailhead emerges from a dense thicket and cuts across the prairie terrain. The trailhead is composed of a punctuated rammed earth wall proportioned on the Fibonacci sequence, a meandering path guiding visitors toward the wooded hillside through a subtle shift in the wall, and a sun-shading canopy hovering above the horizon.

The trailhead's defining element is its 122-foot long, two-foot thick punctuated rammed earth wall extending perpendicularly from the slope of the hillside. The presence of the wall registers the land's gentle topography.

It makes explicit the relationship between ground and horizon while the canopy extends the woodland shadows and modulates the presence of the sky. The canopy's charred louvers evoke the annual burning of the surrounding tallgrass prairie while the choreographed stratification of the rammed earth wall echoes geological forces.

Winding further north through the sloping prairie terrain, visitors pass through a gateway at the entrance to the Field Station headquarters.

The Field Station Gateway frames and is drawn from the surrounding environment. This place is characterized by transition—an intersection between county road and tree-lined entry drive as well as an edge mediating between the western prairie and the eastern woodlands. A rammed earth mass transitions from the prairie with an emphasis on the ground and horizon to a sense of verticality as it

FIGURE 6.4 A rammed earth gateway capped by a thin timber plane greets visitors to the Field Station headquarters, *Field Station Gateway*, Lawrence, Kansas, 2013
Source: Matthew Benfer

FIGURE 6.5 A broad rammed earth mass emerges from the grasslands and transitions to a vertical wall foregrounded by a tree-lined drive, *Field Station Gateway*, Lawrence, Kansas, 2013

Source: Matthew Benfer

FIGURE 6.6 A series of rammed earth walls reinforcing the new entry sequence leads to a timber sunshade canopy, *Armitage Pavilion*, Lawrence, Kansas, 2014

Source: Matt Kleinmann

is foregrounded by a tree-lined drive and demarcates the threshold into the headquarters complex.

Coming to rest just above the top of the rammed earth mass is a charred timber plane, once again evoking prairie fire.

After passing through the gateway and tree-lined drive, the visitor sees a hint of the final intervention of *Prairie Earth* nestling behind a small demonstration prairie. This third set of rammed earth walls guides visitors along the renewed primary-entry axis into the headquarters building.

The pavilion, framing the Kenneth and Katie Armitage Education Center, is a multipurpose gathering space eloquently synthesizing the disparate latent forces and forms present on the site. The once overheated and underused western-facing patio in a neglected corner of the main building has been transformed into a welcoming entry sequence and a cool, shady place to gather. Students again used the familiar and evocative palette of rammed earth and reclaimed timber to reconstruct and reimagine the entry, which includes a canopy and a screen that shield the exterior space from both the intense prairie sun and the erratic winds that blow across the site.

While the overall rectilinear plan geometry of the canopy reinforces the off-axis orientation of the headquarters building, a series of five rammed earth walls emerge from the edge of the prairie and reinforce the primary north-south entry

FIGURE 6.7 A timber sunshade canopy cantilevers over an existing patio while rammed earth walls create a simultaneous sense of refuge and prospect, *Armitage Pavilion*, Lawrence, Kansas, 2014

Source: Matt Kleinmann

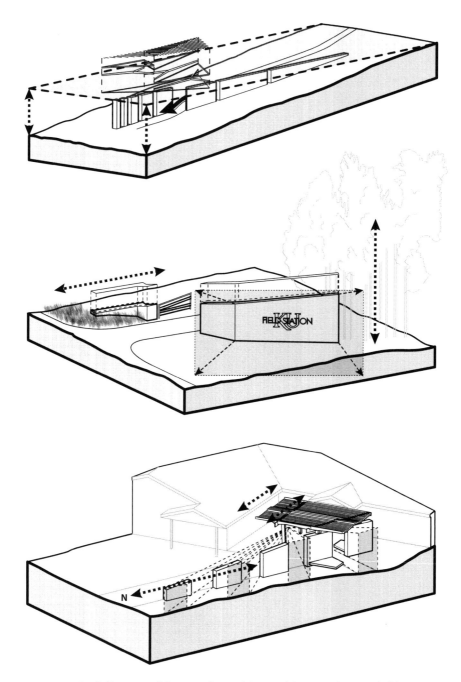

FIGURE 6.8 Parti diagrams of three modest architectural interventions nestled into an ecotone landscape of eastern Kansas, *Prairie Earth*, Lawrence, Kansas, 2012–2014
Source: Chad Kraus

axis, thus acknowledging and bringing into coherence the existing conflicting geometries. These five walls frame selected views of the landscape. A ribbon of red earth darts and threads playfully across its masses. Two raised timber platforms fan out from the rammed earth beneath a timber sun-shading canopy; one fanning out to the eastern interior side to formally serve as a speaking platform during outdoor teaching events and informally as seating, the other fanning out to the western exterior side to serve as a perch to enjoy the surrounding natural environment. A double cantilever of timber slats held in equilibrium using tensile steel cables spans over the existing patio and provides ample shade. The canopy slats undulate in height and angle in deference to the rippling surface of the adjacent tallgrass prairie.

There is nothing radical about the architectural interventions of the Field Station. Neither the interventions nor the forms originate from complex ideas. The work simply draws from and in turn reinforces fundamental phenomena of the natural world—the ground, the sky, the horizon, light, shadow, wind, earth, and fire, what John Keats called *ethereal things*.[16] These works of architecture, as interventions in a natural landscape, serve to gather people and nature together, meaningfully.

FIGURE 6.9 A comparison between an early conceptual rendering of a stone surround, a photograph of students attempting to plug-and-feather a stone into blocks, and the resulting solution using a "floating" timber cap

Source: Chad Kraus

Salutary Failure and Other Opportunities

In architectural details, as Marco Frascari observed, we find an intimate relationship between the construction of a work of architecture and the construing of its significance—the real and the perceived, the necessary and the articulated.[17] In the designbuild studio, students begin to understand the relationship between the two. Through a type of corporeal osmosis, students learn to extend their construing beyond broad-stroked napkin sketches.

A lesson that I love to observe students learning is that materials can be ornery and that awareness of appropriate tolerance is absolutely critical. My students are generally not experienced craftspeople and consequently errors are not uncommon. While this can certainly be a liability, there is virtue in imperfect craft. We humans acknowledge—through mistakes, discrepancies, and accidents—that something has been made. Whether in the awkward mortar joints that preserve the whole brick in Sigurd Lewerentz's St. Mark's and St. Peter's churches or Le Corbusier's desire to immortalize the passage, "Here has passed the hand of man" beneath a mistake made during the construction of the monastery of Sainte-Marie de la Tourette, errors and evidence of craft make our architecture as vulnerable and as relatable as we are.[18] We empathize with these *works*. We feel the presence of the maker's hand. There is a raw beauty in the unpredictable imperfections of a rammed earth wall freshly stripped of its forms. We each hold our breath as the form is pulled away, eagerly awaiting the manifestation of countless hours of working the earth, layer by layer. When we create something tangible in the world, something stirs in us. We come closer to the kind of truth that philosopher Giambattista Vico describes as *verum-factum*.[19] Vico understood that we can only know as truth that which we have made.

Students expand their knowledge and begin to build a durable confidence. A former student observed, "Designbuild offers many things to the student. However, the most important thing it can offer is confidence in one's ability to design."[20] Through these designbuild experiences, students become active, creative agents who shape and structure the experience of others and in the process, begin to understand what it means to have *an experience*.[21]

The synthesis of designer and builder allows the designbuilder to adapt and evolve according to whatever may arise during construction. The design is understood as provisional and contingent; the designer is provided the opportunity to hesitate and to fail and to recover from failure. The designer becomes truly opportunistic. Failure, in this sense, becomes productive, not merely because it imparts the difficult but unforgettable lesson, but because, in the misalignment with what the mind conceived and what the hand produced, in that sliver that we call failure, something unexpected and delightful can bloom. Sociologist Richard Sennett refers to this type of failure as *salutary failure*.[22]

During the construction of the gateway, the studio had planned to plug-and-feather local limestone boulders into ashlar blocks to serve as a cap and edge banding to protect the rammed earth mass. Trial after trial resulted in a series of disheartening failures, as veins in the stone invited the breaks to follow unexpected paths. This setback reignited an earlier debate about the best course of action for the capping element over the rammed earth wall. The stone solution had been chosen partly due to budgetary constraints (the stone was dredged from a nearby pond and thus free); however, with this less expensive option seemingly off the table, the studio quickly turned to earlier solutions. With our best-laid plans thwarted, the studio designed, on the fly, a charred timber cap that would hover two inches above the rammed earth mass, supported by a series of stainless steel threaded rods made possible by a last-minute clutch donation. The virtue of the alternate design was that it unbound the rammed earth mass, as the studio had originally intended, and reintroduced a woodland presence.

The ultimate value of salutary failure in the designbuild studio is that it provides *the necessary resistance against default decisions*.

Similarly, resistance and constraints are understood to be empowering. This understanding is beautifully articulated in the axiom attributed to Leonardo da Vinci, "Art lives from constraints and dies from freedom." Stated another way, through the heat of friction fire is born. As with salutary failure, constraints reveal unexpected and, occasionally, superior solutions to seemingly intractable problems. In the case of the pavilion, the studio was given a pre-existing patio, over which we were tasked with providing shade while leaving ample space for gathering. Over the course of several weeks, the design evolved to be a simple-span canopy

FIGURE 6.10 A comparison between an early design sketch, a later study model, students presenting a prototype, and the resulting rhythmic shadow play
Source: Chad Kraus

106 Chad Kraus

supported by a rammed earth wall on the west and a series of column supports near the headquarters building to the east. This scheme risked disrupting the natural circulation through the patio and potentially compromising the amount of gathering space beneath the canopy. To address these concerns, the column supports were reduced to two and shifted west to reinforce the main entry axis and provide unobstructed gathering space on the patio. In order to provide sufficient shading, the canopy was redesigned to cantilever beyond the column supports. This resulted in a canopy design that would be comprised of long timbers with a simple span in the center bay to serve as the necessary back span for the significant cantilevers on either side.

Around this same time, the studio secured a generous donation of reclaimed telephone-pole timbers of non-uniform species, quality, and length. Despite our gratitude, the reality was that the timbers posed significant challenges. Few of the timbers were of sufficient length to achieve the span and cantilever we had designed. Through a series of design iterations brought on by serious budget constraints, a desire to be resourceful, and real material limitations, the studio developed a novel double cantilever scheme in which the center bay would simply span from one beam, located over the top of the rammed earth walls, to another beam, spanning over the top of the two timber column sets. The outer bays on either side would be offset in plan from the center bay, but aligned with each other, so that the members fitted together like a finger joint along the beams. These outer bays would cantilever without the benefit of a back span due to a tensile cable connection that tied the two cantilevers together so that they acted as one. The result is that, when standing beneath the center of the canopy, a beautiful alternating rhythmic shadow-play of timber slats and steel cables fall on the patio surface below . . . much to the community partners' and the students' delight.

While the pedagogical benefits of designbuild education are numerous, I have chosen to focus on only three—the valorization of hand-made things with their attendant empathetic qualities, the potential to seize on the productive capacity of failure to advance a project forward in the face of adversity, and, lastly, the realization that constraints and limitations are powerful points of departure for engendering creativity. While these types of lessons can be discussed conceptually in the design studio, it is not until the student comes face to face with the stark reality of the material world that the lessons can be truly embodied.

Life Is Tasted through the Kneading of Hands

Dewey believed that "the poetical, in whatever medium, is always a close kin of the animalistic."[23] It is with this attitude that I guide the students of the Dirt Works Studio to think, design, and build poetically, by which I mean to reach down into the pre-reflective depths of the human condition and find there sufficient material to make meaningful change in the world. Drawing upon quotidian experiences, the studio creates *an experience* for those who encounter the work. The direct, hands-on engagement of the designbuild studio aligns with and reinforces the principles I set out to instill in my students. These principles are made more explicit and accessible to my students through this experiential manner of education. It has never been my intention to educate the next generation of designbuilders. Rather, through the best of what designbuild education has to offer, I believe that future architects gain a greater capacity for empathy and an appreciation for the value of *tasting life through the kneading of hands.*[24]

Notes

1 David Versteeg, e-mail message to author, January 10, 2016.
2 Geoff W. Gjertson, "House Divided: Challenges to Design/Build from Within," in proceedings of the Association of Collegiate Schools of Architecture (ACSA) 2011 Fall Conference.
3 Jared Pechauer, e-mail message to author, December 27, 2015.
4 Martin Heidegger, "Building Dwelling Thinking," *Poetry, Language, Thought*, trans. Albert Hofstadter (New York: Harper & Row, 1975).
5 John Dewey, *Art as Experience* (New York: Capricorn, 1958), 13.
6 K. Michael Hays, *Architecture's Desire: Reading the Late Avant-garde* (Cambridge, MA: MIT, 2010), 12.
7 Fumihiko Maki, "The Art of Suki," *A+U* 10 *Carlo Scarpa* (1985), 207.
8 Relph, Edward, "Modernity and the Reclamation of Place," in *Dwelling, Seeing, and Designing: Toward a Phenomenological Ecology*, ed. David Seamon (Albany: State University of New York Press, 1993), 38.
9 Bjarke Ingels and Kelly Loudenberg, "Bjarke Ingels: Architect as Midwife." *NOWNESS*. N.p., 13 Sept. 2012. Web.
10 J.H. van den Berg, *Things: Four Metabletic Reflections* (Pittsburgh, PA: Duquesne UP, 1970).
11 Christian Norberg-Schulz, "The Phenomenon of Place," *Architectural Association Quarterly* 8.4 (1976), 3–10.
12 Sandra B. Rosenthal and Patrick L. Bourgeois, *Pragmatism and Phenomenology: A Philosophic Encounter* (Amsterdam: Grüner, 1980), 25.
13 Edmund Husserl, *Cartesian Meditations*, trans. Dorian Cairns (The Hague: Martius Nijhoff, 1960).
14 Gianni Vattimo, *Dialogue with Nietzsche*, trans. William McCuaig (New York: Columbia University Press, 2006), 123.
15 Ibid., x.
16 Dewey, *Art as Experience*.
17 Marco Frascari, "The Tell-the-Tale Detail," *Theorizing a New Agenda for Architecture*, ed. Kate Nesbitt (New York: Princeton Architectural Press, 1996), 500–514.
18 Philippe Potié, *Le Corbusier: Le Couvent Sainte Marie De La Tourette* (Boston: Birkhäuser, 2001).
19 Giambattista Vico, *Vico: Selected Writings*, ed. Leon Pompa (Cambridge: Cambridge University Press, 1982).
20 Jared Pechauer, e-mail message to author, December 27, 2015.
21 Dewey. *Art as Experience*.
22 Richard Sennett, *The Craftsman* (New Haven: Yale University Press, 2008).
23 Dewey, *Art as Experience*, 29.
24 Paraphrasing a passage from Le Corbusier, *Le Poème de l'Angle Droit*, trans. Kenneth Hylton, (Paris: Fondation Le Corbusier, Editions Connivences, 1989).

7

THE ACTION OF POETRY

Lori Ryker

Many years ago, I had the romantic notion that I needed to go in search of a mentor to help guide me through my early professional choices. It had to be someone I had yet to meet or read about, given that I had no one specifically identified. Yet, I had in my mind that I would share the discovery of this mentor in a book. The search led to Samuel Mockbee and Coleman Coker. The year I started writing the book, *Mockbee Coker: Thought and Process*, was the year Mockbee started Rural Studio.[1] While working on the book I had the opportunity to speak often with Mockbee about his ideas and commitment to Rural Studio. Although the idea of Rural Studio originated from inside Mockbee's practice with Coker, the program was tied to Auburn University from the beginning. What I could not know at the time was how strong an influence Mockbee would have on my life's choices—not so much about the launch of my own designbuild program, but more due to his demonstration of our discipline's responsibility to put beliefs into action to benefit society. An interview Randy Bates and I conducted for the book left a profound impact on me. During the talk Mockbee stated: "If you aspire to a higher, more meaningful quality in your work, I think you can unify your interests and concerns by way of your personal life."[2] Mockbee stood up for and acted on his beliefs. He was eternally in search of the good in humanity and expressed this goodness through his mythic sense of the world, a search I could relate to. The commitment to "take on" is one of the great life lessons I gained from him and that grounded me when I explored the ideas that became the foundation for Remote Studio.

At Remote Studio's core lay two long-time preoccupations of mine. Early in my teaching career, I recognized when discussing the natural world with students that they either employ the word "nature" or the phrase "the nature." The presence or invisibility of "the" when discussing nature seems to present differences in their point of view or relationship to the world. Why would this be, that some people speak of nature around them using "the," such as, *I find the nature is inspiring?*

FIGURE 7.1 Remote Studio, exploring the Beartooth Mountain Wilderness
Source: Steve Harrop

Using "the" in the context of explaining an experience of nature provides a title to the word or phrase, such as "The Tower of London" or "The World Series." I believe that using the article "the" answers to an experienced sense of separation. This practice tends to distinguish people who conceive *nature* to be *us* from those who conceive nature to be *outside of us,* not a part of who we are. When nature is perceived and talked about as something distinct from us, I believe it carries evidence of the practices of an environmentally disengaged society.

Parallel to my preoccupation with nature is the consideration of the practicable differences between beauty and aesthetics. Beauty has an ancient history, recognized as a transcendent, intrinsic quality and partner to poetic expression.[3] From the Enlightenment forward, most philosophers were preoccupied not with the transcendent nature of beauty, but with questions of where beauty lies—with the person, in the object, somewhere between, or in the exchange of the experience.[4] These more recent concerns of beauty arose with the adoption of the scientific method and the shift that privileges objective knowledge.[5] Insistence on measurable facts and the repeatability of empirical knowledge relegates beauty to the unknowable because beauty cannot be measured. And because of this condition, beauty has lost its presence in our considerations of reality, discussions of experience, and what we understand to make up the world.

Aesthetics on the other hand, codified during the Enlightenment era when beauty suffered the inability to be analyzed, provides a way to speak about beauty's objective qualities. Through all variety of analysis of physical form, conditions, and characteristics, the taxonomy of aesthetics has been established to speak around beauty, shifting the consideration of beauty from an experience to something objectified.[6] People feel comfortable with analysis that provides tangible, observable, and repeatable conditions.[7] Today we speak about and teach aesthetics while we disregard beauty itself. With inquiries and education redirected toward aesthetics that result in distancing from experiences with the world, we lose the ability to understand the origin of poetry.

We teach aesthetics, yet poetry does not come about from the application of aesthetics. Rather, poetry is born from our involvement with and our being a part of the world, an experience that also brings forth the experience of beauty.[8] As long as our conception of reality is dominated by the Enlightenment Era's intellectual perceptions and objectifications, we will continue to struggle with and yearn for a deeper sense of belonging to the world as well as struggle with an understanding of the origins of poetry.

These two preoccupations, nature and beauty, are prime motivations of Remote Studio. Specifically, the program was developed to help students gain experience through the lived inspirations of beauty, poetry, and the sense of being in the world.

Nature and beauty can be experienced in most places—cities and wilderness alike. However, the distractions of the modern world, particularly urban and suburban environments and all of their trappings, combined with the investment we make in abstract intellectual and physical constructs, have a powerful impact on our psyche, making an unmediated experience with self and nature nearly impossible. This difficulty affects how we understand ourselves, why we make the choices we do, and our faltering ability to understand and create poetic, integrated, and place-based environments. To provide students direct and unmediated experiences

FIGURE 7.2 Remote Studio, hiking into Pine Creek Lake, Absaroka/Beartooth Wilderness

Source: Lori Ryker

of nature and beauty, Remote Studio occurs in a unique area of the Northern Rockies. The Greater Yellowstone Eco-Region is a remnant of wild landscape that holds some of the last large great predators in North America, a place where the modern world is mostly absent. A place you can truly get lost in and never return from.

For most people who have never experienced an *untrammeled landscape*,[9] it is difficult to comprehend the feel of such a place. To gain some understanding of the *lived* experience of Remote Studio, it is helpful to consider the conditions where most of us live and work every day. Most of our lives are negotiated and held between and within buildings with very definite boundaries. Consider how often or how many hours a day or a week we leave these environments to be out of doors.[10] What is the quality of these places and experiences? What are we doing when we are outside—jogging, playing tennis, or golfing? Or are we in the forest, ocean, desert, or mountains, just *being* with nature?

Consider the differences between the more articulated cultural out-of-doors experience that we refer to as recreational and the experience of *being* with nature.[11] Imagine if the constant experience of walls, roofs, and mechanical systems that enable us to presuppose that *we do not need to know what is beyond the walls* were to disappear. And instead of elaborate articulations, separations, and distinctions, we only had a thin piece of cloth between nature and us. Imagine this feeling for a

FIGURE 7.3 Remote Studio students on the Ridge of Gallatin Mountain Range
Source: Lori Ryker

112   Lori Ryker

night, a week, or for two months. The experience of walls and the definite separation from nature disappears, reliability is tested, and conditions are constantly changing.

The lived experience of "thinness" between what could be called civility and wildness provides students with the immediate and dynamic *experience of place*, not simply *thinking about place* through mechanisms that separate and abstract. The intent of experiencing the "thin" distinction between civility and wildness during Remote Studio is not to demonstrate that the world is unstable, but to provide opportunity for students to gain an intimate relationship with nature and to learn the difference between experiences "about" from experiences "of." *About* and *of* convey two different mindsets for how we conceive self and interact with the world. *About* indicates thoughts, feeling, and/or actions in relation *to* a place, person, or thing, while *of* connects us to something else. *About* is external and discursive (separate from) while *of* is intrinsic (connected to). *About* suggests that the world is perceived and known through analysis and abstractions that become objectified facts presented as verifiable knowledge parlayed into information to understand and apply. *Of* suggests rich, interrelated, and connected experiences with place, person, or thing. These different ways of thinking, speaking, and understanding ourselves in relation to the world concern me because I believe that the overreliance on the *about* mindset undermines our ability to be *of* (connected to) the world.[12]

The *about* mindset results in shallow thinking and feeling and is evidence of being disengaged from the world. Disengagement results in the collection of possessions that stand in for relationships and experiences with the world. The loss of the sense of being a part *of* the world also contributes to the loss of sensed value, specificity, and necessity of the world. From the *about* mindset the world is comprehended in generalized terms—earth, plants, and animals—easily becoming resource and amenity that make palatable and acceptable our activities that destroy the world. To live in a reality that is only understood in terms of *about* is to live in a reality in which poetry is seldom made or experienced.

Remote Studio's pedagogical experiment provides the opportunity to counter the overreliance on abstraction and disconnection, and encourages connected life practices and living *of* the world to experience all its roughness and refinement. The program is structured to provide experiences from which students learn of self and the world simultaneously as a continually lived relationship of the foundation for poetic inspiration and expression.[13]

The current configuration of Remote Studio runs for eight weeks every summer with eight to twelve students from universities throughout the United States. Any given semester, students from Montana to Bahrain, from Louisiana to Japan, from Korea to Mexico, from Texas to Saudi Arabia and elsewhere, attend the program for their "off campus" semester experience.

Remote Studio begins with two weeks of exploring, reading, discussing, making, camping, and hiking in some of the most physically challenging landscape of

The Action of Poetry **113**

North America, not in order to become an accomplished hiker, but to provide students the opportunity of personal experience with the world. In preparation for what can be gained from these experiences, and the semester overall, three concepts are employed from which to discuss the philosophical core of Remote Studio and introduce the idea of a personal worldview.

Worldview and personal motivation are difficult subjects to broach in modern society because it is easier to operate from a less reflective and intimidating place. Yet, awareness of our experiences in the world, learning to express ourselves and understand the intentions that guide our actions, is critical for creative practice.[14] Jim Harrison's essay, "Nesting in Air," offers a glimpse into his worldview: "I think it was Santayana who noted that all people seem to have a secret religion hidden beneath, perhaps surrounding, their more public worship."[15] Harrison continues, "I wake as a mammal . . . as my consciousness begins its paintjob I frequently, but not always, go outside and bow to the six directions, mindful of the ironies involved. I don't mind if the gesture would appear absurd to someone else as I eventually have to die all by myself."[16] The honest and unapologetic words of Harrison stir something within us encouraging the consideration of our own beliefs and actions. His words provide a way to understand mindfulness, the halting of actions for a moment before going forward—physically and mentally.[17] Engaging in mindfulness while hiking and camping connects us to an expanded sense of the world, resulting in greater awareness of the consciousness of life itself without reflection or words.[18]

"Twenty minutes from my house, through the woods by the quarry and across the highway, is Hollins Pond, a remarkable piece of shallowness, where I like to go at sunset and sit on a tree trunk."[19] Annie Dillard is telling her story about meeting a weasel. "I would like to learn, or remember, how to live. I come to Hollins Pond not so much to learn how to live as, frankly, to forget about it."[20] So much of our lives are focused on the retention of information and facts leading us to believe that without objective knowledge we cannot operate properly in or *know* the world. Replaying them in our mind requires reflection and projections, disengaging us from the immediacy of the world. Forgetting, in the way that Dillard suggests, brings us into the present and benefits creativity and the creative process.[21] "[I] might learn something of mindlessness," she writes, "something of the purity of living in the physical senses and the dignity of living without bias or motive."[22] Mindlessness, the state of preconsciousness, is required for poetic intuition, the unity of mind with spirit. The philosopher Alfred Whitehead refers to this experience as "participating in the extensive continuum," the practice of being "present in another entity."[23] We most often experience mindlessness when we stop worrying about the facts and reflecting on our experience, and instead simply move through the world. The unmediated moments of being in the world lead to the spark of creative intuition and self-discovery, the "flash" of inspiration, that becomes the idea we make into poetry.[24] We all know what these moments feel like, but we seldom recognize their role in our creative process. Mindfulness also

FIGURE 7.4 Remote Studio students encamped
Source: Eric Lundeen

has a role during these experiences, providing pause to recognize the power of the feeling and the spark of creative intuition. This momentary pause creates a memory of the experience and the feeling that serves the crafting of poetic intuition, what we call poetry. However, if we ignore the spark, we lose the potential for the expression and making of poetry.

The experience of the world also results in bruised feet, sore muscles, and hunger. The unhappy voice inside our heads after a long day on the trail can result in trudging. A state of mind that is not unique to hiking, but easily recognizable when carrying a heavy backpack on a trail. Trudging, we all know. When the voice inside our head tells us that what we are doing is too hard, that we cannot do it, that we do not want to do it. Trudging is the loss of engagement and the death of *being* in the moment, the lack of valuing where you are and being *of* the world. A straightforward reminder to keep ourselves from simply trudging through the world ensures that we do not miss the beauty that is always around us, and that we do not miss the potential spark of creative (poetic) intuition.

Mindfulness, mindlessness, and trudging serve to illustrate three ways of *existing* in the world, and support an understanding of how engaging in two of these experiences cultivates poetic intuition and creative expression. Discussions of these modes of existence are supported by the students' own experiences in the first few weeks of the program. Somewhere between blisters, moments of awe, miles on feet, and learning how to cook on an open fire, we read, we talk about what we read, and students begin to think about themselves and come into their own country. Who they have been, who they want to be, where they may go in their lives commingles with mindfulness of where they are—in reflection at the end of a day or during a pause for water next to a creek.

These experiences are translated into the student's expressions of self in relation to the world through the making of vessels, hand-crafted material "containers." In an effort to support the connection between experience, mindfulness, and the creative spark, vessels are often created in the backcountry, in the moment, without the opportunity to reflect or project, but simply to make. Situating vessels in the landscape where we hike, live, or work supports the immediate expression gained from the sensed intimacy of place. The making of vessels is typically restricted to found materials, bare hands, or hand tools to teach about the critical relationship craft has to the expression of an idea, and the necessary connection between mind and hand. Asking each student to explicitly relate their sense of the world through the vessels they make helps them gain an appreciation for the value of honesty and integrity, as Jim Harrison so gracefully demonstrates in "Nesting in Air." The discussions also provide an opportunity to learn how to speak about crafting intentions. This *out-of-the-box* and *out-of-the-classroom* approach lays the foundation for understanding that creative intuition and creative process are alive in all creative work, and not only in a studio process.

FIGURE 7.5 Vessel of Aspen and grass by Patricia Flores
Source: Patricia Flores

FIGURE 7.6 Vessel of river rocks and driftwood built by Charlie Dickson, Eva Hughes-Rodriguez, and Alek Hoffman at the West bank of the Snake River for the Inaugural Rendezvous Park project supported by Jackson Hole Land Trust and the LOR Foundation

Source: Hance Hughes

Some years after completing Remote Studio, Nash Emrich wrote of his experience,

> reading environmental essays, and simply sitting, reflecting by the riverbank, I felt like I was seeing the natural world through new eyes. I became acutely aware of my surroundings, and in turn, extended that awareness to what I was doing at Remote [Studio] and would be doing in my career. By immersing myself in nature, I not only formed a deeper appreciation for it, but more importantly, learned that our built environment must live in harmony with the natural world. To this extent, Remote Studio inspired my passion and responsibility to ensure that our future impact on this landscape is a sustainable one.[25]

While Nash's observations may seem straightforward, for most students, who have only ever known the creative process through formal architectural education, this realization can be expansive and liberating. For many it changes how they live in the world and the focus or method of their creative work. For some, the result may be poetry.

For the remaining six weeks of Remote Studio the students shift from the wilderness and making vessels to a community designbuild project that allows them to put into practice their recent experiences and inspirations. The "thin" separation between wildness and civility continues as they sleep in wall tents and eat as a group, sometimes with a full indoor kitchen, but most often out of doors with a grill or Coleman stove. The earlier experiences gained from backpacking and hiking as a group not only serve to ground their consideration for the community project but also provide context and support for the collaborative working conditions required of the project. Their design explorations occur in flexible places such as community rooms of coffee shops or out of doors.

Reflection on their experiences in the wilderness supports the student's growing comprehension and integration of mindfulness, mindlessness, and the engagement of creative intuition during the design process. The exploration of the specific location for their project is enriched from practicing mindfulness, resulting in a more inclusive consideration of local plants, animals, people, land, water, and phenomena, combined with the full landscape context and the community's sense of place. From their experiences of immersion in the place, a more immediate and tangible understanding of environmental responsibility influences the student's consideration of the qualities of the site and search for material expression of their ideas. While not all Remote Studio projects achieve poetic expression, those that do, develop from the organic flow of the student's subconscious combined with the group's openness for a process that cannot be fully explained in rational terms. Allowing their creative intuition to guide them during design explorations pushes out preconceptions and assumptions of architectural outcomes and the post-rationalization of ideas recede from both their work and discussions. The formless inspirations that come about through intuition are engaged with mindfulness to develop form and materiality that embodies the student's sensed experiences of world, place, and landscape. From the beginning of the design process to the end of construction, the student's core architectural ideas that come from creative intuition grounds the final expression and provides the greatest potential for poetry.

In the search for material expression of their ideas, students learn what is available in lumber and steel yards as well as which materials are local and what is immediately available from the environment. Discussions of materials available in the surrounding community and landscape—willow, stone, reclaimed timber from a local mill or hand collected—expand their understanding of how these materials can reduce the labor and time required for the construction process while also generating an embodied tie between idea and place. Their expanding knowledge of materials provides a framework from which they gain the specificity of expression for the design. The search for appropriate techniques of construction encourages them to consider what unique abilities they already have that can be incorporated into the process. Over the years, weaving, knot tying, climbing, or a certain comfort in bartering for materials with a local resident have all played a part in each project's design. This work, a scaled-up version of the vessel process, results in the environmentally specific and often handcrafted aspects of Remote Studio projects.

Revisions and alternative solutions to the determined expression of the materials and details occur as the students are confronted with time constraints and the unanticipated realities of construction. These experiences can provide some of the best

FIGURE 7.7 Meghan Hanson and Tyler Swingle weave rope on the enclosure of the Tree Fort built by Remote Studio Summer 2012 for St. John's Episcopal Church, Jackson Hole, Wyoming

Source: Lori Ryker

lessons for creative practice and manifesting poetry if the students are reminded to return to their initial inspirations before acting. During this process, considerations of being in the world combine with the recent experiences of making vessels. They gain understanding for how to best express their idea when selectively choosing what to include and what to leave out.[26] Through this process their idea transforms into a physical expression, and perhaps poetry emerges.

There is a difficulty in demonstrating the success of a process that aspires to manifest poetry, much like the difficulty in objectively demonstrating beauty. Photographs of work, so often used as proof of certain evidence for architecture, only provide second-hand experience, and at their best may conjure some poetic presence. Perhaps a perceived sense of beauty transfers across the image when combined with the viewer's empathy and imagination. Yet, I believe, as Jacques Maritain does, that poetry (beauty) is not in the object or held by the perceiver, but arrives from the experience.[27] If, as Maritain asserts, poetry can only be known directly, what I offer is an invitation to visit the work, a few photographs, and some observations.

Years ago when the students were completing a shelter for watching quail in the mountains of West Texas a visitor came up to me to tell me of his experience. He told me that the evening before when the sun was setting he came to sit in the shelter to watch for birds. When sitting in the carved out place and experiencing the surrounding landscape from eye level he said he felt as if he were a part of

FIGURE 7.8 Fall 2012 students installing the shade trellis under the polycarbonate roof of the Reading Pavilion at the City of Livingston Yellowstone River park
Source: Lori Ryker

the place. His explanation was stated simply and straightforwardly, and accurately described the students' intent for the design of the pavilion: to help people feel they are a part of the place, not simply observing.[28]

Similar stories of belonging or being a part of place have been told to me from visitors to the Pine Creek Pavilion, built for the United States Forest Service at the edge of the Absaroka-Beartooth wilderness in 2006. There are many aspects of the pavilion that provide a feeling of being a part of the place, including the articulation of the structure that follows the angling of the surrounding tree trunks, the use of wood milled from the site, and soil for the rammed earth wall that came from the edge of the Yellowstone River. But the transforming experience recounted by visitors comes from the roof form. When developing the roof, the students were attentive to the boundary that could be experienced between the Forest Service campground, where their structure was sited, and the wilderness that lay just beyond and in view from the site. The students' aspiration was to bring about an experience of "awe" for visitors, and to make the sense of place tangible with the spectacular mountains visible from the pavilion. They accomplished their aspiration by lowering the roof at the entry and raising it up toward the mountains. The roof, while powerful on its own, exists as part of the whole. The pavilion is a response brought about from poetic intuition and the students' intimate experience of the place articulated through choice of material and brought into a sensed relationship between structure and landscape. These

FIGURE 7.9 *Pine Creek Pavilion*, Remote Studio Fall 2006, USFS Pine Creek Campground, Park County, Montana
Source: Audrey Hall

relationships are where poetry exists, when the spiritual and physical qualities of the world come together to be experienced.

I have had my own experiences of the students' work, similar moments to those described above. In these instances, when I return from having been off site to retrieve a missing bolt or broken drill bit, what was a pile of wood and metal, or hand-collected sticks or rocks, or spool of rope, has been brought together to create an experience of the place that is magical. What exists is more than what was present in the place when the students began. The idea of a wall is now physical and vibrates at the end of the day with light slipping through woven willow, or a steel frame wraps a tree with a floating feeling for those who travel across its open weave, or the sketched shape of a simple shed form comes together to hold the harvest of a farmer's garden while collecting bits of the mountains beyond through sliding screen doors.

The presence of poetry during these experiences feels similar to those Rick Bass describes in his book, *Fiber*.

> You spy a fallen tree just a little bit out of your reach, and at the bottom of a steep slope. You have to cross a tangle of blowdown to get to it. It's a little larger than you should be carrying and a little too far from the truck—you've already hauled a day's worth—but all of these things conspire within you, as you stare at the log, to create a strange transformation or alteration: they

reassemble into the reasons, the precise reasons, that you should go get that log. And always, you do, so that you will not have to go to bed that night thinking about that log, and how you turned away from it.[29]

The making of poetry comes from engaged living in the world and can only be known through immediate experience. Poetry is always ephemeral, momentarily physical, and lives in our memories.

These are the concerns of Remote Studio and the ongoing experiment of each student's life.

FIGURE 7.10 A portion of the Reflection Point on the Yellowstone River, Remote Studio Fall 2008, City of Livingston Yellowstone River park
Source: Lori Ryker

Notes

1 Lori Ryker, *Mockbee Coker: Thought and Process* (New York: Princeton Architectural, 1995).
2 Ibid., 91.
3 James S. Taylor, *Poetic Knowledge: The Recovery of Education* (Albany, NY: SUNY Press), 39.
4 John Hospers, ed. *Introductory Readings in Aesthetics* (New York: The Free Press, 1969).
5 Taylor, *Poetic Knowledge*, 93, 112–113.
6 Hospers, *Introductory Readings in Aesthetics*.
7 Ronald N. Stromberg, *An Intellectual History of Modern Europe* (New York: Appleton-Century-Crofts, 1966), 427.
8 Taylor, *Poetic Knowledge*, 15.
9 The word "untrammeled" is employed in the 1964 Wilderness Act and used by the United States National Forest. "The word 'wilderness' represents this social condition, one in which an area is untrammeled and free from human control" www.fs.fed.us/managing-land/wilderness.
10 Richard Louv, *Last Child In the Woods* (New York: Workman Publishing Co., 2005).
11 Aldo Leopold, *A Sand County Almanac: With Other Essays on Conservation from Round River* (New York: Balantine Books, 1966), 261, 269–272.
12 The contemporary social practice "about" is inherited from the abstracting and objectifying Scientific Method of Inquiry.
13 Albert Levi, *Philosophy and the Modern World* (Bloomington, IN: Indiana University Press, 1958), 501, 512.
14 Lori Ryker, *The Creation of Second Nature: The Problem of Making for Students of Architecture* (Ann Arbor, MI: UMI Dissertation Services, 2000), 136.
15 Jim Harrison, "Nesting in Air," in *Northern Lights: A Selection of New Writing from the American West*, ed. Deborah Clow and Donald Snow (New York: Vintage Books, 1994), 262–264.
16 Ibid.
17 Christophe Andre, *Looking at Mindfulness: Twenty-five Ways to Live in the Moment Through Art* (New York: Penguin, Blue Rider Press, 2014), 8–9.
18 Ibid., 9.
19 Annie Dillard, "Living Like Weasels," in *Teaching a Stone to Talk* (New York: Harper Collins, 1982), 12.
20 Ibid., 15.
21 Paul Shepherd, *Nature and Madness* (San Francisco: Sierra Club, 1982). In this book, Shepherd supports the idea that creativity is not a chief characteristic of the human species, but a characteristic of all species.
22 Dillard, "Living Like Weasels," 15.
23 Levi, *Philosophy and the Modern World*, 501–503.
24 Jacques Maritain, *Creative Intuition in Art and Poetry* (New York: Pantheon Books, 1953), 76–77.
25 Nash Emrich, "Benefits of Remote Studio," unpublished essay.
26 Rick Bass, *Fiber* (Athens: University of Georgia Press, 1998), 18.
27 Maritain, *Creative Intuition in Art and Poetry*, 83–84.
28 Ryker, *The Creation of Second Nature*, 175.
29 Bass, *Fiber*, 27.

PART 3

Process

Methodology and the
Tectonic Imagination

8
IN PROCESS

Marie Zawistowski and Keith Zawistowski

Though much of architectural education revolves around theoretical concepts necessary to the development of creative sensibilities, a key curricular component in five-year undergraduate professional degree programs is the obligation to prepare students for the practice of architecture. In this context, designbuild education is a strategy to balance theoretical underpinning with technical aptitude, not to favor one over the other.

In Process is a critical survey of the design/buildLAB, a two-semester studio in which third-year undergraduate architecture students collaborate with community leaders and industry experts to conceive and realize built works of architecture that are both educational and charitable in nature. This initiative, located at Virginia

FIGURE 8.1 design/buildLAB student simultaneously engaged in designing and building, Blacksburg, Virginia, 2012

Source: design/buildLAB

Tech until 2015, resulted in the construction of five community development projects over the course of five consecutive academic years. As the program charts its next five years, we reflect on a pedagogical approach in which students take the lead in the realization of ambitious architectural projects, in a truly collaborative manner, at a remarkably fast pace, and in the public eye.

The Context

The single most important premise of designbuild education is that student competence and confidence will advance exponentially by building themselves what they have conceived in abstraction. Questions of scale, tectonics, and materiality are easily apprehended and assimilated when experienced first-hand. Quite simply, a person does not approach design the same way once he or she acutely understands the concrete implications of a drawn line. If the goal is simply to build, designbuild loses its educational foundation. The learning curve is relatively shallow for a group of students who only conceive a project and have little or no interaction with the builders of their design, or for a group of students who serve as neck-down labor to build (or worse, to finish building) a project, which they did not conceive. To this end, it is essential that the same students who conceived and developed a project be the ones to complete and reflect on the project.

At the design/buildLAB, the balance between project scope and project timeline is the key to achieving this imperative. The design/buildLAB is structured as a two-semester program: a fall design, a spring build (for academic credit), and a summer contingency (for Intern Development Program credit). Because early departure of a student from the project would fundamentally undermine the primary goal of designbuild education—to build the thing that you designed—a solemn pact is made on day one: the team stays complete until the project is complete. The Covington Farmers Market was organized in this way. The much larger and more complex Smith Creek Park was divided into two consecutive academic year phases: The Masonic Amphitheatre and The Smith Creek Pedestrian Bridge. Similarly, the realization of the Sharon Fieldhouse was directly followed by that of the Sharon Baseball Fields, on the same site. Each phase was a stand-alone project conceived and realized in its entirety by its own student team.

While each successive student team has defined for themselves what prefabrication means, the design/buildLAB consistently relies on the simultaneity of sitework and off-site fabrication to minimize the hindrances of bad weather and to compress the construction schedule into a single semester. Generally, this results in students fabricating the intricate or atypical building elements in a controlled environment, while coordinating the work of tradespeople to realize more conventional or labor-intensive elements on site. For the Covington Farmers Market, a series of unique trusses were produced on a computer-controlled factory assembly line. The students, working at a shop on campus, then built jigs and assembled the trusses into complete roof modules. Meanwhile, a steel fabricator was producing structural columns from the students' shop drawings and a mason was pouring

FIGURE 8.2 Crane lowering prefabricated roof modules onto prefabricated steel columns, *Farmers Market*, Covington, Virginia, 2011
Source: design/buildLAB

foundations and stem walls based on students' construction documents. All prefabricated components were trucked to the site and assembled with a crane in a single week.

While this method is specific to the logic of this project, innovative approaches to construction sequencing are indispensable to fitting a complex project into a single academic year.

Designing the construction process reaches beyond the level of understanding that architecture students (and sadly many architects) are typically expected to have. In fact, the design/buildLAB was created as a direct response to the increasing tendency of academia to shroud the making of architecture in mystery,[1] and to the resulting pressure that this tendency places on students to over-intellectualize their work. In such instances, students, whose vocation as architects is to make a tangible impact on the world around them, often find themselves at a loss for a sense of meaning and purpose. Designbuild education is a counterbalance, providing students with the opportunity to deploy their creative problem-solving abilities in the service of real problems, with measurable impact.

Among the many latent values of immersive real-world learning is the opportunity to equip a generation of emerging professionals who whole-heartedly believe that architects can affect positive change on a grand scale. This empowerment of high professional ethics is most robust when students directly experience the transformative outcomes of their imagination and energy.

FIGURE 8.3 *Farmers Market*, Covington, Virginia, 2011
Source: Jeff Goldberg/Esto

At the design/buildLAB, the tenable impact on the common good is a vital project selection metric. To this end, projects are always for non-profit community foundations or civic entities on publicly accessible sites and in communities of overwhelming need. Projects for private entities, benefiting private interests, or for public organizations, simply in search of lower cost development, are never considered, as they are deemed inappropriate use of student and faculty volunteer labor. Further, the design/buildLAB endeavors to identify and partner with organizations that have a demonstrated history of community leadership and success at realizing their mission. In this context, the students and partnering organization share in the challenges of project stewardship and, more importantly, in the tremendous sense of responsibility that stems from serving the public interest.

The Framework

The design/buildLAB is one of two teaching initiatives of onSITE, a design-build architecture practice. The first initiative is "Designing Practice," a professional practice seminar encouraging students to ask fundamental questions about the nature of practice and the role of the architect in society through the design and study of "Practice Mock-Ups," projecting themselves into virtual practice. At the opposite end of the spectrum, the design/buildLAB is a project-based experiential learning program enabling students to concretize the value of the architect in society through the design and construction of community service projects, thereby projecting themselves into real-world practice.

These initiatives were not directed by instructors embedded in typical tenure track positions, where a heavy load of personal research in addition to teaching is expected; nor were they directed by adjunct professors, often young faculty who are offered little to no stability (and therefore credibility). Rather, we (the programs co-founders) were hired as Professors of Practice, a fixed-term teaching appointment for practicing architects, providing us with the autonomy and security necessary to develop experimental pedagogical models.

Beyond the benefits to the school as a unique platform for innovation, one of the goals of the Professor of Practice position was to promote architecture in the region. Instead of research, we were expected to devote a portion of our time to practice. This academic-professional duality was intended to support both a critical architecture practice and a critical pedagogical project—entities positioned to take measured risk in their respective approaches.

The value of this reciprocity between teaching and practice is not to be understated in the context of a community-based designbuild program such as the design/buildLAB. First, because it provided a necessary level of psychological comfort for both students and community entities involved, i.e., knowing that the professors had expertise in the process. Second, our active practice gave the program uncommon access to professional affiliations and resources. In fact, while it is important to say that onSITE's work was kept completely separate from charitable initiatives involving volunteer student labor, all design/buildLAB projects were the results of trusted relationships developed in a professional setting through our firm's own work: professional consultants volunteered, artisans opened their shops, material suppliers provided expert advice and discounts, and former clients vouched for the projects, building support from within the community. Equally valuable (but less desirable) was the students' access to onSITE's entire arsenal of tools, computers and equipment, making the realization of the first projects possible without university investment. Quite simply, the launching of the designbuild program would not have been possible had we not had an active designbuild practice.

The design/buildLAB is not a faculty-led research initiative with student assistants, a practical internship with professional mentors, or a professional apprenticeship with studio masters, nor does it profess an accepted understanding or a common way of doing. Rather, it is a learning environment where students lead projects and faculty are advisors who set the tone, bring resources to the discussion, and refocus or encourage as needed. From a pedagogical perspective, faculty's ability to practice their profession outside of academia limits their predilection to appropriate designbuild projects as a creative outlet of their own; this approach is indispensable because professional fulfillment enables faculty to set aside personal aspirations and to approach student work with an open mind, guiding the process rather than directing it. The point of limiting the faculty's leadership role is twofold: 1) to facilitate students' individual learning, and 2) to avoid circumventing the benefits of creative problem-solving by prescribing solutions. While professional experience and knowledge are valued as assets for the team to be able to draw upon, students react to propositions developed by their peers, and faculty positions matter as much or as little as anyone else in the room. This *laissez faire* approach is crucial during the design phase, because student ownership of the project will maximize their investment in its making. It is a powerful way to build student

FIGURE 8.4 Local residents captivated by students on crane day, *Masonic Amphitheatre*, Clifton Forge, Virginia, 2012
Source: Jeff Goldberg/Esto

FIGURE 8.5 *Masonic Amphitheatre* and *Smith Creek Pedestrian Bridge*, Clifton Forge, Virginia, 2013
Source: Jeff Goldberg/Esto

confidence and to engender exploration and innovation, which can reach beyond the faculty's knowledge, and is therefore not limited by it.

Regardless of faculty input, the most influential factor to student learning is the real-world nature of the project: the reality of the site, the reality of the available means, and the reality of the people who the building is destined to serve. For the design/buildLAB, this was most in evidence at the outset of the amphitheatre project, when a series of interviews conducted by the students with a broad range of community leaders and stakeholders determined the specific program for the project itself. During the design phase, the community continued to be a sounding board for the students and actively engaged in discussions about the conception of the project. These public input sessions set the tone for an open dialog between architecture students, who were valued for their skills and creativity, and community members, who were valued for their worldview and practical feedback.

This discourse contributed to the making of a modern architecture, which is grounded in the unique identity of people and place.

The Team

Collaboration may be one of the hardest things to teach: first, because it is an attitude that can only be fostered; second, because most students and faculty have been indoctrinated through a system where individual creative talent is the primary measure of success. In the prevailing pedagogical models, one either develops a project alone or works in a group, where most often, a few people forge a narrow focus and others provide secondary or tertiary support. In contrast, the design/buildLAB environment is framed to facilitate genuine collaboration.

The two greatest pitfalls in designbuild education are moving forward without overwhelming consensus (leading to a disenfranchised team) and allowing compromise to replace sound decision-making (resulting in an incoherent project). In the design/buildLAB, projects are designed and built by teams of sixteen to eighteen students. After studying the project's physical and cultural context, researching precedents, and working with the community to develop a detailed program, all students make individual design propositions. Through a series of studio pin-ups and community presentations, strong ideas are identified. The students iteratively merge these ideas, creating larger teams and fewer, more fully developed schemes. This process allows for multiple concepts, approaches, and solutions to be simultaneously explored, and for every student to contribute ideas to the discussion. It is imperative that no one scheme be "chosen." Rather, the result is a unified team who organically arrives at a single project for which there is consensus and community support.

In addition to collaborating on the design of a project, design/buildLAB students divide themselves into separate committees tasked with the management of responsibilities that stem from the realization of the project as a team. The Public Relations committee is in charge of project communication strategies. The Logistics committee is in charge of project coordination strategies. The Administration committee is in charge of ensuring that budget and schedule goals are met. Students find themselves undertaking tasks or responsibilities that they may have never considered as the domain of architecture. A student may have to do structural analysis one day, prepare presentation material the next day, and perform material takeoff calculations the day after that. This process of constantly exchanging roles simultaneously enables students to identify their comfort zones, and encourages them to foster empathy by working outside of that comfort zone. In this context, the taboos of architectural education (marketing, management, scheduling, finance, promotion, compliance, etc.) are revealed as valuable tools, the keys to turning a good idea into a good building. Each design/buildLAB team thrives as its members identify and advance their own strengths, and begin to mentor their peers.

When a group of students is faced with the daunting task of realizing the complexity of their first building, learning to respect the contributions of others becomes a necessity. Here, the role of the advisor is to support individual attainment, while ensuring that collective authorship prevails. For the Pedestrian Bridge team—who designed and built their project in only three months—collaboration tools were created to allow timely conflict resolution and prevent unspoken discontent from destabilizing the team. These tools were designed to be fully integrated and self-regulating. One example, a survey box, was made available for team members to anonymously deposit questions, comments, criticisms, qualms, revelations, ideas. The students regularly opened the box and discussed its content, airing tensions before they became problematic and building on positive feedback. A second example, a comprehensive task list, was recreated at each phase of design and construction. Students would take on tasks in order of priority and report daily progress back to the team, allowing for the collective readjustment of individual workloads. Finally, an outline of absurd examples from the previous year's mishaps, satirically called "code of conduct", encourages both students and faculty to initiate frank conversations about expectations.

FIGURE 8.6 design/buildLAB students celebrating teamwork, *Smith Creek Pedestrian Bridge*, Clifton Forge, Virginia, 2013
Source: design/buildLAB

FIGURE 8.7 *Smith Creek Pedestrian Bridge*, Clifton Forge, Virginia, 2013
Source: Jeff Goldberg/Esto

In this collaborative environment, personal and collective accountability prevents students from stagnating in secondary roles and ensures that each individual gains competence in the expected curricular content areas. Individual students are evaluated on measures such as aesthetic development, technical development, presentation skills, management abilities, participation, and critical thinking. The aspiration of this approach is to place the education of the architect in front of the teaching of architecture,[2] and thus to empower students to do what it is that they want to do, as well as they can do it.

The Making

One of the most common critiques of designbuild education is that there is little to be gained from manual labor. While there is some truth to the fact that swinging a hammer will not directly teach you how to draw, there is profound impact embodied in the act of making.

Respected architectural theorists, such as Juhani Pallasmaa, have long argued that there is a valuable link between the careful actions of the hand and development of intellectual thought.[3] Unfortunately, the undesirable social stigma associated with the various construction trades—more often considered as lower-class actors of the building industry rather than respected craftsmen of regarded know-how—generally prevents architects from thinking of the act of building as an integral part of the architectural discipline. This is due in part to a fundamental shift of the profession in the late 1800s to early 1900s, when it intentionally removed itself from the construction site in an effort to both differentiate itself from builders and to establish its authority in protecting the public interest.[4] This shift has had a lasting impact in academia, essentially removing the responsibility to teach the art of building. While today efforts are made across schools to introduce architecture students to construction in a way that is no longer superficial, the separation between conception and construction has become commonplace, and it is highly unconventional for architects to take part in the building process.

What is essential about designbuild education is not the constructive act itself, but the opportunity it provides for students to think through every aspect of their design decisions, exponentially growing their capacity and thus their value as architects. Rather than only considering the end result, designbuild students *design* the construction process. And because they are experiencing the impact of their own design decisions first-hand, they are in an ideal position to evaluate them—often rethinking them for the better. While designbuild students may get less quantitative experience in the initial design process of a project than their peers (who may design three or four projects to schematic level during the time that it takes designbuild students to design one to construction document/shop drawings level), they gain invaluable knowledge in understanding the process of making.

Because building is the most visible—and photogenic—part of the process, discussions about designbuild education often center on the act of building. In reality, design/buildLAB projects are crafted to ensure that building maintains an appropriate proportion within the overall course content and that expertise from an entire interdisciplinary resource team of faculty is available.[5] In this way, concepts uncovered in peripheral courses such as Building Structures, Environmental Building Systems, and Professional Practice can be tested in furtherance of conceiving and realizing a work of architecture.

In the design/buildLAB, students spend the majority of their time at their desks—studying, designing, managing, and coordinating—similar to a professional architect in practice—a kind of practical experience that has often remained the domain of the internship. However, opportunities for students to *practice* their profession within the framework of the academy allow for much greater control of the quantity, quality, and breadth of curricular content, while providing an environment where mistakes—teachable moments—are embraced. The complexities and imperatives of building help students discover the architect's role in dissolving the boundaries between discipline-specific knowledge and in integrating competing interests into a coherent whole.

To be fair, there is such a thing as too much building in a designbuild project, and it occurs as soon as the pressures to finish the project short-circuit the time needed for ideas to mature. At the design/buildLAB, students are constantly reminded that they are studying to become architects, not builders. This is to say that an architect has something to contribute to the building process beyond the execution of repetitive tasks for the sake of building something. There is a fundamental difference between the teaching of a trade (building) and the teaching of a discipline (architecture). The measure of success in architectural education cannot be limited to the quality of the work itself. While the work must strive for excellence, so too must the process of making.

For this reason, project planning must incorporate the understanding that mistakes are expected and embraced. For the Sharon Fieldhouse team, who sought a spare material palette with quiet detailing and limited resonance of the hand, this became a challenge, because the students' ambitions consistently resisted their capacity for mature detailing and execution in a compressed timeframe. While they eventually attained resolution of an exquisite project, some last-minute decisions were inevitably rushed.

Students do not know what they do not know. This is to say that a student who has never taken (or even witnessed) a project beyond schematic design thinks that the work is fully developed and ready for building, when in fact many questions remain to be asked and answered before building can commence. The intensity of real-world project experience differs drastically from the linearity of the learning process in a typical studio environment. Rather than each subject being brought up sequentially, the multiplicity of factors involved results in a range of questions arising simultaneously.[6]

Each requires knowledge from various areas of expertise, which need to be synthesized in practical applications. In this context, *savoir* (knowledge) and *savoir-faire* (know-how) are of equal importance. The imperative to utilize these abilities in tandem results in the forming of durable knowledge: knowledge that is deeply engrained.

FIGURE 8.8 *Little League Fieldhouse*, Sharon, Virginia, 2014
Source: Jeff Goldberg/Esto

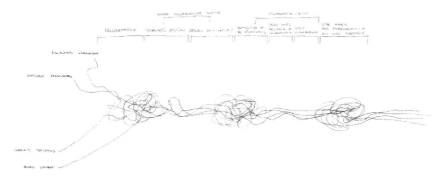

FIGURE 8.9 Process diagram
Source: design/buildLAB

The Impact

The educational and benevolent values of community-based designbuild programs such as the design/buildLAB are undeniable. In five years, the program was able to provide architecture students with an unparalleled educational and character-building experience, one that profoundly impacted their personal and professional development. At the same time, the program provided economically distressed communities with state-of-the-art public facilities, dramatically improving their prospects for the future.

Paradoxically, the qualities that make this mix a success also define the limits of its educational reach. Because these projects are realized in a charitable setting—for real communities with real needs and limited resources—they can never be truly experimental, and therefore their innovative potential is limited. While students are allowed to stumble, failure is never an option. Eventually, if the building did fail, who would be responsible? In such a context, educators are faced with a tremendous dilemma, one that is almost impossible to resolve: what is best for the public is not necessarily best for the education of the students, and vice versa.

For example, to allow students to execute unconventional construction details of their design means taking a risk on the long-term maintenance needs of the building for the community. Yet, not allowing them to do so would limit the students' growth as creative professionals. Community-based projects have the potential to put the faculty in constant contradiction with the premise of the educational experience itself—for the students to lead the realization of a project that they designed—because the faculty may have to intervene to avert potentially catastrophic decisions. To give the students the freedom to innovate is to face the inevitable long-term pressures of the community once the students are gone and adjustments are needed. This requires a tremendous personal commitment, one that cannot be imposed on any given team of faculty.

Another potential pitfall to continued community activism is project saturation: how much change can a community handle, and how many projects can it build support for? For the design/buildLAB, this is partially addressed with careful selection of the building sites, purposely removed from each other geographically. However, the realization of projects within a single county still calls upon the participation of the same pool of people, local businesses in particular. Keeping the community involved and engaged in the process of realizing projects becomes increasingly more challenging when they repeatedly occur in the same place, for a simple reason: by building the trust of the community in their ability to make the projects happen, students and faculty can unintentionally build an expectation of inevitability.

The design/buildLAB experienced this symptom for the first time through the realization of the Sharon Fields, built to expand the impact of the Sharon Fieldhouse, the year immediately following its completion. Because the Fieldhouse was already in use and because the previous team had demonstrated such determination in making the extraordinary possible, the sense of challenge seemed to be removed from the collective mindset, and the community showed significantly less initiative to participate in the endeavor.

In a recent interview, Canadian architect Brian MacKay-Lyons recalled Italian architect Giancarlo De Carlo (a proponent of participatory design) imparting the wisdom, "to serve is not to be a servant."[7] No matter how well intentioned, charitable initiatives should not contribute to community passivity. On the contrary, they should be the catalyst to stimulate additional positive change from within the community itself.

While design/buildLAB projects are funded largely by capital and material sourced from an aggregate of public, private, foundation, and corporate

FIGURE 8.10 design/buildLAB students adjusting the alignment of their prefabricated press box as a crane lowers it onto its concrete stem-walls, *Little League Fields*, Sharon, Virginia, 2015

Source: Jeff Goldberg/Esto

organizations, with an equally diverse set of philanthropic, community development, marketing, and research interests, the most treasured contributions come from the communities themselves. When design/buildLAB students move on site at the end of the spring semester to assemble their prefabricated building elements, the outpouring of generosity from local families, businesses, and tradesmen is overwhelming. For all design/buildLAB projects, communities have organized themselves to participate in labor-intensive tasks, to store tools and materials, to lodge the students in their homes, to provide meals, and even to wash students' laundry. By taking ownership of the effort to make the building, the communities became vested in the independent maintenance and long-term vitality of its civic architecture. Over the years, the momentum created around design/buildLAB projects has both propelled latent community enterprises, such as the creation of an art school and the rehabilitation of a century-old theatre, and sparked private development, such as inns and restaurants. Design/buildLAB projects have become unprecedented ambassadors for the value of architecture and architects, and the process of realizing them will remain in the collective memory of these communities for years to come as an inspiring example of what is possible.

Taking Stock

Since most student work will never be built, the prevailing pedagogical models rely on drawings and models to simulate the complex process of developing an idea from conception to realization.[8] The designbuild approach to teaching architects is simply a strategy to remove this abstraction. This approach is at its best when 1) the project is a work of architecture, 2) the project is designed by the students, and 3) the students, themselves, direct its realization. Beyond technical skills, design/buildLAB students undoubtedly experience "what the process of making concrete things reveals to us about ourselves."[9] The teaching of architecture is, after all, the empowering of students to develop and own their process.

The design/buildLAB offers students real-world experience where education is the primary driver. Students have less difficulty connecting with course content because they understand how they will deploy it in their own unique futures. The making of their project not only requires them to hone skills in design, construction, communication, and administration, but also exposes them to the plurality of disciplinary concerns like social consciousness, environmental stewardship, poetics, and craft. Above all, the design/buildLAB is an initiative with a tangible impact on people, resulting in the education of architects about the value of the public, and the education of the public about the value of architecture.

At a time when architects are increasingly interested in the production of images, and the public is increasingly skeptical about the value architects offer, the academy has a responsibility to ask critical questions of the profession, and to drive constructive change. Such optimistic approaches are critical to the reshaping of architectural education—and thus, to the reshaping of the profession.

Notes

1 Brian Mackay-Lyons, *Ghost: Building an Architectural Vision* (New York: Princeton Architectural Press, 2008).
2 Frank Weiner and Shelley Martin, "The Education of An Architect: 3 Points of View: Rowe, Hejduk and Ferrari," *Association of Collegiate Schools of Architecture 93rd Annual Meeting, The Art of Architecture/The Science of Architecture* (2005).
3 Juhani Pallasmaa, *The Thinking Hand: Existential and Embodied Wisdom in Architecture* (Chichester, UK: Wiley, 2009).
4 Bernard Marrey, *Architecte: du maître de l'oeuvre au disagneur* (Paris: Editions Du Linteau, 2014).
5 Charles Burchard, "A Curriculum Geared to the Times," *AIA Journal*, May 1967.
6 Ibid.
7 Marie Zawistowski, Keith Zawistowski, and Brian MacKay-Lyons, "Design Dialogue," *Inform*, 26 September 2014, http://readinform.com/design-dialogue/design-dialogue-brian-mackay-lyons.
8 Scott Marble, David Smiley, and Marwan Al-Sayed, "Student Work at Columbia: A Discussion with Kenneth Frampton," preface to *Architecture and Body, The Special Project from Precis, Columbia Architectural Journal* (Rizzoli, 1989).
9 Richard Sennett, *The Craftsman* (New Haven: Yale University Press, 2008).

9

EMBODIED MAKING

Designing at Full Scale

Terry Boling

> *The way to true architectural empathy is through an understanding of weight, material, and assembly. That the way to form is through material . . . in short, that the way to a spiritual understanding of a building is through a constructional understanding.*
>
> —Edward Ford[1]

In a period of architectural production giddy with the euphoria of computer-generated form, the messy facts of construction—weight, material, weather, touch, and smell—have been supplanted by clean virtuality. Gone are the nuances and inflections of the hand and body leaving indelible traces of time, place, technique, and humanity in the work—the resistance of real material cannot be experienced in the realm of the digital. The prevalence of MDF, polyurethane foam, and plastics as the primary prototyping materials in many digital fabrication labs underscores the desire for *virtual* materials that respond predictably to computer-controlled machining. It is likely that this recognition fuels the fire in experiential learning and design-build studios across the country today. Students are hungry for the directness and physicality of the constructed artifact—made even more cogent as a result of our increased dependence on digital tools and our disconnection from manual ones. Several architecture schools have responded to this rift by embedding the teaching of construction, materials, and methods in a studio environment, where students design something and then construct it themselves. While this exposure to construction can certainly contribute to the understanding of the complex relationships between the work of the architect and the work of the builder, the process is typically linear—design followed by construction. The pedagogical position outlined here, however, is that making at full scale is not simply a means to an end, but is actually a powerful design tool that can provide specific feedback distinct from other modes of design inquiry. Particularly at the scale of the detail, the process of enabling the simultaneity of design and construction as a technique can illuminate and reveal the forces of mind and hand working together, embedding tectonic qualities directly in the work itself.[2]

Drawing Conclusions

My own spark for making ignited in the late 1980s when I was a student of architecture, comfortably enveloped in the seductive veil of architectural theory and representation that defined many architectural schools at that time. Discovering the work of people like Steve Badanes and Jersey Devil, Michael Cadwell, and shortly thereafter Dan Hoffman had an enormous impact on me. Their work posited an alternative to the detached, academic provocations I was taught and instead embraced construction, craft, and place as the true content of architecture. Of particular interest for me was the shift in emphasis from the abstractions of drawing (which were my only tools) to the constructed fact. In describing his own passion for making, Michael Cadwell laments the lack of meaning in the conventions of plans, sections, and elevations, as he no longer knew what the abstractions stood for, yearning for what he calls "sensual knowledge" that embraces the tactile and the temporal.[3] Much like a musical score or a recipe, an architect's work is primarily abstract and meant to be interpreted by someone else, a unique combination of words, graphics, and numbers used to accurately fix location and relationships of constituent components—"a set of instructions for realizing a building."[4] Robin Evans, in *Translations from Drawings to Buildings*, recognizes the distinct problem of representation for architects—that the work of an architect is always through an intervening medium, most often the drawing, while artists and sculptors work directly on their objects. Evans notes that perhaps the real potential of the medium of drawing in architecture is actually in its *difference* to the thing it is representing rather than in its similarity.[5] The ephemeral qualities of drawing stand in stark contrast to the corporeal properties of the things made. Evans suggests that architects might use the "transitive, communicative properties of the drawing to better effect."[6] Instead of a one-to-one relationship between drawing and building, new relationships can be constructed that critically interrogate drawing as a generative tool in the process of design. This notion of the expanded role of drawing seems especially clear in the work of Carlo Scarpa, whose drawings were never hollow instructions for making, but mediated between descriptive geometry, perspective, analysis, and technical detail all in the same space, presenting manifold possibilities and readings rather than one fixed and complete representation of an *a priori* idea.[7]

Position

Scarpa's re-working of the conventions of drawing might encourage us to similarly position a way of thinking and constructing that also breaks out of the rigid confines of representation. This might be akin to sketching with material—working at full scale, responding to the conditions, resistances, and tolerances of actual materials, searching for the latent and serendipitous rather than being bound by an abstract set of explicit instructions. Must a constructed architectural artifact always be the material consequence of a pre-determined idea—fixed and delineated by someone and then constructed by someone else—or can the act of making itself be generative, exploiting the dense, fertile ground of difference that Evans is implying and that Scarpa demonstrates in his drawings? I propose a way of building that uses the transitive power of iterative prototyping to advance the tectonic qualities in the work. This is not simply to say that the architect's direct involvement in the work is any guarantee of success—only to suggest that the gap between the abstraction of drawing and the constructed outcome has been neglected as a source of inspiration and meaning. A robust period of material and assembly explorations, full-scale prototyping, testing for fit on site, all combined with simultaneous refinements and modifications, constitute a significant part of a holistic and empathetic design process that has somehow disappeared in the work of most architects.

This is a difficult proposition today, as the days of the master builder are well behind us. Our current academic, professional, and legal constructs make very clear distinctions between intent, which is the architect's charge, and means and methods, which have been disconnected from the architect and have become the responsibility of the builder. The absurdity of this separation is brought to light by Nader Tehrani in the foreword to Michael Cadwell's book, *Strange Details:*

> How can one not, for instance, differentiate between a cast-in-place concrete wall and a pre-cast one, without simultaneously broaching significant material and philosophical questions? Severing the architect from the means and methods of construction is somewhat like permitting the writer to use a certain vocabulary, but disassociating it from the very alphabet from which the text emerges.[8]

The roles of architect and builder, as well as other highly specific offshoots such as construction management, product design and development, and materials science, are now all defined as separate and distinct professions, each having their own education, licensing, and legal ramifications. As a result of these fractures, many architects have been marginalized as image-makers, steadily losing control of the increasingly complex outcomes of the design and construction process.

The bifurcation of idea and its subsequent manifestation in architecture is nothing new. Although the rift between draughtsmanship and craftsmanship began during the Renaissance, the digital age has served to make the separation even more pronounced. As digital technologies replace manual ones, the interpretive or transitive possibilities in the design process appear to have been completely diminished. Building Information Modeling allows the entire building to be *constructed* virtually, composed of individual components embedded with information pertaining to their structural properties, performance specifications, and costs. The models can be seductive, yet deceptive; they *appear* complete yet lack any of the physical and haptic characteristics that connect them to a constructed reality. Our ability to virtually define forms and surfaces quickly with multiple-decimal-point accuracy is increasing exponentially, yet our intimate knowledge about materials, construction, and assembly has continued to atrophy. While not longing for a nostalgic return to craft, we must know much more about the behaviors and latent qualities of materials and processes if we intend to orchestrate them—through architecture—in a meaningful and critical manner.

Making It

Schools of architecture across the country have responded to the gap between the virtual and the real by offering students opportunities to engage in real construction through designbuild studios. Many of these studios adhere to a model of relationships that parallel traditional practices—the client who directs objectives, the architect who designs and documents, and the builder who executes the instructions. The distinctive feature of most of these studios, however, is the conflation of the designer and the builder—providing students with direct involvement in both the generation and the execution of the design. The consequent building process in these studios is typically linear and hierarchical, following the professional model, as students learn to procure materials, negotiate schedules, organize trades, and countless other practical tasks that comprise the role of the builder. I have taken a different position with my studios by not simulating this kind of practice model, but rather expanding a particular moment in the designbuild process that is often overlooked. I am not only concerned with teaching the students to build, but rather to encourage them to design *through* building—engaging the fertile gap between thinking and making.

The goal of the work in our studio is to eliminate the hard distinctions between the virtual and the real through the introduction of full-scale material and assembly prototyping as a generative force in design thinking. Instead of moving from general to particular, from abstract idea to physical manifestation, the work emphasizes the constructed material joint—the detail. Especially true in American architectural education, details are simply means to an end and, in most cases, operate primarily as technical solutions to problems of form. In marked contrast, Marco Frascari's seminal work, "The Tell-the-Tale Detail," describes how the architectural detail can be understood "as the minimal units of signification in the architectural production of meanings."[9] Details in this definition can be understood as generative—containing the embedded *DNA* of their own making—and can anticipate future constructions by positing explicit material and intellectual strategies that can be applied across a multitude of situations.[10]

Because the students at the University of Cincinnati are part of an educational system that integrates experiential learning through working in practice as part of the curriculum, our approach to the designbuild process is not modeled on the traditional relationships between client, architect, and builder, but operates more like sponsored applied research.[11] In the beginning of each project, the studio enters into an agreement with a partner that is willing to support a design investigation with mutually beneficial constructed outcomes. What the partner gains in return is a commitment from the studio to produce design research in the form of full-scale working prototypes. The prototypes are owned by the partner, and are often used to advance larger scopes of work in the future. Many organizations engage with the studio based on our previous work, some hoping to simply create a buzz around a particular event (Louder Than a Bomb) or a place (Five Points Alley).

The programmatic and performative expectations of the prototypes are articulated loosely in the beginning of each studio (seating, portable and transformable objects, exhibition space, performance space, lighting, etc.), yet no final products are defined until midstream, as potentials emerge from the constructions. It is important to note that the outcomes of each project, many of which are fairly comprehensive, should be considered incidental to the primary objectives of the research process and learning objectives. In this sense, the work is liberated from strict adherence to certain conventional architect/client responsibilities while engaging more actively with others, such as research and innovation. It is made clear that innovation, curiosity, and sensuality are as valid criteria as budget, schedule, and program. The work produced is speculative, and operates at the intimate scale of the architectural detail and assembly rather than at the scale of the building. The scope is intentionally myopic—it is critical to take on projects that will allow the students time and space to experiment, reflect, and refine at full scale in the space of a semester.

FIGURE 9.1 The studio worked with local high school students to design and build performance environments for Louder than a Bomb, the world's largest youth poetry competition. Shown is a student poet during the final competition. *Louder Than a Bomb*, Cincinnati, Ohio, 2015

Source: Nikki Weitz

FIGURE 9.2 A series of site installations for a neighborhood redevelopment organization to reclaim an abandoned interstitial space bound by several alleys. Integrated LED lighting was used extensively to make the space feel safe. Shown is a bench made from reconstituted wooden pallets, acrylic, and a stone cornice from a demolished building in the neighborhood. *Five Points Alley*, Cincinnati, Ohio, 2014
Source: Petar Mitev

Process

One of the first steps in the studio is to get all of the students certified on all of the tools in the college's fabrication shop. Woodworking, tool safety, and shop protocol are followed by several more advanced certificates for welding and metalwork.[12] The transformation from thinker to maker is tangible, as students that had previously never made more than a chipboard model exude confidence after mastering a few basic welding and forging skills.

The ensuing work begins as open-ended experiments, addressing both the intrinsic and extrinsic factors pertaining to material and assemblies. As the work is funded primarily through small donations from non-profit organizations, projects typically have extremely low budgets allocated to purchase materials. Instead of

FIGURE 9.3 Students are shown heating and bending metal on a custom fabricated jig to achieve a series of complex bends in 1/2" plate steel. *School of Architecture Bench*, Cincinnati, Ohio, 2012

Source: Tyler Walter

starting by defining form abstractly and then substituting an appropriate material, work commences with things that are simply at hand, or readily available as sources of inspiration. We found a steady source of free wooden pallets, often made from sturdy white oak and richly colored Douglas fir that were disassembled and re-worked as raw material. The university press gave us access to all of their old newspapers, tile companies donated stacks of remnant VCT tile, and we made weekly trips to the metal scrapyard in search of inspiration. This frugal attitude about material has regional roots: Cincinnati, my adopted hometown, is also home to Proctor and Gamble, a global company that started out using waste from the thriving livestock industry to make soap and candles. This attitude about material exemplifies a unique Midwestern work ethic of making something from nothing—a kind of industrial alchemy that defines a particular material culture. The transformation of something banal into something precious is at the heart of our own work in the studio.

It is possible to re-inscribe value and meaning to material through a process that is not industrialized, but crafted. This definition of craft is not simply the consequence of skilled labor, but results from a convergence of intellectual and physical operations, leaving indelible traces of processes, techniques, and humanity embedded in the work itself. "The authenticity of architectural experience is grounded in the tectonic language of building and the comprehensibility of the act of construction to the senses."[13] This quote by Juhani Palaasmaa and the previously cited work by Marco Frascari recognize the importance of a certain legibility of construction that is manifest in the work itself. The *mark of the maker* is evidence of the mind and hand at work in concert.

The beginning steps are structured to work with the simplest processes and materials—wood, steel, paper, plastics, etc.—are subject to operations like burning,

Embodied Making 147

FIGURE 9.4 Pallet wood was processed, assembled in modules, and then finely sanded with an industrial sander. The surfaces were then flame treated in a gradient pattern across several modules. The modules were then assembled in a steel angle frame. *Louder Than a Bomb*, Cincinnati, Ohio, 2015. Modular stage components
Source: Daniel Kruk

FIGURE 9.5 Corner detail showing modified hurricane tie strap at existing picture rail, and steel stud secondary structure. Vitrine is composed of opaque and transparent acrylic with dovetail joints and embedded aluminum clip angles and LED lighting. *School of Architecture Exhibition Vitrine*, Cincinnati, Ohio, 2012
Source: Terry Boling

bending, sanding, and cutting. Materials are worked, studied, hacked, coveted, set aside, and re-worked. Our primary interests are in the unexpected behaviors, resistances, tolerances, material limits, and serendipitous discoveries that can only be realized through this heuristic method.

The use of conventional architectural drawings and processes are minimized in favor of working through the materials directly. The design and construction of the work is intended to be simultaneous, creating a *feedback loop*—a unique phenomenon of learning through making.[14] This methodology can be difficult for many students to comprehend; because their world is increasingly driven by abstractions and images, the students are not usually accountable for connecting the design process with actual material consequences. Some students in the studio initially resist the iterative technique and fall back on habits—modeling ideas virtually before constructing them. A digital model is precise, predictable, and without gravity, tolerances, or mechanical connections. The deficiencies of the *design-then-build* technique are evident immediately, as the myriad tangible problems of simple construction face off squarely with an idealized concept. Thinly sawn wood profiles—crisp, clean, and straight in the model—sag under their own weight when spanning. Brutish bolts and screws appear where two pieces of material somehow seamlessly joined and connected virtually. The recognition of the difference between thought and action as an integral part of the design process is critical. Risk and failure are essential, as no innovation can happen without them. In fact, the discoveries made here are among the most enlightening, as happy accidents move the design in unexpected directions.

FIGURE 9.6 A series of experiments with 1/8" steel bar stock. The material was heated, twisted, and bent to test deformation and accuracy. *Louder Than a Bomb*, Cincinnati, Ohio, 2015

Source: Megan Gotsch and Daniel Kruk

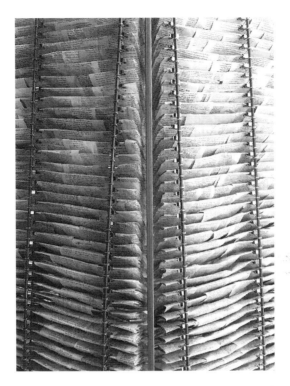

FIGURE 9.7 Book pages were cut out, stacked, crumpled, folded, and then fixed to a steel tube and rod armature with binder clips to create an enclosure with rough paper edges on the interior, and smooth folded striations on the perimeter. Louder Than a Bomb, Cincinnati, Ohio, 2016

Source: Terry Boling

Shay Myers, a fourth year undergraduate student in one of the studios, notes:

> The trial-and-error process is also a practice in efficiency—testing structure and connections while continually refining details. This also requires a high degree of discipline, to be able to delay making certain design decisions prematurely and instead trusting that the material explorations and the techniques that are discovered will ultimately yield something significant.[15]

Eighteenth century Italian philosopher Giambattista Vico's dictum "Verum Ipsum Factum," or truth through making, is poignantly realized as students begin to understand the limits, tolerances, and opportunities embedded in the materials and techniques of construction with their own hands. Even though the operative nature of the studio in schools of architecture is about making and invention in contrast to pure observation, the spirit of Vico's statement places the significance directly on the *thing in itself* rather than on its representation.

150 Terry Boling

After a long process of starts and stops, failures, and misdirections, repertoires of detailed moments emerge from the accumulated stock of experiments and slowly congeal into recognizable positions.

These are magic moments, when the vibe of the studio is set and the design direction is materialized. There are no longer only individual and personal investigations, but a communal collection of sympathetic work.

The great pianist Bill Evans wrote about group dynamics and the improvisational process in his liner notes for Miles Davis's masterpiece "Kind of Blue." While also noting that the "direct deed is the most meaningful reflection," using Japanese parchment painting as an example of improvisational art, he illustrates the problem of group improvisation in jazz: "Aside from the weighty technical problem of collective coherent thinking, there is the very human, even social need for sympathy from all members to bend for the common result."[16] This particular necessity in improvisational jazz music best describes the way students work together at this juncture. They must look, feel, listen, yield, and respond with varying degrees of individual and collective voices to create work that is truly coherent as a group composition. With the exception of group site models and research projects, students are generally accustomed to working on design individually and have little experience in collaborative design thinking. From a student's

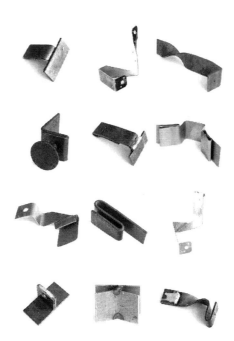

FIGURE 9.8 Bent steel plate clips and fasteners were developed as a family of details across the studio and used to assemble and connect components to each other. *Louder Than a Bomb*, Cincinnati, Ohio, 2015

Source: Megan Gotsch, Daniel Kruk, and Shay Myers

Embodied Making **151**

FIGURE 9.9 Forged steel leg and strut assembly of bench and exhibition wall. Bench constructed from reconstituted, laminated, and shaped pallet wood; paper panels held with twisted steel straps; and reclaimed leather sleeves at floor. *Louder Than a Bomb*, Cincinnati, Ohio, 2015

Source: Shay Myers

FIGURE 9.10 Exhibition wall with edge-lit and laser-etched acrylic panels with laminated and sanded newspaper panels beyond. Hand-written lines of poetry from the high school competitors were laser etched onto the marbleized surface of the paper. A serendipitous mistake in the laser settings burned through the paper, allowing light to come through the backlit panels. Louder Than a Bomb, Cincinnati, Ohio, 2015

Source: Terry Boling

152 Terry Boling

perspective, "working across groups was definitely one of our biggest challenges; the best strategy we found seemed to be figuring out what our common design opportunities were between projects and finding a shareable solution."[17]

Building Conclusions

> The process of designing and building at full scale has transformed my understanding of architecture. Now when I design, I can't draw two materials next to one another without thinking about how they will meet. Thinking about design in this way has unlocked my perspective from zoom extents, forcing me to consider questions of material, assembly, and weathering, alongside questions of site, programming, and form.
> —Pooja Kashyap, designbuild studio student[18]

Embodied making is a way of re-discovering what has been lamentably obscured in the education of the architect—the rich dialogue between intentions, materials, techniques, and form. Focusing on the scale of the hand—or detail—is a technique that enables this kind of experience to be a manageable part of any curriculum in a relatively short amount of time. As many schools of architecture contemplate the possibility of integrating designbuild in the curriculum,[19] it is important to note that the empirical evidence generated in an environment that supports full-scale material and assembly investigations can have a profound impact on students, regardless of scale.

Notes

1 Edward Ford, *Five Houses, Ten Details* (New York: Princeton Architectural Press, 2009), 26.
2 Eduard F. Sekler, "Structure, Construction, Tectonics," in *Structure in Art and in Science*, ed. Georgy Keppes (New York: George Brazziler, 1965), 89. The word *tectonic* here refers to Sekler's definition as what "cannot be described by construction and structure alone. For these qualities, which are expressive of a relation of form to force, the term tectonic should be reserved," as distinguished from a Semperian understanding of tectonics as pertaining exclusively to the frame and lightweight linear construction.
3 Michael Cadwell, *Pamphlet 17, Small Buildings* (New York: Princeton Architectural Press, 1996), 4.
4 Stan Allen, "Notations + Diagrams: Mapping the Intangible," *Practice: Architecture, Technique, and Representation* (New York: Routledge, 2009), 41. Nelson Goodman's distinction between the allographic and autographic arts is introduced here to explain the unique role of drawing in the making of architecture. The autographic arts are characterized by a direct relationship between author and object, while the allographic primarily involves notation.
5 Robin Evans, *Translations from Drawing to Building* (Cambridge: MIT Press, 1997), 154.
6 Ibid., 160.
7 Marco Frascari, "The Tell-the-Tale Detail," *Theorizing a New Agenda for Architecture*, ed. Kate Nesbitt (New York: Princeton Architectural Press, 1996), 500–514.
8 Nader Tehrani, "A Murder in the Court," in *Strange Details* by Michael Cadwell (Cambridge: MIT Press, 2007), vii–xi.
9 Frascari, "The Tell-the-Tale Detail," 500.
10 Frascari, "The Tell-the-Tale Detail," 509. Carlo Scarpa would often invent details without particular architectural responsibilities—only to discover the correct fit after using it several times in various contexts.

Embodied Making **153**

11 The University of Cincinnati is well known for their co-op program, where students alternate semesters of coursework with practice, equipping the students with exposure to contemporary office culture. While this kind of experiential learning plays a significant role in the students' education, many still lament the lack of connection to construction—both in the curriculum as well as in the field. To address this deficit, the school has offered several hands-on fabrication opportunities throughout the years in graduate elective courses, but due to the constantly shifting student population (students are in school for one semester, followed by a work semester, then school, etc.), projects were small in scope and lacked continuity in the curriculum. In 2012, William Williams, the director of the school, established a task force to implement designbuild pedagogy as a core part of the curriculum and appointed Michael Zaretsky as the director of the designbuild effort. MetroLAB was formed as a program within the university's School of Architecture and Interior Design that combines students and faculty from the school, the college, and the university with local, national, and international communities, developers, and stakeholders that support the infrastructure and development of the built environment. MetroLAB focuses on three pillars: learning through the process of making, applied design research, and community engagement.

12 Students are also encouraged to use our rapid prototyping center, which includes laser cutting and etching, CNC routing, and 3D printing. These technologies are best utilized after a sound understanding of the manual interface with material properties and the tools that shape them. In addition, our rapid prototyping facilities are shared with several other schools in the college and are run professionally. As there are no student-operated machines to experiment with directly, the studio objectives of simultaneity of design and construction and instant feedback are difficult to achieve. Our goal is to provide more direct access to these important tools.

13 Juhani Pallasmaa, *Eyes of the Skin* (West Sussex: Wiley, 2005), 64.

14 Instead of a linear process where all output is judged against an ideal set of conditions (a drawing or model, for example), the iterative process of making allows new criteria to enter and alter the outcomes. In the studio work, these are commonly accidental discoveries that are not anticipated yet often influence the final work.

15 Shay Myers, student of architecture in designbuild studio, email message to author, November 29, 2015.

16 Bill Evans, "Improvisation in Jazz," liner notes for "Kind of Blue," by Miles Davis, 1959.

17 Nikki Weitz, student of architecture in designbuild studio, email message to author, November 29, 2015.

18 Pooja Kashyap, student of architecture in designbuild studio, email message to author, November 27, 2015.

19 Geoff W. Gjertson, "House Divided: Challenges to Design/Build from Within," in proceedings of the Association of Collegiate Schools of Architecture Fall Conference 2011: Local Identities/Global Challenges. Here Gjertson outlines the challenges of integrating designbuild into the curriculum. Of particular note are the structural difficulties brought about by time, resources, and potential faculty alienation and burnout. Limiting the scale and scope of projects is one way to achieve the pedagogical goals of designbuild without sacrificing quality.

10

PRACTICING THE DIGITAL VERNACULAR

Raising a Barn and Raising Questions

James Stevens, Ralph Nelson, and Natalie Haddad

Introduction

We are perpetual students of architecture, makers with a passion for designbuild experiences that test the capability of our skills, our thinking, and our tools. As educators we continually craft learning experiences for our students and collaborate with them on a range of designbuild projects. We value designbuild education for the immediate and natural consequences of its process and its outcomes. As author David Pye has noted, "Design, like war, is an uncertain trade and we have to make the things we have designed before we can find out whether our assumptions are right or wrong."[1] Our pedagogical strategy is to lead students through experiences that simultaneously engage the real and the representational in a productive tug-of-war.

Our theoretical framework, the *Digital Vernacular*, guides our pedagogy.[2] It is a theory defined by practice and inspired by Yogi Berra's recognition that "in theory there is no difference between theory and practice. In practice there is." We recognize that digital tools are embedded in contemporary design practice and are rapidly being integrated with all phases of construction. We also recognize that designbuild traditions are embedded in vernacular architecture with principles founded in the memory and transfer of community knowledge and collaborative processes of construction. Clear examples are the barn raising traditions of the Midwest, which persist to this day, and the institutionalized examples such as that realized by Habitat for Humanity or the designbuild projects at schools of architecture throughout North America.

In this essay, we illuminate the origin and premise of the *Digital Vernacular* through the lens of a specific designbuild project, *The Barn*. We reflect on the questions raised through the process and outcome of this project and through lessons learned that have influenced students and faculty.

Illuminating the Digital Vernacular

We believe that sound education and meaningful design is based on learning from the past and fully engaging with the present. Design innovation emerges when time-tested principles are synthesized with available technologies and unique circumstances of time and place. These ideas are often contrary to contemporary design and academic practices that place primary emphasis on digital tools in the service of free-ranging expression and abstract representation. Global digital unification has generated a powerful desire to express new ideas in architecture independent of regional place and time, which has fostered a voracious appetite for a new global architecture built around common ideas, not common places or techniques. Students and faculty are influenced by these desires. We have found that designbuild education challenges digital hegemony with physical tangibility and feedback to provide a more critical focus and meaningful perspective.

The practical capabilities and seductive qualities of digital toolsets for design and fabrication have transformed the practice of architecture and altered the historic traditions of designbuild, which originally privileged the hand skills and learned traditions of the maker within a local context. To reconcile the contradiction of an abstract digital environment with concrete local circumstances, we have developed a theory and mode of practice we call the *Digital Vernacular*. The *Digital Vernacular* is an idea that combines vernacular design principles of the past and digital technologies of the present with goals of joining widely available digital tools with community knowledge to generate appropriate innovation in a contemporary design context. By vernacular we specifically mean the common building morphologies, construction preferences, and material availabilities that have developed in a particular culture, place, or climate. The use of the term digital embraces both numbers and fingers. We should foster the use of computers and computer driven tools as well as use of the most accessible tool, the human hand.

Prior to the Industrial Age, when *design* and *making* were aligned, master craftsmen within the vernacular trades created most architecture. The Industrial Age, and most recently the Information Age, shifted the role of the architect away from that of *master craftsman* to professional *knowledge worker*. As a result, a divide between design and making in the practice of architecture occurred. This shift changed an essential part of the architect's role in the process and also the way in which architects and students of architecture learn to design. By degrading the symbiotic relationship between mind and hand and limiting the exposure to immediate design consequences, students and architects have become the operators of tools that often only represent design, not tools that produce tangible design outcomes. By immersing students in designbuild processes and activities there is greater opportunity to operate the tools for both design and making in productive harmony.

Our design decisions only come to bear on us directly when we build. By building what we design, we must take responsibility for the immediate consequences of our decisions and our actions. The computer has leveled a new complexity on the student and architect. It can too easily remove from us an awareness of scale, tolerance, and tactility by providing a universally scaled world that is always level, square, and untouchable. The computer, in effect, dictates that the world should match the abstract coordinates of our software, which we all know is never true.

Technological developments have shifted the current economic model of architectural design and making by providing the opportunity to reestablish this lost connection. They have provided new opportunities for designbuild work-flows supported by digital tools. The innovative processes used to create digitally fabricated architecture are just now emerging with some clarity, and these parallel the confluence of readily accessible digital technologies with traditional construction methods. These technologies call for a more robust understanding of not only romanticized notions of the future but of sound design principles rooted in the historical and evolutionary development of architecture. We believe it is important for students to internalize this perspective in their educational experience.

To practice the *Digital Vernacular*, an architect must initially establish, through careful observation and analysis, one or more guiding vernacular precedents. Principles may be gleaned from a precedent through the recognition of design responses to particular circumstances. A vernacular design principle must be time-tested and be part of common or populist knowledge. Once a valuable precedent is selected, these principles set in motion a *Digital Vernacular* design process unique to each situation and context. It is not especially important which valuable vernacular precedents are identified or which principles are recognized, as long as they are clear, relevant, and interesting to the designer. What is most important is what the designer does with the precedents and principles and how they guide the definition of a design or designbuild proposition.

For example, in 17th century England, it was common to remove clay from pre-fired bricks in a process called "cut and rubbed" or gauged brickwork. Brick makers would take a standard unit and, using a wood jig, would rub the clay to remove material to create a unique profiled shape with specific practical and aesthetic characteristics. This process created brick units that could form twisting chimneys, roof coping, and other ornate masonry features common at that time. Using a *Digital Vernacular* design process, an architecture student can study this historic example (precedent), identify that it is a thoughtful and measured removal of material to create custom units that perform a specific role (principle), and then propose a new masonry design employing a removal process from a cast unit using digital tools and techniques (proposition). This process guides the student to achieve mass customized masonry units using sound principles and processes established in the vernacular tradition while employing appropriate traditional and contemporary digital tools.

The *Digital Vernacular* is a pedagogical approach that provides specific insights into the process of design, fabrication, and construction of physical outcomes. The

FIGURE 10.1 Bent number two prepared for raising, *The Barn*, Lawrence Technological University, Southfield Michigan, 2015
Source: Natalie Haddad

selected project, *The Barn*, demonstrates the variability and resiliency that digital fabrication provides in terms of scale, character, and construction methods guided by vernacular precedents and principles.

Barn Raising

The Barn project began with a small grant from the Coleman Foundation to support entrepreneurial activity within a design curriculum. Students and faculty framed the proposal collaboratively to explore new methods of construction with economic viability that could be applied to a simple building typology. The practical objective of *The Barn* was to design, develop, iterate, and fabricate an architectural structure built solely out of plywood sheets, digitally fabricated primarily with a student-built CNC tool, then finished and assembled with hand tools.

We were limited by the most readily available tools and materials. The pedagogical objective of *The Barn* was to provide students an opportunity and experience to develop an architectural experiment from initial design through fabrication and construction. It was to be based on simple vernacular precedents and principles and realized by alternating back and forth between, and engaging with, both digital and hand tools. These conditions were set so that students would be able to understand how vernacular principles can influence new work and demonstrate how an outcome is influenced by tool choice and use.

A programmed use was not defined for *The Barn*; rather the structure was imagined to accommodate a range of possible functions like most vernacular buildings. We expected our budget would not even allow us to build a full building, though we could create some prototype sections that could be

FIGURE 10.2 Architecture students assembling components of a bent on site
Source: Andreea Vasile

extended longitudinally. The sectional width of *The Barn* was initially defined relative to the estimated structural spanning limits of the plywood construction and by the size limits established for construction modules that could be moved or lifted by two or three people. The goal was to be able to accomplish any process from digital design to prototyping and fabrication without the use of heavy machinery or complex tools. The factors of weight and size guided the limits of element and component profiles. They were consistently discussed as variables throughout all iterations.

Students began the process by researching platform and balloon framing. Both have long been the dominant techniques in the construction of vernacular wood-frame buildings in North America. The systems use wood studs placed in frequent succession, which are then sheathed with boards or sheet goods, forming a structural diaphragm for lateral stability. This method has persisted because of the relatively low cost of new-growth lumber and sheet goods such as plywood, and also the persistent vernacular knowledge of wood framing. Dr. Larry Sass, a professor and researcher at M.I.T., transformed this system through the use of digital technology. In the *YourHouse* project, Dr. Sass replicated a New Orleans shotgun house using only CNC-cut plywood and assembled it using only friction-fit joinery.[3] Platform framing and the *YourHouse* project served as the initial precedents for *The Barn*.

Engaging these initial precedents, students digitally replicated significant details of the precedents and considered how they could be adapted to a new construction context. The students wanted to maximize the material potential of plywood, and they initially questioned the spacing of the structural elements. In traditional platform construction the studs are typically placed at 16" or 24" on center. For *The Barn*, the initial structural modules were considered at 24" to take advantage of the modular size of the plywood.

This led to exploratory models of four repetitive structural components—the wall, the eave, the roof, and the ridge.

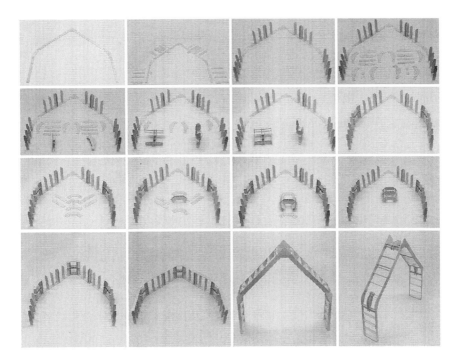

FIGURE 10.3 A scaled prototype assembly sequence
Source: Anthony Printz

Focusing on the structural conditions of the ridge and eave led students to a precedent study of pre-engineered steel buildings, which typically are defined as rigid *portal frames*, created by structural sections known as *bents* that taper following the load paths.[4] In simple terms, form follows force. Most manufacturers taper the steel sections to allow the width to increase at the eaves in response to the maximum moment at the eave. By understanding the structural principle of the vernacular portal frame, the students were able to integrate the principle into their design. What resulted was a digitally fabricated plywood bent that influenced a new type of structural prototype, assembly strategy, and the formal configuration of a clear-span building section.

With major details and challenges identified, the next step was to prototype, at full scale, an eave and ridge condition in response to the moment and shear forces. These prototypes allowed comparison of the scaled fabrication model to the full-scale component and to test its strength against structural calculations. The eave and ridge components were compression-tested to determine their shear and moment strength.

Tested in a controlled environment, both components resisted more than twice the estimated force load from the structural analysis. The structural tests allowed the students to observe how and where the details failed and also how well the connections worked in resisting the reaction forces.

FIGURE 10.4 Two plywood bents assembled and lifted into position
Source: Natalie Haddad

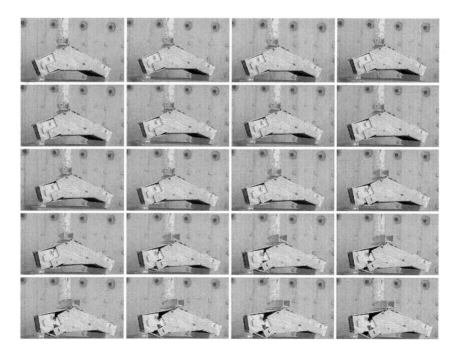

FIGURE 10.5 An eave moment prototype being tested for shear strength
Source: Anthony Printz

FIGURE 10.6 A 5'x10' DIY CNC machine cutting component parts
Source: Natalie Haddad

The test affirmed that the connections were the most vulnerable to failure. The students responded to the test data and created a new iteration that reinforced and reconfigured the areas of previous failure.

The final components of *The Barn* were fabricated using only 4'x8' sheets of plywood milled on a three-axis 5'x10' CNC machine.

The final building construction system was comprised of 4' wide structural bays of interlocking plywood sheets—joined with friction-fit tab-and-tenon connections and minimal screw fasteners to articulate continuous space and form. Each structural bay was subdivided into the wall, roof, eave, and ridge components that were limited by the overall dimensions of the 4'x8' plywood sheet. The weight of each component and bay module was considered for ease of transportation to a site and for lifting by two or three persons into position. Once on site, in the construction yard at our school, each bay was tilted up into place.

A significant constraint on *The Barn* project was the absence of a crane. Faced with plywood modules that weighed over 1,000 pounds, the students sought ways of lifting the units into place. Two 1,000 pound capacity wall jacks were used for lifting in combination with guidelines tied to the ridge and temporary wood stops that prevented each module from tipping beyond its resting point. The jacking points were located at the outer edge of the eave moment, evenly distributing the weight between the width and height of the structure.

The hand cranking of the jacks was a slow and sometimes scary process, but ultimately the gable end was lifted to a point where the guidelines could be pulled by two persons to settle the module into place. The process, relying on the precision of the digitally fabricated structure and the strength of a common jack, made for a stressful but effective "barn raising."

The module raising exposed the students to the virtues and potential drawbacks of digital pre-fabrication. The experience demonstrated David Pye's distinction between the craftsmanship of risk and the craftsmanship of certainty.[5] The

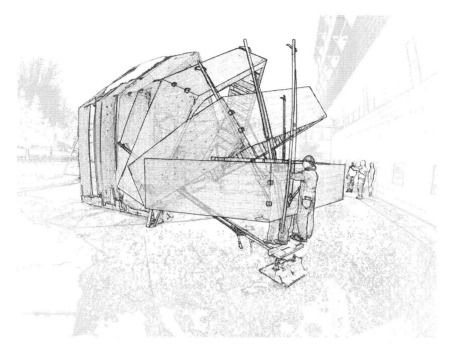

FIGURE 10.7 Barn raising process drawing
Source: Natalie Haddad

craftsmanship of risk is a process where the quality of the result is frequently at risk during the process of making and is dependent on the judgment and care exercised by the maker. The craftsmanship of certainty requires comprehensive planning of the process prior to fabrication and erection with all components pre-determined and pre-tested to the greatest extent possible.

The process of making *The Barn* exhibited traits of both certainty and risk, the barn raising leaning heavily toward the side of risk. The students had worked for months to design, test, fabricate, and assemble components in multiple iterations. They were confident and certain that the fabricated components would perform as expected once lifted into position. Standing on site on a cold Michigan night, the students faced the reality of lifting the modules into place and the actual risk that this entailed.

The prospect of failure was tangible. The reality of their design decisions came to bear as the jacks lifted a module into place. The students discovered that even the craftsmanship of certainty is fraught with risk and when experimenting with a new idea all the upfront planning can never remove the responsibility to exercise continual judgment, care, and creative improvisation.

Balancing certainty with risk introduced the recognition of tolerance as an important factor for all construction, and especially critical for digital fabrication. If a wall or module is not placed square and level, it will be difficult to adjust

FIGURE 10.8 Architecture students lifting a bent using wall jacks and guidelines
Source: Andreea Vasile

unless tolerance is designed into the component and the erection process. To further complicate the issue, each bent, even if square, true, and stable prior to lifting, could develop slight settling and misalign the joint between multiple panels. To correct this problem is not as simple as shimming an 1,800-pound assembly. The misalignments in the foundation proved to be an issue when attaching the modules together. There were slight shifts in all directions due to the differences between the precision in the plywood structure and a student-built foundation. This required adapting the design to account for this necessary tolerance. The students introduced a new set of holes at the base of each module at strategic points for the insertion of circular drift pins to assist with alignment of the modules and accomplish smoother transitions from bent to bent.

The Barn prototyping was completed after raising three full-section modules over a foundation. Students considered interior and exterior cladding applications as well as insulation strategies, though these were beyond the scope of the initial grant-funded research. Students covered *The Barn* in tarpaper to protect the plywood and monitored the structure over the winter to observe changes in response to temperature, humidity, snow load, or connection failure. *The Barn* was dismantled following the observation period. Its components and lessons are being reapplied in a project currently in progress in which students are designing, digitally fabricating, and building a house for a local chapter of Habitat for Humanity.

Question Raising

The most significant outcome of *The Barn* was the questions that the project revealed and inspired, which are now guiding new student designbuild projects.

Not surprisingly, most of the challenging questions resided in the paradox between the digital realm and the haptic world. Working within a design-build context allowed this paradox to present itself on a frequent basis, providing a broad range of learning opportunities. Designbuild pedagogy should be structured to allow these questions to be both posed and addressed by students immersed in hands-on work.

Are Construction Drawings Necessary for Digital Fabrication Designbuild?

Robin Evans states in *Translations from Drawing to Building* that "[denying drawn communication] would be possible, yet seems very unlikely to occur because, for architecture, even in the solitude of pretended autonomy, there is one unfailing communicant, and that is the drawing."[6] Traditional construction techniques require interpretation of design drawings by builders; the drawings are only a representation of what is intended. Yet, digital fabrication processes remove the builder's interpretation, via file-to-fabrication, providing an outcome directly fabricated from a digital file. Despite these factors, the students discovered that new sets of information were necessary to effectively communicate and document beyond the construction drawing. The students questioned traditional construction

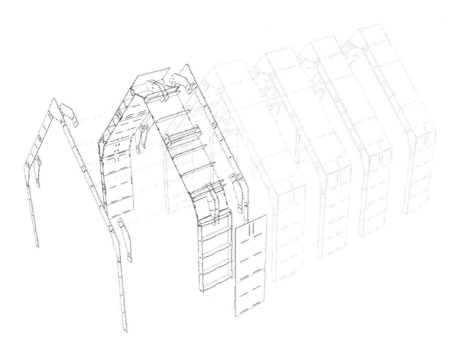

FIGURE 10.9 An isometric drawing showing parts of a bent
Source: Ergys Hoxha

documentation by supplanting many standard orthogonal drawings with exploded isometric drawings focused on major points of assembly.

As educators trained in traditional practice and the rigorous application of graphic standards for construction drawings, this was a teaching challenge. Designbuild pedagogy should allow students to discover what drawings are necessary and how the drawings are used in the designbuild process.

What Advantages are Offered by Designbuild in the Context of Digital Design?

An advantage to physically making what you digitally design is the ability to understand material, tool, and construction issues that may arise and must be addressed in the design process prior to and during construction. The students are in control of the design, fabrication, and assembly process; and this full scope of responsibility profoundly influences their approach to design. A digital workflow provides an opportunity for timely on-site adaptation and allows changes to continually cycle through the full design, fabrication, and assembly process. As educators, we recognize the importance of the students' ability to work in a continuous fluid motion between design and making. This advantage comes with a caution. It takes time, skill, and effort for the students to reach a fluidity of making necessary to achieve the advantages of digital fabrication. This is only realized toward the end of a student's education. Designbuild pedagogy must be designed to immerse students into digital fabrication with appropriately managed and limited complexity until they achieve a skillful fluidity of thinking and making.

How is Complexity Handled in a Designbuild Digital Fabrication Project?

One of our students, Jia Liu, notes that the digital finger is prone to fatigue and the digital computer is prone to stamina. In her words, digital tools "push human production capacity to unprecedented heights" to deal with an overwhelming "mass of accuracy of information." The computer's stamina far exceeds the threshold of the number of component locations and orientations that one student can memorize. Since most digitally designed and fabricated designbuild projects have some form of uniqueness, the unfamiliarity provides a need for clarification and review before the assembly process commences. The students are able to identify and conceptually determine the location and orientation of individual components at any stage in the making process. However, the students agree that the complexity of the design and the efforts required to communicate the location and orientation of all components at all times is an overwhelming task. Designbuild educators need to engage students in challenges that test new ways of managing complexity. These investigations will need to go beyond drawings and documentation and reach into the simulation of assembly and management of workflow.

FIGURE 10.10 Students preparing for assembly
Source: Natalie Haddad

How Important is Tolerance in Digital Designbuild?

All successful construction techniques have a tolerance, without this they fail to respond to an inexact world. Material limits need to be defined, and a student needs to understand what this limit is and how it may change for each material and environmental condition. Given that digital fabrication lends itself to the control and creation of multiple components and assemblies, tolerance knowledge is essential. It is important for designbuild educators to understand that most students are aware of the need and consequences of tolerance but few are able to skillfully make the necessary accommodation. Mastery of the tolerance variable is of paramount importance and requires rigor and time.

Conclusion

As educators we are fully committed to designbuild projects in academia because the learning experiences for students are challenging, meaningful, and distinct from design-only studios and conventional coursework. The demands of designbuild inherently require students to fully engage tangible circumstances that promote honesty, integrity, and a robust work ethic. Students become familiar with a range of design and construction limits and begin to respect their value as catalysts for creative thinking and action. We believe it is important to develop designbuild pedagogy around a guiding framework of sound principles and clear strategies for processes such as that provided by the *Digital Vernacular.*

We believe that contemporary digital tools for both representation and fabrication have opened up new avenues of design exploration and work-flow management that now make designbuild both more accessible and more enriching than ever before. But these digital tools must be utilized within a practical and ethical perspective that demands greater understanding of how not only something can be made but also why it is made. We recognize the continued importance of designing and building by hand, to maintain a tangible connection to work that may be conceived in an electronic realm but must live in the haptic realm.

We have deep respect for vernacular architecture and the principles that have guided the vernacular in the long and continuing evolution of design activity. We are continually inspired by the "native genius in anonymous architecture" as described by Sibly Moholy-Nagy in her seminal book of this title.[7] The vernacular is a powerful expression of cultural forces, and the scope and scale of vernacular architecture is affected by the inherent conditions of labor, tools, knowledge, and infrastructural resources.[8] We believe that drawing from the well-spring of vernacular architecture provides a meaningful and useful guide in the creation of new architecture, and an antidote to much of the abstract and formal experimentation that guides much of contemporary architecture with little regard for the past, the present, or collective values. Perhaps most importantly, we have found that the vernacular provides both solid footing and accessible ideas for our students, who then transform these ideas through the power of their intellect and creativity. As the filmmaker Jean Luc Godard has said, "it is not where you take things from— it's where you take them to" that really matters.[9]

Notes

1 David Pye, *The Nature and Aesthetics of Design* (New York: Van Nostrand Reinhold, 1978), 27.
2 James Stevens and Ralph Nelson, *Digital Vernacular: Architectural Principles, Tools, and Processes* (New York: Routledge, 2015).
3 Lawrence Sass and Marcel Botha, "The Instant House," *International Journal of Architectural Computing* 4.4 (2006): 109–123.
4 Henrich Engle, *Structure Systems* (New York: Van Nostrand Reinhold, 1981).
5 David Pye, *The Nature and Art of Workmanship* (Cambridge: University Press, 1968), 20–29.
6 Robin Evans, *Translations from Drawing to Building and Other Essays* (London: Architectural Association, 1997), 153–193.
7 Sibly Moholy-Nagy, *Native Genius in Anonymous Architecture* (New York: Horizon, 1957), 19.
8 John Brinckerhoff Jackson, *Discovering the Vernacular Landscape* (New Haven: Yale University Press, 1984).
9 Austin Kleon, *Steal Like an Artist* (New York: Workman Pub, 2012).

PART 4

Practice
The Academic-Professional Bridge

11

SECOND NATURE

Embedded Knowledge through Designbuild Education

Tricia Stuth

The practice of architecture is complex and becoming more so. Newly developing construction techniques, the expanding information management requirements of data-rich modeling and documentation software, and the growing imperative for addressing the performative characteristics of the built environment all put pressure on contemporary practitioners while not relieving them of the architects' role as a creator of culturally significant artifacts. The melding of art and science, long understood as the territory of architecture, today requires a broader range of knowledge than was necessary even a few decades ago. To gain expertise in these emerging areas of professional concern is laborious. Yet, as with any realm of knowledge, for such expertise to fully inform the design process, the practitioner must develop a level of facility with the information such that it becomes *second nature*. Only then will these concerns become integral to the work.

The process of developing such embedded understandings of these complex issues presents difficulties for both the profession and the academy. For practitioners, significant development of new expertise cannot be undertaken with each project. It is simply too costly. Some reasonable percentage of work in a professional office must be accomplished with well-understood processes that are reliable and efficient. Within schools of design, the development of the functional knowledge needed to grapple with the expanding field of professional concerns (familiarity with construction technologies, ability with analytic software, and a working knowledge of the principles of building science) suffer from a perceived lack of criticality and are routinely seen as mere vocational skills.

A Case Study for Applied Research and Education

The New Norris House (NNH), a *designbuild-and-evaluate* project at the University of Tennessee (UT), recognizes these criticisms and allows participants to develop embedded knowledge in ways that overcome impediments in the profession and the academy. The project produces a single-family dwelling that is modular, prototypical, resource efficient, and located on a previously developed infill lot in Norris, Tennessee, a New Deal town created by the Tennessee Valley Authority (TVA).

One of the first planned communities in the United States, the town is on the National Register of Historic Places. Key to the community were the Norris Houses, homes built as models of modern, affordable, and efficient living. These homes integrated new technologies of the time—municipal electricity, water and sanitary systems—and incorporated new materials and building techniques. The NNH commemorates the 75th anniversary of Norris and reconsiders its agenda.

Honored with LEED for Homes Platinum certification, an AIA COTE Top Ten Green Award, an ASLA Honor Award, and a Residential Architect Design Award, the NNH pursues high performance buildings through traditional and innovative means. Stewardship and the betterment of society were central to the original Norris project and serve as touchstones for the NNH.

The NNH is less than half the size of the median US house and sited on a 0.3-acre lot. A Norris House plan informed the NNH's 24'x32' footprint.[1] The 768 square foot home (1,006 square feet including a loft) can allow one, two, or three sleeping rooms and includes one bathroom.

Natural, durable materials that improve with weathering resonate with the historic context. The placement of apertures is optimized to enhance spaciousness, balance connections to the public street and forest preserve, and leverage useful solar gain and natural ventilation. Off-site construction led to a seventy

FIGURE 11.1 Montage of original Norris Houses beyond and in window reflection of the New Norris House, *New Norris House,* Norris, Tennessee, 2010

Source: The University of Tennessee College of Architecture and Design

Second Nature **173**

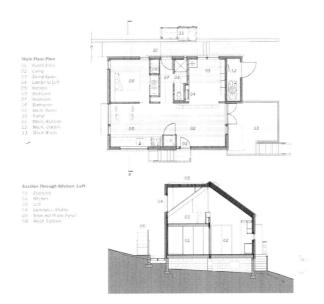

FIGURE 11.2 Main Floor Plan and Cross Section, *New Norris House*, Norris, Tennessee, 2010
Source: The University of Tennessee College of Architecture and Design

FIGURE 11.3 Interior view looking toward Oak Road, *New Norris House*, Norris, Tennessee, 2011
Source: Ken McKown

percent diversion of construction waste. Advanced framing resulted in a seventeen and a half percent reduction in lumber, increased insulation, and decreased thermal bridging. A ventilated rainscreen façade resists moisture and decay while highly insulated walls reduce heat transfer. Active systems are minimized by passive design. Efficient equipment includes ductless heat/air systems, energy recovery ventilation, ceiling fans, and solar hot water heating. Collected roof water is treated for non-potable uses and greywater and stormwater are managed on site.

The NNH is also regarded for its educational methods. Recognition for pedagogy includes: the US Environmental Protection Agency's P3 Student Design Competition; an NCARB Prize for the Creative Integration of Education and Practice; and the ACSA Design/Build Award. The NNH was conceived for students to learn about sustainability through direct engagement with the built environment. Within the context of the research university and the project's historic setting, this pedagogy relies on interdisciplinary education and research and models for collaborative practice.

Design Education and Sustainability

A design studio paired with a co-requisite technology seminar is a long-standing hallmark of the UT curriculum. This course pairing allows for faculty input necessary to integrate structure, construction, and environmental systems in the design of a hypothetical building. The school also values learning through physical making, with seminars exploring design through construction dating back to the 1970s. In 2007, UT faculty voted to support the 2010 Imperative and the 2030 Challenge.[2] Many viewed increased integration of sustainable design and technology in the studio pedagogy as vital to this challenge.

Spurred by this position and supported by grants for two designbuild projects (including the NNH), designbuild education at UT rapidly scaled up in size and complexity around this time. These efforts represented the desire of the faculty to practice, teach, and research collaboratively and broadly—to achieve the highest levels of design excellence, environmental performance, and social responsibility. Previous designbuild projects were modest, and small teams led by faculty relied on hired or volunteer consultants and help from building science instructors. Yet the NNH project required a broader range of knowledge, skills, perspectives, and intense collaboration. The diverse expertise and modes of inquiry were essential to engaging with the issues that the project would encompass.

Forming a diverse team of faculty, students, and non-academic contributors is among the central challenges of designbuild projects. Financial, structural, and philosophical, this challenge is exacerbated by conventional studio formats and teaching assignments. Architecture students normally learn design by developing individual theoretical projects. Architecture professors typically guide students' processes in studio where classmates are also architecture students. In such settings the integration of technology and the implications for failing to address environmental imperatives often remain abstract propositions. A studio that offers opportunities to actively synthesize technology and design is critical to the development of such abilities. Designbuild impels students to synthesize design and technology and begin to embed skills and knowledge that ultimately give rise to intuitive understanding of technical concepts. Delaying such experiences delays second nature modes of working, which merge technology with creative processes.

Sustainable Practice and Design

The NNH conceptualizes issues of sustainability broadly and develops knowledge through execution and evaluation. The project location, twenty miles from UT, was chosen for its regional context and place in US history. The Tennessee Valley Authority Act was one of the most ambitious of the New Deal programs. It established the Tennessee Valley Authority (TVA) in 1933 to manage the Tennessee River watershed and generate electricity supplied through dams and power stations along the river.[3]

Yet, the TVA's goals were more comprehensive, including "flood control, improved river navigation, increased fertilizer production, better agricultural practices, natural resource conservation, [and] industrial promotion."[4] Modernization transformed life in the Tennessee Valley, and the TVA was conscious of its planning agenda and associated social aims. Planning for a region was unprecedented, and planners, engineers, architects, landscape architects, and artists were organized

FIGURE 11.4 Norris Dam and Powerhouse, Norris, Tennessee, between 1933 and 1945
Source: U.S. Farm Security Administration/Office of War Information Black & White Photographs

176 Tricia Stuth

to work cooperatively with construction divisions. Capitalizing on the need for housing at the site of the first dam, the TVA used Norris to devise, construct, test, and evaluate a series of housing types that sought to integrate the practical, technical, and beautiful for the benefit of the region and enduring use and enjoyment by its people.[5]

We took cues from the TVA's work at Norris as an essential criteria for our work: interdisciplinary cooperation; shared responsibility; and assessment of decisions relative to the region and its temporal, spatial, regulatory, economic, sociocultural, and environmental conditions. In this effort faculty and students filled multiple overlapping roles: 1) developer/owner and property manager, 2) designer/engineer, and 3) contractor/builder. This structure provided students with direct experience acting from concerns specific to each role *and* to a shared objective— sustainable dwelling.

In *Integrated Design in Contemporary Architecture*, Kiel Moe notes that "sustainable architecture" has become a vague concept while suggesting that

> 'Integrated Design' is a term that characterizes what architects and architecture students do when they incorporate the energy, site, and climatic, formal, construction, programmatic, regulatory, economic, and social aspects of a project as primary parameters for design. The result is often better building design and building performance on account of a fundamental engagement with these multiple often complex, contexts that condition contemporary architecture. In doing so, practitioners engender what could be more sustainable modes of practice. If architecture becomes more sustainable, it is because its practices and building will become more integrated.[6]

The NNH posits that sustainability is achievable only through processes that serve to integrate diverse and complex issues. Such processes require a range of contributors. It is valuable to examine the partners and processes that enabled particular achievements in sustainable design and integration—and make the NNH notable for its comprehensiveness perhaps more than its innovativeness. In the following sections, three areas of focus are organized around partnerships and processes that led to successes in construction and project delivery, high performance, and stewardship.

Construction and Project Delivery

An early goal of the project was to use experimental materials, building assemblies, and construction techniques to make affordable, resource efficient housing that reinterpreted vernacular dwellings.[7] Other objectives emerged from the region's history and resources, namely to use Integrated Project Delivery (IPD) to factory-build a home that is prototypical yet site specific; and to combine on- and off-site fabrication to respond to climate and place.

The site, part of the 1933 Plan of Norris, included a derelict Norris House. Lack of a formal designbuild curriculum meant students would be enrolled in unrelated classes on campus far from the site. This challenge was addressed through an industry partnership. Clayton Homes, the nation's largest producer of manufactured and modular housing, is headquartered in the area. Working with Clayton helped address the difficulty of the remote site and introduced significant expertise as well as significant constraints arising from its manufacturing processes, assemblies, and materials. An eight-member team of architecture, civil and structural engineering, and environmental studies students set high performance targets and potential strategies. Tours of the factory and detailed inventories of historic Norris residences provided the context to understand temporal, social, material, and technical matters.

At mid-semester, students made a presentation to partners at Clayton that effectively communicated the project's complexity, potential, and integral conception. This established credibility and convinced Clayton of the project's value. The term concluded with a full-day charrette with Clayton which identified numerous challenges including: an under-supported hinged roof; optimized framing; details with precise aesthetic, systems, and performance criteria; a high performance thermal envelope; benign material specifications; green technology integration; and modular installation. The team grew to twenty-one architecture, structural engineering, and landscape architecture students. Concerns that crossed scales and disciplines and drove the original Norris Project were apparent. Work focused on preparations for a five-day factory line and site installation the following September. The lengthy process provided time to reflect on the surrounding region and New Deal landscape. Learning centered on effective communication to coordinate what would be done, by whom, and how and when portions of the work would meet.

Working with Clayton, students developed detailed shop drawings and specifications. These instruments recorded a process of negotiated agreements rather than the assignment of liability or responsibility. Students worked closely with Clayton's purchasing department to source materials to meet regional, recycled, and sustainably harvested criteria. Particular effort was required to control glues and sealants used in the factory. Requirements for transparency in material content represented new ground both for students and some suppliers. Fine-grained integration included material substitutions. For example, Clayton uses a thin layer of luan over framing to increase rigidity during transport. Instead of this tropical wood, the NNH used dense cardboard.

Experience with prefabrication extended to student-built components. In constructing decks, ramps, stairs, a dormer, and mechanical housing, students modeled Clayton's processes in anticipating and timing factory and site components, planning for systems integration, and building with tight tolerances. Following the spring semester, five paid summer assistants worked to ensure design quality and consistency. Three assistants continued the following year and focused on

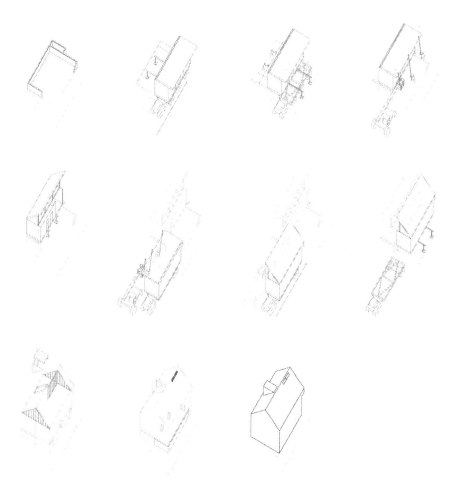

FIGURE 11.5 Diagrams illustrate sequence for installing modules and work completed on site, *New Norris House*, Norris, Tennessee, 2012

Source: The University of Tennessee College of Architecture and Design

1) factory construction/systems coordination, commissioning, and monitoring set-up; 2) on-site supervision; and 3) off-site supervision.

Students and faculty from civil engineering, structural engineering, and landscape architecture provided expertise to prepare the site and to achieve integration and performance goals. The university required a contractor to oversee site work and footings, and to subcontract with mechanical, electrical, and plumbing trades, providing students with exposure to construction administration. By fall 2010 coordination with Clayton was largely complete. A student team learned to do masonry and built foundation walls—finishing this work after the modules were set, but not lowered. Other teams refined roof details and built custom doors and windows. During the week of the factory-build, all students witnessed parts

FIGURE 11.6 Factory-built modules were completed at the site, *New Norris House*, Norris, Tennessee, 2010–2011

Source: The University of Tennessee College of Architecture and Design

of the production. Two assistants remained at the plant to answer questions and to photograph for LEED documentation. On September 29, 2010, students observed and assisted the set team. In one day the modules were set, roofs raised, temporarily blocked, and tied down. The next day, the set team helped students install the panelized dormer, and together they finished dry-in and secured tie-downs. Construction of this shell provided learning through off-site making and on-site completion.

High Performance and Water Resources

In 1933, the Tennessee Valley was the poorest area of the US and the least likely to have electrical service.[8] Water quality was a major concern, and few rural households in the region had indoor plumbing. By 1936, municipal electricity, water, and sanitary systems served all homes in the Town of Norris. The TVA collected data on these novel practices, assessing, for example, the benefits of new materials, insulation, and ventilation and heating systems. The analysis informed future construction and was publicly disseminated.

Again taking cues from the TVA's work, the NNH examined emerging paradigms in water infrastructure. The NNH pursues complementary performance and design intentions where water systems provide greater independence from the central grid. Design goals included: collecting, treating, and reusing rainwater; greywater infiltration on site; and managing one hundred percent of the run-off and stormwater on the site.

The NNH seeks the appropriate balance between public and private services as they relate to safe, convenient, efficient, and environmentally responsible water use. Roof run-off is collected and treated for use in the house and landscape. One year of water quality and quantity data demonstrates the ability to collect, treat, and provide water that is safe for human contact by EPA criteria, meets drinking water standards, and is sufficient in quantity to meet thirty percent of a two-person household's needs. Greywater is allowed to infiltrate the site in a below grade terrace (existing sewer connections remove blackwater). Primary benefits of on-site greywater management include reducing municipal energy to transport and centrally treat wastewater and recharging the local groundwater

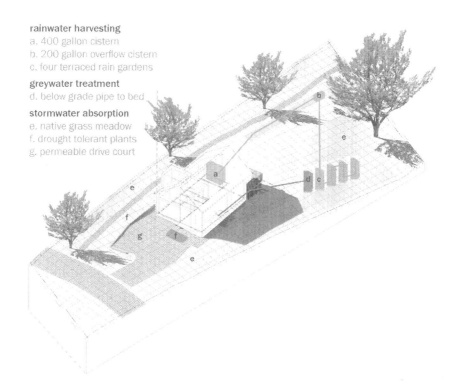

FIGURE 11.7 Site diagram of integrated water systems, *New Norris House*, Norris, Tennessee, 2010

Source: The University of Tennessee College of Architecture and Design

through infiltration. All stormwater generated from on-site impervious surfaces is managed on site. Practices include use of treated rainwater for in-home use and irrigation and on-site infiltration of untreated cistern-overflow.[9] Water (and energy) use was monitored during a two-year residency and the results disseminated.[10]

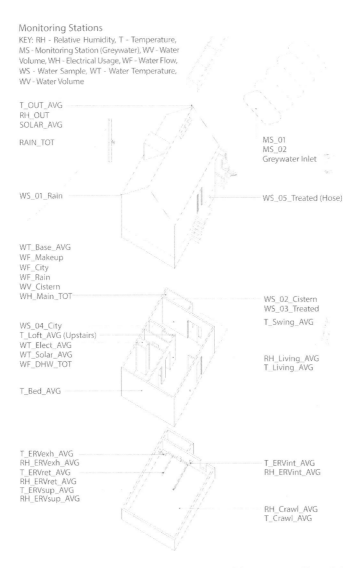

FIGURE 11.8 During post-occupancy evaluation over fifty sensors collected data on climate, performance, and occupancy patterns. Oak Ridge National Laboratory's Buildings Research and Technologies Integration Center supported the UT team. *New Norris House*, Norris, Tennessee, 2011

Source: The University of Tennessee College of Architecture and Design

182 Tricia Stuth

These goals required a multidisciplinary team. Civil/wastewater engineering and landscape architecture students brought passion for and knowledge of water-, soil-, and plant-related issues and critical input from departmental advisors. The team applied principles of integrated design to create the scheme and challenged technical, economic, legal, and aesthetic concerns affecting implementation. In his semester-end summary report, an engineering student remarked that it was the "largest collaboration to date between disciplines, [where you] start to understand synthesis, conflicts, and ways to remedy."[11] Calculations at one end of the table often informed design decisions at the other end, an occurrence that one architecture student cited as a highly valued experience.

The team also worked to detangle a regulatory knot that hampered implementation of the designed systems. For example, state and local codes prohibit treated rainwater use in the home, and the equipment supplier does not guarantee its system will produce potable water. The team worked to obtain variances for limited use of treated rainwater (toilet flushing, clothes washing, and hose bibs) and to revise city ordinances. However, the main authority for greywater rested with the state. Therefore the team orchestrated a presentation to state officials that resulted in the issuance of a two-year operating permit.

If one assumes the future of infrastructure (including water, energy, and food) will include lower energy solutions pushed down to the level of the site, then society has a long way to go toward implementation. Projects that combine education, research, and community outreach, like the NNH, are effective vehicles for beginning those conversations and exposing students to these questions. Such demonstration projects bring together the parties affected so that problems can be encountered, resolved, and the results disseminated.[12]

Cultural and Environmental Stewardship

Immersion in Norris and its history allowed students' work to inhabit this unique greenbelt town. Adopting the place allowed assessment of residents' appreciation for its past and present, and speculation on its future. Until 1948, the TVA held all land in common. The residue of its care for the quality of materials, sensitivity of siting, and approach to public infrastructure is apparent. The team's experience parallels Michael Sorkin's thoughts on his visit to Norris:

> The vibe is tender, though—even moving. Kids are wandering the pathways at dusk. Neighbors are chatting in the commons. . . . Here, I thought to myself, was a genuine town. . . . there's a lingering aura of purpose that exceeds the site planning. The plan conveys a way of seeing spaces as continuities, flowing in scale from the town to the river to its watershed to regional topography to the organization of the nation and beyond. Its rationalism is gentle and its layout curvy. Those curves—understood as the contour-following outgrowth of a compact with nature—reflect a strong feeling for the welfare of the environment: an ecological vision, an idea of sympathy, not of discipline.[13]

Students negotiated contradictions between tradition and change. While residents recognize the benefits of growth and modernized dwellings, they are concerned about the possible adverse effects of development. A student-led workshop revealed residents' enthusiasm for new technologies, more daylight, and connections with nature, along with reservations about density, form, material, and aesthetic deviations. Relationships with local government officials and residents grew organically, helped by regular encounters at the solitary café. Norris's unique mail system—pick-up occurs only at the branch post office—creates a speaker's corner where exhibited work in progress generated public criticism and conversation about design.

Further to the students' experience, blogs maintained by NNH residents living in the house during the evaluation phase described comfort and enjoyment, eating from the garden, rainfall, and appreciation for seasonal changes. Complementary blogs by graduate researchers focused on post-occupancy evaluation. Engagement continued beyond construction with an online continuing education course, invited lectures and exhibits, community meetings, and tours for widely diverse audiences.

Informed by these experiences, NNH students practiced a regionalist form of sustainability. Vincent Canizaro describes this approach to sustainability as one which emphasizes "attention, awareness, and thinking in terms of local places (or regions) experientially, ecologically, and in terms of their social and cultural construction."[14] Sustainable design in this sense is the construction of a setting

FIGURE 11.9 Exhibit of work in progress outside the Norris Post Office, Norris, Tennessee, 2009

Source: The University of Tennessee College of Architecture and Design

FIGURE 11.10 East elevation of the New Norris House, *New Norris House*, Norris, Tennessee, 2011
Source: Ken McKown

that enhances everyday life. For the students, Norris is not an idealized past, nor is it a place that requires a utopic future. "By providing a pragmatic, intimate, culturally enriching, participatory, and everyday relationship with their local or regional environment, the abstractions of sustainability and sustainable techniques are made direct and personal."[15] It is hoped that the experience working on the NNH embedded a sensibility toward regionalism where local culture, climate, and resources temper technical solutions.

Conclusion

Beyond pedagogical goals and research questions lie issues for further investigation. The NNH is a relatively expensive house on a relatively inexpensive street where homes are mostly original, close together, minimally updated, and in various states of repair. The NNH estimated values vary considerably: $155,500 appraised market value (2013); $180,000 estimated cost to build (2011).[16] For comparison, an original cottage of similar size cost $6,500 to build—the equivalent of $113,900 today. It was intended for lease by a small family for accommodation in four rooms, one bath, and 600 square feet. An appraisal required for the public auction of the NNH was difficult to obtain given practices that rely on nearby comparable properties. A prospective buyer worked with seven appraisers before withdrawing a purchase offer. Greywater and rainwater systems present additional legal and financial burdens for prospective buyers as permits were granted for the experiment only if UT is overseeing their operation—despite data and precedent that demonstrate safe use and, in parts of the US, legal use.

The designbuild educational model is also costly. From 2008–2012, the NNH cost nearly $450,000 for instruction and construction in addition to faculty salary, university facilities, and donations of time and material. Faculty critics point to the profession's responsibility to educate young designers about construction and environmental technology. Meanwhile, the growing complexity in contemporary practice demands interns with a much broader range of knowledge. Fortunately, even modest designbuild experiences instill facility with the various concepts and technical integration that lead to embedded knowledge and give rise to *second nature* understanding.

Notes

1 In 2011 in the southern United States, the median new single family house was 2,430 square feet and the median lot 0.21 acres, according to "2013 Characteristics of New Housing," https://www.census.gov/construction/chars/pdf/lotsize.pdf.

2 Architecture 2030 is a non-profit founded by Edward Mazria, FAIA, to address climate change by establishing programs to reduce fossil fuel use and emissions caused by the built environment.

3 For further history of the TVA, see: "Tennessee Valley Authority," *Architectural Forum*, no. 08 (August 1939): 73–114; John H. Kyle, *The Building of TVA* (Baton Rouge: Louisiana State University Press: 1958); Arthur Morgan, *Making of the TVA* (Buffalo, NY: Prometheus Books; London: Pemberton Books, 1974).

4 Carroll Van West, *Tennessee's New Deal Landscape* (Knoxville: The University of Tennessee Press, 2001), 9.

5 For further history of the Norris Project, see Daniel Shafer, *Norris, TN 1933–1983* (Norris Historical Society, 1993); Michael J. McDonald and John Muldowny, *TVA and the Dispossessed* (Knoxville: The University of Tennessee Press, 1981); and Louis Grandgent, *Houses at Norris, Tennessee,* a TVA report to Earl S. Draper, Director of Land Planning and Housing, dated March 14, 1936.

6 Kiel Moe, *Integrated Design in Contemporary Architecture* (New York: Princeton Architectural Press, 2008), 6.

7 See Avigail Sachs and Tricia Stuth, "Innovation and Tradition: Eighty Years of Housing Construction in Southern Appalachia," *Construction History* 28.1 (2013), 65–82, for further reading on the regional history of house construction beginning with TVA's Norris House and concluding with UT's NNH.

8 Tim Culvahouse, ed., *The Tennessee Valley Authority* (New York: Princeton Architectural Press, 2007), 55.

9 For details on NNH water research see Tricia Stuth, Samuel Mortimer, Valerie Friedmann, and John Buchanan, "A New Norris House: Making Criteria for Sustainable Landscapes Visible," *The Visibility of Research: Proceedings of the 2013 ARCC Spring Research Conference*, http://www.arcc-journal.org/index.php/repository/article/view/220.
10 Ibid.
11 Matthew Snyder, undergraduate student, Civil Engineering, University of Tennessee-Knoxville.
12 A UT Design Build Evaluate website contains information on the NNH and UT designbuild projects, including project blogs and publication links. See http://dbei.utk.edu/projects/new-norris-house/ and http://dbei.utk.edu/evaluate.
13 Michael Sorkin, "Sorkin finds a model in a Tennessee small town with a genuine sense of purpose." *Architectural Record* 189.7 (July 2001): 63–64.
14 Vincent B. Canizaro, "Regionalism, Place, Specificity, and Sustainable Design," in *Pragmatic Sustainability*, ed. Steven A. Moore (New York: Routledge, 2010), 151.
15 Ibid., 152.
16 See Samuel Mortimer, "A New Norris House," *PLEA 2013—Sustainable Architecture for a Renewable Future Conference*, 51/192 for NNH project cost assessment.

12

LABOR-INTENSIVE

Innovation by Necessity

Erik Sommerfeld

It is often assumed that designbuild programs in the academic environment mirror professional practice; however, the disconnection between the profession and designbuild education in North America is significant. Educational designbuild programs are often tied to academic calendars further complicated by building departments and multi-headed constituents. Academic programs require a tremendous amount of setup by faculty and administrators to ensure projects are delivered within the semester and on budget. Bound to these academic calendars, designbuild programs do not have the luxury of extending project timelines. Project funding is often difficult and can occur as projects are being developed.

Colorado Building Workshop, the designbuild program at the University of Colorado Denver, has embraced these challenges and allowed them to craft how design solutions are engaged. Limited budgets force material and structural experimentation where labor costs are low and material costs *are* the budget. This leads to labor-intensive building that has allowed students to create innovative approaches to prefabrication, material reuse, and lean construction delivery methods. Limited skillsets from students in the earliest stages of their design education facilitate unique interdisciplinary professional collaborations and university partnerships, such as teaching students the importance of Integrated Project Delivery (IPD). Using this method of delivery, and embracing the ideas that emerge from this process, gives architecture students a fresh perspective on the core architectural issues of context, material, climate, structure, and natural light. These ideas become the foundational constructs for the design, leading students away from their preconceptions and towards greater innovation.

History

In 1992, Professor Phillip Gallegos founded the designbuild program at the University of Colorado Denver (CU Denver). Over the course of the next decade, graduate students designed and built projects from the western slope to the eastern plains of Colorado. The work impacted small communities and urban centers with designs that emphasized structural expression and resourceful construction techniques. Professor Gallegos' departure to the University of New Mexico in 2008 nearly marked the end of designbuild education at CU Denver. Even with an eighteen-credit designbuild certificate embedded in the curriculum and one of the longest running designbuild programs in the country, the college was considering shuttering the program. Without any leadership, the college found it increasingly difficult to find community partners interested in working with students and qualified faculty dedicated to providing a one-semester designbuild experience. This pivotal moment in the program's history signifies that designbuild education is rarely about the institution offering the program, regardless of its history, but rather the people passionate about running it.

Colorado Building Workshop and DesignBuildBLUFF

While acting as the Associate Chair for the Department of Architecture, I took over the designbuild certificate program in 2009. During the first semester under my direction Rob Pyatt and I guided twenty students through the design and construction of the museum store, entry lobby, and west gallery at the Boulder Museum of Contemporary Art (BMoCA). Although we did not know it at the time, this would be the first project for CU Denver's Colorado Building Workshop. The following semester Hank Louis, founder of DesignBuildBLUFF, approached CU Denver with a vision to expand DesignBuildBLUFF beyond the University of Utah. He would provide the project, funding, housing, tools, and construction supervision if the University of Colorado Denver could provide the design faculty and students. In the program's first year Professor Louis selflessly allowed me to explore my pedagogical approach while mentoring me through the complexities of DesignBuildBLUFF from Utah. Over the next five years, the Colorado Building Workshop collaboration with DesignBuildBLUFF completed five homes and two cabins on Navajo Nation in southeastern Utah. During that same five-year period, Colorado Building Workshop completed five community projects in various locations across the state of Colorado. It was an unprecedented twelve projects in five years that reestablished designbuild at the University of Colorado Denver, moved me into the position of Director of Design Build Initiatives, and solidified my approach to designbuild education.

Design Approach

Colorado Building Workshop focuses on IPD, which carries with it the advantage of distributed authorship. Distributed authorship is not only a fact of architectural production but also a safe haven that architectural Live Projects can support and cultivate.[1] For the IPD team to create this distributed authorship, the focus of the early design dialogue is focused on how the building functions in relationship to the core issues of context, material, climate, structure, and natural light, purposefully avoiding any stylistic discussion. The goal, adopted from the design philosophy of the Office of Metropolitan Architecture, is to establish a number of core issues, and in collaboration with the client and integrated project delivery team, identify joint positions.[2] The core issues and joint positions are a way of establishing important ideas without attaching preconceived imagery to the project. Since the IPD team includes the consultants and client, this process creates early architectural buy-in. This buy-in is valuable in later stages of the design process as it builds trust and often leads to the client accepting more innovative architectural solutions.

Before meeting with the client to present these design solutions, students work collaboratively on architectural morphologies. The morphologies are a response to the joint positions established by the IPD team. Weekly design critiques, led by the students, provide constructive feedback on how the designs need to evolve. At the end of each critique the students select one or two designs to develop for the following week. These designs are adopted by the entire studio and subsequently redesigned for the following critique. This process requires that students set aside individual egos and focus their energy on solving the design based on the joint positions. They know that to have their ideas accepted by the group, and ultimately the client, their design has to meet the criteria agreed upon by the IPD team. One could visualize this approach to design selection in a *Darwinian* way. Only the strongest designs survive the week, but everyone gets a chance to try to evolve the selected design through the following week. Through this process, individual ideas are folded into the larger design solution, strengthening it and all but eliminating the possibility of a single author. As the semester progresses and the morphologies develop, the projects are strengthened with the added realities as students increase their understanding of context, climate, program, material, structure, and natural light. By creating this framework and asking students questions that lead to investigations that are project appropriate, we can reach a clearer design solution. This clarity helps students avoid solutions that rely on design trends rather than on contemporary architectural discourse.

Labor-Intensive

The motivation of architecture students to see their design ideas realized is powerful capital. Engaged students help offset low project budgets through hands-on skills and labor-intensive investigations. A look into a material culture[3] often reveals historic techniques that use regionally sourced materials—such as adobe, rammed earth, and straw bale construction in the Four Corners region. The difficulty lies in improving the material performance of these historic traditions and modernizing them in accordance with contemporary expectations. Locally sourced materials should not be oversimplified into material selections based on proximity to the building site alone. Often there are cultural and environmental reasons for the selection of each material. An example is the desert climate of southeastern

Utah. With its large diurnal temperature swings, mass materials such as earth and concrete protect the inhabitants from harsh winds and take advantage of the thermal mass to regulate indoor temperature. During the design process, students were asked to identify strengths and weaknesses of a selected material. The research included data from the region and global examples that share similar climates. This research leads to more innovative design solutions.

Raine House, one of the Navajo home collaborations with DesignBuildBLUFF, was an investigation into slow-pour, thermally broken concrete. This project is an example of how graduate student research into regional and global climates reveals how passive design solutions can be combined with labor-intensive material investigations to produce new regionally appropriate design solutions. The result is a climate-responsive home that eliminates the clients' reliance on fossil fuels to heat and cool their home.

The studio collaborated with the National Renewable Energy Lab (NREL) and engineering students from the University of Southern Utah to design the home. Using energy modeling software developed by NREL, the integrated project delivery team was able to test a number of different designs, settling on the design that pragmatically accommodated the family's needs while maintaining the best possible passive solar strategies. During an IDP meeting, concrete walls were proposed as an affordable and durable wall construction assembly; however, concerns were raised that the diurnal temperature swings would not be enough to keep the home cool in the summer and warm in the winter. The fear was that

FIGURE 12.1 *Raine House*, Navajo Nation, 2012
Source: MC Burns

once the concrete warmed up in the summer, or cooled down in the winter, the daily temperature swing alone would not be enough to regulate the home's temperature. To better control the temperature and isolate the mass from the interior space, a thermal break was proposed. The concrete wall was divided into two walls separated by two inches of rigid insulation. The new thermally broken concrete wall created a durable outer layer and an isolated interior layer that would help stabilize temperature swings. The concrete walls in this system coupled with the concrete floor slabs collect solar rays and maintain a year round internal temperature between 62 and 82 degrees Fahrenheit without the need for additional heating or cooling. The students were encouraged by the energy models but now had to solve the construction of the concrete walls.

The nearest concrete plant was over an hour drive away, and concrete formwork was cost prohibitive to purchase or rent. It was determined that all the concrete would have to be hand mixed on-site. This labor-intensive design constraint meant that cold joints would form before the next batch could be mixed. The advantage of this constraint was that less formwork would be required. By only pouring six inches of concrete at a time the formwork could be moved up after the concrete cured. The students researched this technique and found that Peter Zumthor had used a similar method in the construction of the Bruder Klaus Field Chapel.[4] They consulted the IPD team to ensure the concrete as detailed could accommodate the cold joints and received approval to proceed. After building a series of mockups that helped them better understand the reinforcing, students were confident enough to incorporate the solution into their design.

The final design hurdle would be protecting the structure against heat loss in the evenings. The energy model showed that covering the windows at night could reduce the heat load on the building by an additional 20 to 30 percent. Seeing

FIGURE 12.2 Construction of the slow-pour concrete walls, *Raine House*, Navajo Nation, 2012

Source: Erik Sommerfeld

FIGURE 12.3 Insulated sliding doors in the kitchen, *Raine House*, Navajo Nation, 2012
Source: MC Burns

value in additional insulation, the students designed and fabricated interior sliding panels that cover the glass curtain wall and windows in the evening, providing an additional R-9 of insulation for the home. During the day these panels nest along the walls in the living room, opening up views to Red Mesa and collecting solar radiation.

Material Reuse

Material reuse is a well-established way to reduce project costs and respond to limited construction budgets. Whether in the form of agricultural waste or material up-cycling, student designbuild projects often explore alternative building assemblies. Richard Sennett, in his book *The Craftsman*, discusses an engaged material consciousness; he notes that we become particularly interested in the things we can change.[5] The architecture student's thinking follows this logic.

Their interest in material reuse lies in what the material *can be* versus what the material *is*. However, this exploration can be a risky endeavor. Without proper research, blind experimentation can lead to unsustainable design practices that result in buildings with poor indoor air quality, mold, and structural deficiencies. As instructors guiding these students, we must ensure that experiments are not being carried out on underserved communities in the name of architectural education. Research into best practice and material standards are necessary. For these reasons, students at CU Denver are asked to focus their material reuse on proven methods of construction.

The Skow Residence is perhaps our most measurable example of material reuse. At the beginning of the project, when the students arrived on-site to meet the client, they found a pile of building materials. The clients had already received a typical *home build kit* from their local chapter house on Navajo Nation. The clients were disappointed in the home kit's design but had already completed a CMU foundation. At the request of the client, and as an exploration into a more site-specific response to housing in the Utah desert, the students decided to redesign the home, incorporating the existing foundation and virtually all of the build kit materials stockpiled on the site. It was clear from the beginning that the trusses would be the most difficult part of the kit to reuse. Simply keeping them in the orientation that they were engineered for would not only recall the *white man's house* that the client was adamantly opposed to, but it would also disconnect the inside of the home from the view of Monument Valley in the distance. By inverting the trusses,

FIGURE 12.4 Exterior of the home showing the reused inverted trusses, oil pipes, and aluminum fascia, *Skow Residence*, Navajo Nation, 2013

Source: Jesse Kuroiwa

the students were able to raise the ceiling height at the perimeter of the house, allowing better views and better solar gain in the winter. The inverted roof also provided a water catchment system for the home.

The trusses were reengineered to hang from a series of reclaimed Douglas fir beams assisting in the distribution of loads with minimal redesign to the webbing. The beams were connected to a series of reclaimed steel pipes allowing the perimeter wall of the home to be a façade free from any structural load requirements. This was an important design consideration because the exterior walls were mainly constructed from straw, a non-load bearing material. The remainder of the structure was clad in a custom designed, student manufactured, reclaimed cedar curtain wall. Since the lumber for the curtain wall was not graded, the engineer could not count on it to carry any of the load.

The curtain wall was fabricated using orientation-specific glazing that allows the sun into the structure on the southern side but reflects the majority of the solar radiation on the western side of the structure facing the view.

This was an important design concept since the floor is made of compressed earth block and the roof on the south overhangs the façade to block solar gain in the summer but allows it into the building and onto the floor in the winter. The ceiling of the home is clad in reclaimed cedar tongue and groove boards reclaimed from a home renovation in Sun Valley, Idaho. A large deck wraps the western and

FIGURE 12.5 Interior curtain wall with reclaimed cedar mullions and reused cedar ceiling, *Skow Residence*, Navajo Nation, 2013

Source: Jesse Kuroiwa

Labor-Intensive **195**

southern sides of the home and brings the *livable* space outdoors for much of the year while an eastern entry porch provides shaded outdoor space to gather during summer afternoons.

Prefabrication

Prefabricated building systems can be traced as far back as the seventeenth century when a panelized wood home was shipped from England to Cape Ann to provide housing for a fishing fleet.[6] This early example of prefabrication focused on a delivery model as a necessity. Similarly, Colorado Building Workshop employs prefabrication out of necessity. Large student groups can be difficult to manage during construction, and safety quickly becomes a major concern. Many of the job sites are remote, and projects are often built in less than ideal climates. Cranes can be cost prohibitive and in certain cases impossible to bring to the job site. Long Colorado winters filled with snowstorms and inclement weather coupled with tight deadlines often necessitate various forms of prefabrication.

The micro cabins for the Colorado Outward Bound School (COBS) required a variety of prefabricated techniques due to the remote context and tight delivery timeline. In 2015, Colorado Building Workshop was asked to design, build, and deliver fourteen unique cabins, each under 200 square feet, to the COBS campus in Leadville, Colorado. The timeline for the project, from meeting the client to the final delivery of the cabins, was just under nineteen weeks.

Sitting on a sloping site at an elevation of 10,200 feet above sea level, the location and scope of work made it impossible to construct the project without some level of prefabrication. To satisfy the clients' lodging and storage requirements and to facilitate completion of on-site construction in four weeks, the cabins were conceived as two separate elements, a *box* and a *frame*. The *frame* acts as a storage device for the educators' bikes, skis, and kayaks while simultaneously housing the cabin *box* and covered porches.

To construct the frame, 136 unique steel columns and beams were prefabricated to accommodate the slope of each site. Over 500 cross bracing tabs, girder plates, and beam tabs were welded to the columns to reconcile the different frame designs. This forced students to explore parametric modeling, just-in-time delivery methods, and scheduling tools to keep track of changes and communicate the design intent to the students assigned to fabrication. Each of the columns and beams was individually marked and fabricated accordingly to drawings provided by each group building the cabin. The fabrication of each column occurred no more than one day ahead of the steel's scheduled erection date. This reduced the columns' exposure to ground snow present on the job site and allowed students to make design changes up to one day before steel erection. Since the project was located in a lodgepole pine forest, cranes were not able to access the site. This system of prefabricated parts allowed the team to erect between five and six steel frames each day, drastically reducing fabrication time and minimizing the danger of students

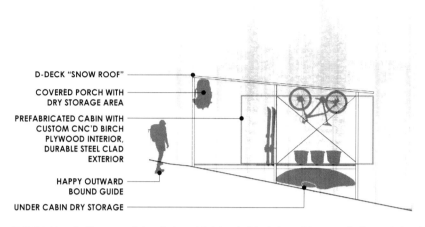

FIGURE 12.6 A diagram of the design thinking behind the cabin morphology, *Colorado Outward Bound Micro-Cabins*, Leadville, Colorado, 2015
Source: Holly Paris

working on scaffolding and around heavy equipment. After the *frames* platforms were constructed, the box could be brought in and assembled.

The flat-packed prefabricated cabin *box* rests in the frame under the protection of a snow roof. This second roof is designed to keep the winter snow load off the waterproofed EPDM roof of the cabin directly below. The walls of the cabin were prefabricated in Denver using a modified advanced framing system. The system was designed to minimize the lumber required and align the studs with the CNC-fabricated birch plywood interiors. Each panel was designed to be light enough so that four students could easily move it from the fabrication facility onto the trucks and from the trucks onto the *frame* platform in Leadville.

The CNC-fabricated birch plywood interiors were developed using software originally designed to manufacture custom cabinets. The students reconsidered its use and scaled it up to construct the interior of the cabin. The furniture and storage elements were designed in SketchUp, imported into the Cabinet Vision Software and manufactured using a CNC router. The cabinets interface with the wall, roof, and floor system and click together in place, drastically reducing on-site fabrication time. The majority of the cabin interiors took two days to assemble—a timeline that simply could not have been replicated without the use of this innovative flat-pack prefabrication method.

In the end, the project deployed three different types of prefabricated building components specific to each building material and unique building assembly it served. The students understood the appropriate applications for each different assembly and utilized various computer applications to help facilitate its delivery. The three different types of prefabrication had to interface with one another in less than one month of on-site construction and were implemented in fourteen different cabins.

Labor-Intensive **197**

FIGURE 12.7 Cabin number two looking south, *Colorado Outward Bound Micro-Cabins*, Leadville, Colorado, 2015
Source: Jesse Kuroiwa

FIGURE 12.8 A view of the prefabricated CNC'd furniture in the interior of cabin number eleven
Source: Jesse Kuroiwa

FIGURE 12.9 Exploded axonometric drawing of the prefabricated building components, Colorado Outward Bound Micro Cabins, Leadville, Colorado, 2015
Source: Ken Roberts and Kit Piane

Lean Construction

Lean Construction or Lean Project Delivery (LPD) demonstrates students' understanding of the project at every level of design and construction. It requires the project team to minimize the cost and maximize the value of the project for the benefit of everyone involved. This resonates with the desire of students to give back to the community, explore architectural ideas, and learn how their ideas translate into built works.

Lean Construction is explored at each phase of the design with the IPD team. In the early stages of the design process, production strategies, structural concepts, and material investigations are questioned. The goal is to find strategies for students to explore that synthesize the joint positions of the group by simultaneously creating the greatest return on the project's budget. Before submitting for permits, the design is considered again. At this phase the team questions material sizes and proportions to maximize material usage and minimize waste. Adjustments are made to the overall dimensions as students reconsider how different material standards interface and how the design can maximize the use of each material. During construction, prefabrication and just-in-time delivery methods are utilized to compress timelines and increase student safety.

An example of how IPD led to the implementation of Lean Construction is evident in the Lamar Station Classroom for Urban Farming (LSC). The Planned Unit Development that the LSC serves is adjacent to the newest light rail line in Colorado, the W line to Golden. The housing authority in charge of the project approached Colorado Building Workshop about designing a classroom to educate the residents about urban farming. Given the up-and-coming character of the neighborhood, visibility into the classroom and vandalism were major concerns.

This led the students to investigate durable translucent skins that would appear opaque from some angles and transparent from others.

During an IDP team meeting Andy Paddock, the structural engineer on the project, suggested that if a bar grate skin was used, the loads from the roof might be able to be carried through the skin of the structure and reduce the number of columns required to hold up the roof. The students were already considering bar grate as a skin. They noted that the privacy increased when using this skin, because as one approaches the structure on the path the building becomes more oblique and, therefore, gets continually more opaque with the vertical louvers of the bar grate.

A finite element analysis of the structure revealed that not only could the number of columns be reduced, all the vertical webbing in the roof trusses could also be omitted. This reduced the overall cost and weight of the project and increased the transparency. Prior to submitting to the building department for approval, the project was redesigned to maximize material sizes. The length and width of the structure were placed on a 2' 11 13/16" grid to match the width of standard bar grate. This drastically reduced the fabrication timeline by eliminating any horizontal cuts that would have been required on the bar grate. The grid also spaces the bar grate evenly between panels to ensure an evenly spaced skin across the entire façade.

Each interior truss was considered in the same way as the exterior skin. Students assessed the pragmatic requirements of the space below and worked with the structural engineer to minimize waste. The scupper that drains into the vegetable

FIGURE 12.10 The seamless modularity of the load-bearing structural bar grate skin, *Lamar Station Classroom for Urban Farming*, Lakewood, Colorado, 2014

Source: Jesse Kuroiwa

washing station and herb garden becomes a structural scupper supporting the roof. In the roof over the table, webbing is replaced by plate steel forming the skylight. To counter lateral loads, shear walls are integrated into the steel plate connecting the interior and exterior walls. The implementation of these Lean Construction strategies saved time and material but, more importantly, allowed the students to explore a more innovative architecture.

Conclusion

Many of the building techniques described in this chapter do not translate from academia to the profession; however, this is not our ambition. The point is to educate architecture students to identify the necessities of the project and be innovative in the way they think through a design solution. They may never again intensely engage the labor of construction, but we are not training students to be builders, we are educating them to be better problem solvers. We are educating them to collaborate and question the very nature of the project. This can only happen if the students who design the projects are allowed to build them; otherwise it is not designbuild. They must be allowed to fully analyze the complexity of the issues at hand, craft a design solution to the positions they identify, test it with mockups, construct it at full scale, and have time to reflect on what they have done.

Notes

1 Harriet Harriss, "Co-Authoring a Live Project Manifesto," in *Architecture Live Projects: Pedagogy into Practice*, ed. Harriet Harriss and Lynnette Widder (London: Routledge, 2014), 41.
2 Joshua Prince-Ramus, "Behind the Design of Seattle's Library," TED Talk (February 2006), https://www.ted.com/talks/joshua_prince_ramus_on_seattle_s_library?language=en.
3 Brian MacKay-Lyons, *Local Architecture: Building Place, Craft, and Community* (Princeton Architectural Press, 2015).
4 Peter Zumthor, *Peter Zumthor: Buildings and Projects, Volume 3 1998–2001* (Zurich: Scheidegger & Spiess, 2014), 121–122.
5 Richard Sennett, *The Craftsman* (New Haven: Yale University Press, 2008), 120.
6 Allison Arieff and Bryan Burkhart, *Prefab* (Salt Lake City: Gibbs Smith, 2002), 13.

13

FROM SCRATCH

How to Start a Designbuild Program

Eric Weber

Creating a new designbuild program from scratch is an exceptionally challenging, but highly rewarding process. Numerous questions must be answered before starting the process, and many more appear as the program takes shape. This essay outlines the specific experiences of initiating the David G. Howryla Design+Build Studio at the University of Nevada, Las Vegas (UNLV) School of Architecture, but many of the issues uncovered and lessons learned may prove useful for others.

One of the first tasks that must be undertaken is to determine a funding source; this may have a major impact on the type of projects that can be accomplished. In UNLV's case, the school's director contacted an alumnus who is a partner in a successful designbuild firm, and the firm's interest in hiring qualified practitioners led them to provide seed funding for the program. The donation was specifically earmarked to cover tools, equipment, facility upgrades, and materials necessary to jumpstart the program's development. However, the donation was not intended to fund the projects themselves, so project funding would need to be secured elsewhere.

Once a funding mechanism has been identified, the next task is to determine the legal framework that applies to the potential program. The School of Architecture contacted UNLV's Office of General Counsel to begin this process, and counsel asked numerous questions regarding the scope and size of the program, the program's purpose, and how involved students would be in the actual construction processes. Having answers to these questions in advance of meeting with general counsel saves valuable time. In this case, the school determined that there would be a need to limit the studio to 12 students for organizational reasons. The assumption was that a larger student group would be difficult to supervise and effectively teach while still maintaining a high level of craft. Subsequent experience has substantiated this assumption, with the notable exception during the design development and construction documents phases of the UNLV

Solar Decathlon house, in which four graduate students assisted in managing the undergraduate student project team.

General Counsel informed the Design+Build Studio coordinator that UNLV is self-insured, and that the university would cover students working on design-build projects, with an important caveat: students would only be covered for work done on campus. Off-campus work would not be covered except in very special circumstances, on a case-by-case basis. This meant that the proposed designbuild program would either be limited to doing work for on-campus facilities, or the work would need to be off-site construction for other clients. This determination impacted the projects that have followed, as well as the regulatory structure necessary to complete the projects.

A review of the Nevada Revised Statutes by counsel also determined that electrical and plumbing work would need to be done by licensed contractors. It was determined that it was pedagogically important to have students do as much of the work as possible, but working with professionals when necessary is an excellent teaching opportunity.

In Nevada, all habitable buildings constructed off-site are required to be reviewed by the state government's Manufactured Housing Division, which further requires any applicant for a permit to carry a manufacturing license.[1] As an educational program, rather than a commercial manufacturer, the Division recommended that the Studio work with an established firm as a Manufacturer of Record; this ultimately was the route taken. UNLV entered into a partnership with a local manufacturer, PKMM Inc., and their interest in working with the designbuild studio was to support the university, as well as to have access to the lessons learned from the Studio's projects.

The Solar Decathlon: Opportunities and Challenges

The UNLV Design+Build Studio determined that the first project should be something highly public, as this would assist in generating support for the program. The U.S. Department of Energy's Solar Decathlon appeared to be an ideal opportunity. The Decathlon requires university-based student teams to design and build solar-powered housing prototypes, which must be transported to a competition site for testing. This requirement was consistent with the university's insurance requirement for on-campus (and thus, off-site-constructed) building, and the School of Architecture surmised that the emphasis on solar power might prove compelling to prospective donors to the program.

The Department of Energy gives teams that are accepted into the competition $100,000 to assist with defraying the cost of competing, but this money cannot be used for building the house. Teams must raise all of the money necessary for constructing the house on their own. The team solicited donations from local industry for materials and services, as well as funds to cover the remaining competition costs.

After determining insurance, regulatory approval processes, and funding, another key component is determining the appropriate construction location and acquiring the necessary equipment for completing construction. As on most university campuses, space was at a premium on the UNLV main campus, but the university was able to allocate a site on the university's Paradise Road campus, approximately one mile from the School of Architecture. The site was slated for a turf reduction project, so the university's facilities manager was amenable to its use for temporary construction. The Design+Build Studio was required to pay for bringing temporary power and water to the site from nearby hookups, as well as temporary construction fencing. In addition, strict limits were placed on construction vehicle access and parking, and the site was required to be completely vacated by the time of the Solar Decathlon competition. While this was a workable situation, the stipulation to clear the site by the start of competition created significant difficulties, as all of the students participating in the Decathlon had to travel with the house to its competition site for coordination, setup, and testing. This condition resulted in the decision to utilize the School of Architecture's building yard for future designbuild projects whenever possible. At the time of the Solar Decathlon build (spring and summer 2013), the building yard was fully occupied with test cells for a research project. The yard has since been cleared for designbuild projects, provided they fit its access constraints and physical size. These constraints limit building module sizes to those that will fit on a typical semi trailer, approximately 14 by 50 feet.[2] A maximum of two modules could occupy the building yard at the same time, according to state regulations.[3] These constraints are expected to meet the Studio's needs for the foreseeable future.

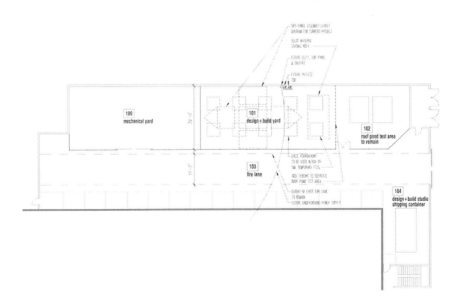

FIGURE 13.1 *UNLV School of Architecture Building Yard Plan*, Las Vegas, Nevada, 2015
Source: Eric Weber

204 Eric Weber

Acquiring tools and equipment for a designbuild program is a challenging task, since it is important to have many of the tools in place before a project starts construction. Anticipating which tools will be necessary when it is unclear what may be possible with the students' skill sets and the time constraints inherent in an educational setting may seem daunting, but a few key decisions help to clarify the priority list.

Determining the likely primary structural system will have a major impact on tool selection. The designbuild educator's own skill sets will affect the selection of other tools. An expert cabinetmaker would need tools such as a mortiser, joiner/planer, and other millworking tools. Welders and other metalworking tools may also be appropriate, especially since nonstructural welding is a very expensive task to subcontract, and can be taught fairly readily. Structural welding is likely to require certifications, depending on the local jurisdiction. Taking careful stock of the tasks the designbuild studio is likely to undertake on a regular basis, versus those done less frequently, can lead to major savings on equipment. In the Design+Build Studio's case, concrete cutting, coring, and finishing tools are unlikely to be needed as often, due to UNLV's insurance rules, so it is better practice for us to subcontract foundation work.

Another challenge that may not be immediately apparent is how much space will be available for tool storage, and whether access to the designbuild tools will be made available to the school as a whole. Tool security can be a major problem. The UNLV School of Architecture's administration initially made many of the tools purchased for the designbuilders available to the school's shop facility during down time between projects. Loss, damage, and simply not having necessary tools at hand when needed became increasingly difficult challenges to manage. Ultimately, the school decided to keep the major designbuild-specific tools, such as carpentry tools and cordless hand tools, separate from the main tool storage room. The Studio purchased a used shipping container to store all of the designbuild tools, and has had no problems with tool losses or damage since this was implemented.

Safety is a significant challenge for designbuild programs. The Occupational Safety and Health Administration's (OSHA) 10-hour safety-training course is mandatory for all students participating in the Solar Decathlon. In addition, site supervisors are required to attend OSHA's 30-hour training course. This training is essential for complex projects like a Solar Decathlon house, and sets the stage for situational awareness and the level of professionalism needed when on a potentially hazardous construction site. The School of Architecture has since hired a full-time shop supervisor, who provides basic shop and tool safety awareness training, as well as more advanced training on proper tool usage, allowing the designbuild studio coordinator to focus training on tools and techniques specific to construction projects.

Despite UNLV's success participating in Solar Decathlon 2013, finishing in second place (the only U.S. team in the top three), the experience was not without its challenges.

The most critical of these was when the schematic design documents were completed, and it was time to fully commit to the design in order to complete construction documents on time for the Department of Energy's strict submission deadline. Several student team leaders wanted to explore an alternate design, rather than moving forward with the project as designed, despite the selected design having been vetted in reviews over the course of two semesters. I informed the students that there was insufficient time to revisit the design process, but this resulted in increased friction within the team. In order to preserve team unity, I gave the students the opportunity to propose the alternative design to a third party to see if it might be better than the selected design. When the alternative design was reviewed by a third party, a group of professional architects, it was clear that the original design was far superior, having been developed over the course of eight months of research and development with critiques by architects, engineers, an economist specializing in real estate, and numerous other parties. While this was the expected result, it cost the team valuable time, which made it more challenging to lead the team to a successful outcome. Interpersonal relationships are essential to the success of any designbuild project, and learning to negotiate these challenges is an essential skill for a designbuild educator to master.

Perhaps the biggest hurdle was the expense of competing. UNLV had to raise $650,000 in order to cover the cost of competing, of which $300,00 was used on the house; the bulk of the remaining fundraising was necessary for the infrastructure

FIGURE 13.2 *UNLV Solar Decathlon House*, Orange County, California, 2013
Source: Kevin Duffy

FIGURE 13.3 *UNLV Solar Decathlon House*, Orange County, California, 2013
Source: Kevin Duffy

FIGURE 13.4 *UNLV Solar Decathlon House*, Orange County, California, 2013
Source: Kevin Duffy

needed for a successful outcome. As a state university, this was a monumental challenge, and one of the smallest, youngest academic units on campus, the School of Architecture, was responsible for carrying the heaviest load.

The two-year competition timeline of the Decathlon makes it difficult for students to work on the project from conception to completion; only four students on UNLV's initial team finished the competition. While this made team continuity difficult, the far larger challenge was for the undergraduate students, who were not able to see their project through from beginning to end. One of the key benefits of a designbuild education is the opportunity for students to have the direct experience of building what they have designed.

A surprising aspect of the competition is how much time is spent on tasks other than building the house. In UNLV's case, only the last four months of the 24-month competition were devoted to building the house, and due to this timeline, it was necessary for many more tasks to be completed by professionals than would have been ideal for student learning.

While working with professional subcontractors can be an exceptional opportunity for students to witness the thought processes and challenges encountered in completing a project, the compressed construction schedule meant that a large number of tasks were completed during the summer, after many of the undergraduate students had graduated. Fortunately, the graduate students enrolled in the Studio were able to stay on to manage this phase of the work, and they benefited greatly from the experience. In current and future designbuild projects, construction schedules will be adjusted where possible to maximize the teaching opportunities offered by collaborating with building trades.

Due to the specific requirement that the house had to be placed on a temporary competition site, it had to be moved at least twice; in UNLV's case, the house was moved a third time, to its final home at the Las Vegas Springs Preserve. Designing a building to survive multiple moves adds significantly to the cost of construction; $45,000 of DesertSol's building cost was for a structural steel chassis. Based on calculations by the team's professional cost estimator, if the house had been designed for a single move onto its final site, eighty percent of the chassis cost would have been unnecessary.

With these challenges in mind the Design+Build Studio was reorganized to better serve the School of Architecture's needs. Enabling additional students to benefit from designbuild projects was a priority to the administration, and utilizing the off-site construction infrastructure developed during the Solar Decathlon offered an opportunity to satisfy this desire while simultaneously giving the Design+Build Studio a viable future.

A Sustainable Future for the Design+Build Studio

After deciding not to participate in the Solar Decathlon again, identifying a sustainable funding source for future projects became particularly important. The Studio coordinator had researched successful designbuild programs during the Decathlon,

208 Eric Weber

and this continued throughout the transition to a new model for the program.[4] As UNLV's School of Architecture serves the functions normally associated with land grant universities and is the sole architectural program in the state, its primary purpose is to work for the benefit of the people of Nevada. The Design+Build Studio was interested in leveraging limited state and federal budgets to support this purpose. In addition, Nevada's diverse climate zones offer an opportunity to expand the students' exposure and understanding of how to respond effectively to this complex landscape. In consultation with the School's leadership, the designbuild coordinator made assisting the state's residents in connecting to natural resources, wildlife, and ecosystems a core mission of the Studio. The administration envisioned the program designing and building projects such as forest ranger housing, park cabins, ramadas, viewing platforms, and other similar projects. Interestingly, most of the state parks are in central and northern Nevada, while the majority of the population is in southern Nevada.[5] By demonstrating UNLV's commitment to the rest of the state, designing projects that support visitors to the parks may generate goodwill for rural residents who do not historically support funding for Nevada's universities.

With these assumptions in mind, the designbuild coordinator contacted the head of the regional Bureau of Land Management office, the Forest Supervisor for the Humboldt-Toiyabe National Forest, and the Director of the Nevada Division of State Parks. While there was little success with the Bureau of Land Management, the National Forest's supervisor expressed significant interest. However, project timelines with federal agencies require several years to come to fruition, and a project has yet to be identified. This is a key lesson for prospective designbuilders to keep in mind; while many government agencies may be receptive to working with designbuild programs, the process of developing the necessary relationships and bringing projects to fruition is often a multi-year process. Identifying the appropriate agency and getting into their funding appropriation schedule while simultaneously organizing the aforementioned processes instead of waiting to complete these steps will reduce the time between initiating program planning and beginning an actual project.

The Director of the Nevada Division of State Parks was immediately interested in discussing potential projects, in part because of previous experience working with community groups on small park maintenance and improvement projects. After an initial meeting in Carson City to determine capabilities and whether it appeared to be a mutually beneficial relationship, the primary task was to determine appropriate projects. Many of the state parks are quite remote from population centers, limiting professional interest in small projects; builders need to mobilize significant resources in order to utilize conventional construction methods. The Director immediately recognized that due to the offsite construction processes demonstrated in UNLV's Solar Decathlon house, many of the issues inherent with remote sites are far less problematic. Additionally, there is a strong interest in creating a continuing relationship from the Division of State Parks, as this would greatly simplify their appropriations process. Nevada's state legislature only meets on a biannual basis, so all departments need to plan their budgets for two-year intervals. This is a key reason why the Division of State Parks entered into a Memorandum of Understanding with the studio that formalized a recurring project pipeline.

In January 2015, the Design+Build Studio began work on the first project for the Nevada Division of State Parks, a box office for the Lake Tahoe Shakespeare Festival. The Festival is an annual event at Sand Harbor State Park, Lake Tahoe, Nevada. The project is in a highly public environment and serves as an opportunity to develop the Studio's capability to work in diverse environmental conditions. Construction began in September and was completed in Spring 2016.

The first step in completing the box office was writing a contract proposal. It was determined that the state parks' head of planning and construction would review and stamp the architectural drawings prepared by the Design+Build Studio. Structural drawings were to be completed by a state parks engineer, with mechanical and electrical engineering by a Las Vegas-based private firm. The contract specified that site work and utilities would be prepared by the state parks. Somewhat surprisingly, the division Director offered to use state parks vehicles to transport the box office and associated materials from Las Vegas to Lake Tahoe; the Studio would only be responsible for craning the building onto the trailer, as well as setting the building onto its site-built, subcontracted concrete perimeter foundation.

Due to the box office's small size, construction took place in the School of Architecture's build yard, across from the lecture halls used for technology courses. Off-site construction offers opportunities for students outside the Design+Build Studio to engage the construction process, including students in Construction Technology, Computer-Aided-Design, Building Structures, and Environmental Control Systems courses. By seeing these systems firsthand, students who are not enrolled in the Studio have an unparalleled opportunity to enrich their education with real-world exposure to systems explored in their course materials.

FIGURE 13.5 Site for box office designbuild project, *Sand Harbor Box Office Site*, Lake Tahoe, Nevada, 2014
Source: Eric Weber

210 Eric Weber

FIGURE 13.6 Concept models, *Sand Harbor Box Office*, Lake Tahoe, Nevada, 2015
Source: Eric Weber

FIGURE 13.7 Computer rendering, *Sand Harbor Box Office*, Lake Tahoe, Nevada, 2015
Source: Eric Weber

FIGURE 13.8 Construction at UNLV School of Architecture, *Sand Harbor Box Office*, Lake Tahoe, Nevada, 2015
Source: Eric Weber

There were several lessons learned from the project. The regulatory review process for the project was complex, with reviews by the Division of State Parks, the State Public Works Board, the Manufactured Housing Division, and the Tahoe Regional Planning Authority. The complete process took six months, far longer than expected for such a modest building. Decision-making has been significantly streamlined compared to the Solar Decathlon, primarily due to the fact that the university administration is not involved. In addition, relying on professional engineers resulted in a significant reduction in student workload during the preparation of construction documents. It had been necessary for designbuild students to prepare all engineering drawings as well as architectural sheets during the Solar Decathlon. Without having to engage in fundraising activities, students were also able to focus much more attention on producing professional project documentation.

As the Division of State Parks had limited funding available for the project, the Design+Build Studio engaged the network of contacts developed during the

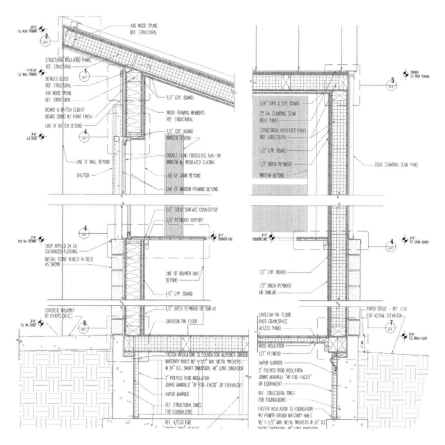

FIGURE 13.9 Wall sections, *Sand Harbor Box Office*, Lake Tahoe, Nevada, 2015
Source: Eric Weber

Decathlon in order to extend the available resources as far as possible. In addition to assisting the Studio with the regulatory approval process, PKMM donated structural insulated panels (SIPs).

The studio coordinator investigated the use of SIPs in the project for several reasons. The lack of construction experience among incoming designbuild students makes it challenging to erect structural framing quickly and accurately, and it was assumed that the difficulty of creating a tightly insulated building would also cause problems. SIPs offer the promise of accurate construction and good thermal performance, as well as comparatively quick erection.

The Design+Build Studio has discovered that while SIPs are in fact quite straight, assembly is not as straightforward as it might appear. One of the lessons learned from assembling the box office is that while the SIPs were readily available from the donor, the manufacturer's proprietary installation screws, sealing tape, and structural adhesive were not available locally. These installation accessories had to be ordered from the manufacturer's representative in Colorado, with a two-week lead time. The need to anticipate lead times and account for waste and student error is a critical skill for designbuilders to develop.

Due to heavy snow loads and the project's location in a seismic zone, the State Park's structural engineer required the use of continuous 4x6 wood splines at two feet on center, instead of the more typical 2x6 splines at four feet on center. This resulted in significant amounts of preparatory work, as the donated panels had to be cut down to two feet wide. It also resulted in much heavier panels to assemble, a particular challenge during the erection of the roof structure.

Conclusion

Establishing a new designbuild program requires dedication, determination, and a good measure of patience. Navigating the complexities of regulatory processes and university bureaucracy can at times seem to be overwhelming, but a careful understanding of the constraints and opportunities is essential to a successful outcome. Developing reliable funding and project streams are also critical to the long-term viability of any designbuild program. While every circumstance is unique, a careful review of the lessons learned by other designbuild educators can assist in avoiding making the same mistakes, while capitalizing on the sometimes-unexpected lessons that can be learned. One of the more surprising lessons for the Design+Build Studio's coordinator was the need to teach students soft skills like constructing clear, concise e-mails to suppliers. Proper phone etiquette, following up on communications to ensure consultants deliver on commitments, and the importance of being early for meetings are a few of the many skills employers expect graduates to know that have become integral parts of the Studio's teaching. Professionals who have hired graduates from the Design+Build Studio have commented to the Studio coordinator that these new hires have much better communication and interpersonal skills than their peers, an unexpected but positive development.

Notes

1 Nevada Revised Statute, Chapter 489, as referenced by the Nevada Manufactured Housing Division. http://mhd.nv.gov/licensing/#license.
2 Ryan E. Smith, *Prefab Architecture* (Hoboken: John Wiley & Sons, 2010), 198–199.
3 Nevada Revised Statute, Chapter 484D, Section 715, *Permit for Movement of Oversized Manufactured or Mobile Home or Similar Structure: Requirements; Conditions; Regulations.* http://www.leg.state.nv.us/NRS/NRS-484D.html#NRS484DSec700.
4 Eric Weber, "After the Solar Decathlon: Creating a New Design-Build Program," in *Intersections and Adjacencies: Leadership in Architectural Technology Education*, Proceedings of the 2015 Building Technology Educators' Society Conference, eds. Jacob A. Gines, Erin Carraher, Jose Galarza (Salt Lake: Building Technology Educators' Society, 2015), 22–24.
5 Paul Mackun and Steven Wilson, *Population Distribution and Change: 2000 to 2010* (Washington, D.C.: U.S. Department of Commerce Economics and Statistics Administration U.S. Census Bureau, 2011), 10.

14

WORK ETHIC, ETHICAL WORK

A Conversation with Designbuild Pioneer Dan Rockhill

Dan Rockhill and Chad Kraus

Editors Note: Over the course of the 2014–2015 academic year, I sat down with my colleague and fellow designbuild educator Dan Rockhill, the founder and director of Studio 804, to discuss his views on designbuild education. Studio 804 has become one of the most respected designbuild programs in the country. Yet, for all of their successes, Studio 804 remains an enigma to many. Rockhill has preferred to let the work stand for itself. On this occasion, I have sought to pry into the workings and theoretical underpinnings of Studio 804. Our conversation is divided into three themes: 1) Holistic Designbuild Education, 2) The Goodness of Labor and Other Designbuild Virtues, and 3) How Designbuild Gets Done.

FIGURE 14.1 An interior view of the auditorium from the lectern, *The Forum at Marvin Hall*, Lawrence, Kansas, 2014
Source: James Ewing/OTTO

Holistic Designbuild Education

> "Studio 804 is a truly comprehensive experience where we as students are responsible for all aspects of building, from design and budgeting to pouring concrete and framing walls. However, the lessons learned in Studio 804 go far beyond the architectural realm into team dynamics and work ethic."
>
> —Sam Florance, Schemata XXIV: East Lawrence Passive House, 2015

CK: *Studio 804, now in its twenty-second year, has become one of the most prominent designbuild programs in the country. The earlier work of the Studio concentrated on single-family homes, which at the time were seen as radically ambitious. Since then, the studio has successfully designed and built five significant architectural projects for institutions of higher learning and has only recently returned to the intimacy of the residential scale. Throughout this time, Studio 804 has served as a model to many of my generation of designbuild educators. Looking back, how do you feel about the impact Studio 804 has had?*

DR: I am delighted that the torch of designbuild education is being handed off. While Studio 804 represents the most extreme version of designbuild education, in the sense that the studio designs and builds every part of what are relatively complex projects, hands-on pedagogies of all kinds have the capacity to dislodge architects out of their comfort zones and to disrupt complacent attitudes about the profession. I cannot see any other way to synthesize an architectural education.

FIGURE 14.2 An exterior view of the shou-sugi-ban sided home, *Prescott Passive House*, Kansas City, Kansas, 2010
Source: Dan Rockhill

FIGURE 14.3 An exterior view of the woven aluminum rain screen, *Ecohawks Research Facility*, Lawrence, Kansas, 2013
Source: Dan Rockhill

CK: *When you started Studio 804 back in 1995, there were only a handful of academic designbuild experiences to be had. It was a pretty rare opportunity. There was, of course, the venerated Yale Building project established in the late 1960s, but that was a fairly isolated experience. Over the past ten years, however, there has been a proliferation of designbuild programs in the United States and elsewhere. Do you believe that designbuild education ought to be an integral and required component of architectural education, or should it remain, as it is today, a marginal (in terms of curricular emphasis) and unique experience for those who happen to be drawn to it?*

DR: I think the culture has changed. When I first started teaching, my students were very different than the students I encounter today. This generation is great in many ways but in an equal number of ways they struggle, to the extent that they often do not even recognize how little they know. Children used to go outside and build rudimentary tree houses, experiencing how to secure supports from which a board can span, or to place boards so that they are more-or-less level. Children today are more likely to play, if they play outdoors at all, in one of those pathetic, plastic, snap-together tree houses that their parents purchased from the store. I use this example only to identify a significant cultural shift, one that I believe contributes to a certain lack of awareness about the world.

CK: *Designbuild, then, is in some ways an antidote to this generation's paucity of integrated tectonic experiences during their formative years?*

DR: [Nodding]

CK: *Perhaps this explains why educators, across disciplines, have been turning to experiential learning models and why we see a reawakening of the "tinkerer" in the Maker Movement. How do you feel about designbuild education in relation to larger societal shifts?*

DR: I feel good about the emergence of experiential learning and service learning models. These pedagogies not only provide greater justification to university administrators for the existence of designbuild programs, they also signal a broader movement. It's good to be a part of a loftier learning experience. Despite successes and increased presence in design schools, designbuild education remains vulnerable. Many architecture educators and administrators feel threatened by it, or feel that it has yet to prove its worth. I think it's changing; you can't help but see, through tangible evidence, the benefits these programs have to students and to the institutions that house them.

CK: *Do you find parallels between designbuild culture and non-academic developments, such as the rise of maker spaces that empower communities of makers to create physical, tangible things?*

DR: It reinforces or identifies a desire that a few academics detected twenty years ago. Today, people are simply growing dissatisfied with going to a big-box store to buy generic things to populate their lives.

CK: *Designbuild programs, such as Studio 804, represent tremendous commitments from both faculty and students. Alongside the rise of designbuild programs across the country, as you say, there are those who question the value of designbuild education. Can you elaborate on why designbuild education is important?*

DR: I do what I do because over the course of my career I have seen a tremendous change in young people. Our contemporary ready-made, snap-together environment has shaped their formative years. They have been denied the opportunity to experience having to put a nail in a tree. I am not simply talking about a poetic sense of tactility, or even the imperative of making. Today our students have not been empowered to make an intervention in the world, *on their own*. They have had little need for imagination or inventiveness because images and inventions could be purchased on their behalf. I am talking about instilling in my students the value of doing more than selecting products from a catalog. We have become so overwhelmed by consumerism that the whole culture of making is rapidly fading away. I am not trying to romanticize what it once was; things are what they are. However, one of the reasons I am drawn to designbuild experiences is that I am not prepared to resign to the pressures of commodification. I witness all the time the effects this cultural shift has had on young people. A case in point: a group of my students were painting structural steel elements for the Forum using a sprayed-on clear coat. After observing the steel beginning to rust almost immediately after installation, I looked into the "empty" five-gallon containers only to discover they had left in the bottom of the containers this white stuff, which, incidentally, is the ingredient responsible for protecting against oxidation. It never occurred to me to instruct them to mix the paint. Despite having consistently intelligent students, surprisingly, this kind of thing happens fairly often. There is a certain kind of savvy that comes with having your hands in it. This kind of learning by doing has become increasingly rare.

CK: *How do your students respond to lessons learned through designbuild education?*

DR: Prior to founding Studio 804, I taught a final-year, two-semester graduate design studio, Arch 803 and Arch 804. Since it was the last studio students would have to take before graduating, it turned out to be the worst studio you could teach. Students already had one foot out the door; they felt I was blocking them from getting on with their lives. Then, a colleague and friend of mine, Professor Harris Stone, was diagnosed with cancer and was soon overcome by the disease. He had been working on the restoration of an old stone schoolhouse called the Barber School. In the summers, students would work with Harris to lovingly breathe life back into the building. During his suffering, before his abrupt and tragic passing, I pitched the idea of finishing what Harris had started to a group of my students. The response was overwhelmingly positive and completely unexpected; I couldn't believe the difference. Fueled by their enthusiasm, I remember wheeling a cart loaded with full-scale steel details into the hospital to share with Harris and to get his approval.

FIGURE 14.4 An exterior view of the historic school house with its new steel frame roof support, *Barber School House*, near Lawrence, Kansas, 1995

Source: Dan Rockhill

Suddenly, my students were engaged and passionate about their work. They were working late into the night, pulling their cars up to the school so they could work in the light of the headlamps. The project flipped a switch; it ignited a fire. The next year we did a small project, and then the next year . . . you know how the story goes.

CK: *Let's explore the relationship between designbuild education and professional practice. Some observers have asserted that designbuild education has the potential to fill an unwholesome divide between academia and practice, a rekindled apprenticeship model, so to speak. How do you see Studio 804 orienting students toward future practice?*

DR: The apprenticeship model is a good analogy; however, most of my graduates will end up in traditional architecture firms. Most will work for several years in that setting before they can appreciate the difference and ask, "Is this it?" while recalling the control over the design they had when they were doing the building as well. The potency of their Studio 804 experiences will hopefully empower them to look toward other ways to find a place for themselves in the profession, perhaps outside of traditional practices. Yet it remains an interesting connection to make and in some ways it feeds the desire to do this kind of work.

FIGURE 14.5 Students installing Alaskan yellow cedar shingle siding, *1301 New York*, Lawrence, Kansas, 2015
Source: Dan Rockhill

CK: *As I mentioned before, Studio 804 has recently returned to the more intimate scale of single-family houses. Why?*

DR: I returned to houses because, compared to the larger institutional projects, they provide a more holistic learning environment—from code compliance, budget management, and property acquisitions, to the design of wall systems and spatial configurations. The single-family house is complex enough to touch on much of what the architect needs to know while being small enough that students can appreciate its complexity.

The Goodness of Labor and Other Designbuild Virtues

> "I won't be spending the rest of my life on a construction site, pouring concrete, framing walls, or welding curtain wall frames, but I hope to spend it designing and drawing those very details, and there is no better way to learn how to draw details than to have to build what it is you drew."
>
> —Liz Pritting, Schemata XXI: Galileo's Pavilion, 2012

> "Understanding the concept of design tolerance is fundamental to what we did: the real world is not as exact as the CAD world. Building materials are not perfect."
>
> —Hayder Alsaad, Schemata XXII: Ecohawks Research Facility, 2013

CK: *Unlike most design studios—which are largely hypothetical—designbuild studios such as Studio 804 serve not only internal pedagogical obligations but also external obligations. These buildings have to perform. How do you balance these obligations? For example, a student is struggling to understand a particular problem. Do you take the time to ensure that the student learns what you have set out to teach them, even if this negatively impacts the schedule of the project, or, given the pressures of completing the project on time and on budget, do you push it forward even if you risk missing a teaching opportunity?*

FIGURE 14.6 Students working to erect the structure and framing, *Ecohawks Research Facility*, Lawrence, Kansas, 2013

Source: Dan Rockhill

DR: I tend to privilege student learning, if nothing else for the sake of quality. I do it by intimidation. There is a lot of work that gets torn out and redone. Fortunately, I have had the experience to know what to look for. I know where the quicksand is. I try to catch them before it becomes a nightmare. We do not do bad work. I am very insistent on that. The work should be done with pride; an element of craft has to be evident. This is one of the more difficult aspects to teach. They need to understand this first hand, and once they do, they can almost always predict what I will say when they show me what they have done. I am insistent that we conduct ourselves as professionals, both through design and construction documentation but also in the actual built work. It takes a while for them to come to terms with that.

CK: *In the design studio, failure can be a viable outcome; some of the best lessons arise when students try something very risky and ultimately "fail" to bring the idea to fruition. There can be a lot to take away from these types of experiences, sort of "failing up," as it were. In the past you have criticized architects for wanting to solve everything on paper and have praised the ability to be agile in the face of inevitable uncertainty during the construction process. In designbuild studios such as Studio 804, is there any opportunity for productive failure?*

DR: Part of the enjoyment of designbuild is that we are afforded the luxury of building at full scale. We can examine multiple ideas through mockups and then stand back and observe it in its final context and test the ideas. I will

FIGURE 14.7 An interior view of the Springfield House, Kansas City, Kansas 2009
Source: Dan Rockhill

usually put a time cap on it—"Let's give this our best half day." We have a building to build, so we just keep pushing. In the case of the East Lawrence House, we built some pretty awful iterations in the process, but we saw the potential and drove the mockups until we were satisfied. Some days I just have to say no and pull the plug on the idea. I am fairly dictatorial. In their professional careers it will not always be their favorite lesson, but it is an important one nonetheless.

CK: *As a designbuild professional and educator, how would you describe your professional philosophy or conceptual framework, and how is that manifested in designbuild pedagogies?*

DR: A clear conceptual framework is essential to designbuild education, because you need to be able to guide a group of strong-willed, novice designers to make good design decisions at all scales. This is particularly true when you are working with students, who honestly do not yet know what they do not know. I draw heavily on my approach to professional practice to guide my students. The work is driven by passive environmental strategies bound to the particularities of a given place. Broad southern exposure, introduction of cross ventilation, highly insulated thermal envelopes, and connections to the landscape and agricultural identity of the region emerge from a sense of place and a desire to do environmentally smart buildings. Understanding the influence of the culture is important to us—vast horizons, wheat, bibles, these beautiful ad hoc assemblies of agricultural and muscular industrial buildings, trains, the tin man, crop dusters, experimenting with materials, being resourceful.

These last two qualities are particularly engrained in my approach to architecture. We repurpose a lot of materials—scrapped steel from a former cheesemaking factory, wood floor boards from a demolished basketball court, stone tailings from a quarry, glass from a failed speculative office building—we build using a lot of recycled and reclaimed material. We do this to be sustainable, sure, but we also do this because our budgets are often a fraction of what these projects would cost if done in a conventional delivery method. We squeeze blood from rocks, so to speak. This allows us to keep our foot in the door to do good and inspired work.

We simply cannot otherwise afford to do this type of work in these communities, so we have to find creative and unorthodox ways. We beat up the building process, dismantle conventions, and look for opportunities. The whole designbuild approach, for me, has been largely born out of necessity. Our heart is in design. Our ability to make the buildings we design allows us to pursue a level of quality that is largely elusive for most architects. In the process, we develop a connectedness to these buildings and the processes of building them so that we are not intimidated from being inventive. This is what I like to refer to as "the presence of the hand."

CK: *One of the primary criticisms of designbuild education has been the lack of evidence that this pedagogical model actually contributes to making our students better architects. What are the most significant benefits of designbuild education you have observed over the more than two decades of teaching Studio 804?*

DR: Sustainability has been a major focus of Studio 804. Equipping young people with a solid knowledge base in sustainable strategies is important, and I take pride in my students' ability to confidently engage in sustainable practices. Having directly experienced sustainable design in all phases of a project, including the post-construction submission of paperwork for LEED and Passivhaus standards, it brings to life the lessons they learn in their support courses. I have no doubt that this emphasis has contributed to fueling real change in the profession.

Aside from the principles of architecture, one of the most important lessons I impart to my students is the value of hard work. It takes hard work to do good work. The act of work—*labor*—is itself a lesson. This is a particularly important lesson at a time when fewer young people experience the rigors of labor as an integral or natural condition of their formative years, a labor that hones and cultivates a thirst for goodness. Students do not have enough experience to know what it takes to achieve truly good work. I stress and try to instill in my students the passion and drive to make something good, and see it through, so that it bears fruit. They often want to take the path of least resistance and do not yet have the designer's judgment to reject the "good enough." They are initially quite willing to accept the mediocre. Once they understand this drive for excellence, they become engaged and the enthusiasm is palpable. Yet, the struggle to impart this particular lesson is becoming increasingly difficult with each passing year, which only galvanizes the need to do so.

Of course, it is difficult to quantitatively measure the benefits of designbuild education. I suppose you could compare my students to those who have not had a designbuild experience, but you would still need to control for a multitude of other variables. What I do see is a lot of anecdotal evidence. I often hear from my former students just how much the Studio 804 experience has meant to them. I also frequently hear from firms who have made a habit of hiring Studio 804 graduates.

How Designbuild Gets Done

"For me, Studio 804 revealed a layer of architecture that traditional academics doesn't touch on, the real world and its variables. Studios I had taken before allowed me to detach architecture from the difficulties of how buildings are constructed and what must happen simultaneously in the background. In my opinion, architecture becomes much more interesting when these complexities are included."

—Benjamin Peek, Schemata XXIII: The Forum, 2014

CK: *The works of Studio 804 have an air of inevitability. Although all who experience them understand that the finished work is but the tip of the iceberg, rarely do we get a glimpse of the rest of the iceberg itself, or if we do, it is through murky waters. Here I want to focus on the logistics behind the curtain. Over the past twenty-plus years, Studio 804 has occasionally operated with the support of your own professional designbuild firm, Rockhill and Associates. How would you characterize this relationship, and in what ways has this support enabled Studio 804 to accomplish what it has?*

FIGURE 14.8 Students erecting the building's timber structure, *The Forum at Marvin Hall*, Lawrence, Kansas, 2014
Source: Dan Rockhill

DR: While I am certain that Studio 804 could have been possible without the presence of Rockhill and Associates, one of the most immediate benefits of this relationship is that the Studio has had access to tools and equipment that are not readily available at the university. For instance, when it came time for a student to fold a piece of sheet metal, instead of trying to convince the administration to purchase a sheet metal brake, I made the metal brake in my shop available. This certainly has made production easier; however, the Studio is resourceful, and there have been times when we have found other ways to achieve our purposes with limited resources. It is true that in the last several years I have brought on my professional partners, Dave Sain and Doug Callahan, because the schedule for the projects never changes but the size of the projects have increased significantly. It helps to have a staff as a safety net when working at that scale. I keep this to a bare minimum, however. With the exception of the Forum it is no more than several hours a month. I have to bill Studio 804 for their time, and we do not have the funds to support much at all. The Forum was a very complex building with many moving parts that all had to come together without a glitch; everybody worked hard to bring that one over the finish line.

One other benefit comes to mind. The permitting process has to go through Rockhill and Associates because of our contractor's license, which is maintained by my employees. Studio 804 cannot maintain the license due to continuing education requirements, which becomes too much of an additional burden on my time. This, of course, can be a serious obstacle for someone who does not have the infrastructure of his or her own design firm to fall back on.

CK: *The reason I ask this question is that many aspiring designbuild educators see the work of Studio 804 and ask, "How does this get done?" Yet the "how" is rarely a focus in public discourse.*

DR: To teach designbuild studios, my recommendation to most people would be to get experience and become comfortable with using your hands, to talk to people in the industry, to work with people in the construction or craft trades. You must find a level of comfort where you can ask questions. That is the great potential of the designbuild experience—to impart to students a level of comfort collaborating with tradespeople. You talk to contractors and learn something about roof membranes or drainage strategies. These kinds of honest interactions are important, because I often observe in our profession a tendency to just cover up what you do not know. Designbuild opens up that world of questioning and asking how. For example, one of my recent students, Sam Florence, had a great experience learning about standing seam roofs while working in collaboration with a manufacturer in Kansas City. Through my coaching, he was able to have these productive conversations that, from a pedagogical standpoint, were wildly successful. After completing our project a group of Studio 804 graduates went out and put a standing seam roof on a project they developed out in Colorado. I love it when they start with so little knowledge and in a short time *I* am in *their* way.

CK: *One of the most challenging issues with designbuild education is the limited and finite academic time frame. Studio 804 operates as a two-semester program, with extensions into the summer when necessary. Earlier you mentioned the permitting process. How does Studio 804 handle the potential scheduling delays of this process?*

FIGURE 14.9 Students installing standing seam roofing, *1301 New York*, Lawrence, Kansas, 2015

Source: Dan Rockhill

DR: I have had enough experience working with city and state officials to know exactly what they want. I can usually anticipate where there may be problems, and we address that before they have to ask.

CK: *Does the permitting process constrain design development since you may have to pull a permit early enough to have time to build?*

DR: The permitting process actually enhances design development, although it depends on what is considered design development. We basically commit to the footprint of the building, and we address all the life safety issues that could be a source of contention. While that permit is being processed, which can take three or four weeks, we continue to develop other aspects of the design, such as detailing. Ideally we can wrap this up by the time the permit is ready and go break ground.

CK: *Are the students involved in every aspect of the permitting process?*

DR: Absolutely. I pride myself on not making a phone call. They do everything. These bigger university projects have been more difficult. I suppose I did field a phone call or two on those projects.

CK: *One of the most common questions regarding the logistics of designbuild education has got to be, "Where does the funding typically come from?"*

DR: Studio 804 is self-funded now and has been since 2009—so for seven of the past twenty-two years—with the exception of a few university-related projects, which were client-funded. What I mean by self-funded is that we use the proceeds of the sale of previous Studio 804 projects to fund the next one.

Prior to this funding mechanism, we had to figure out a way to convince most of the neighborhood associations that it was a good idea for them to support us to fund those projects. In other words, I would ask them to loan me, for example, $100,000, to be repaid in six months at $108,000, and I would sell the house for whatever the market will bear. In this way Studio 804 began to save enough money to buy a piece of property, finance the house, and generate enough savings to start the process again the following year.

CK: *Amazingly then, Studio 804 is not only the designer and the builder but also the developer. Can you explain how the Studio is organized as an academic endeavor and what role does its separate non-profit status, as Studio 804 Inc., serve?*

DR: The Studio is organized similarly to a professional office. Everybody has a specific responsibility, we meet six days a week, and we discuss how everybody will meet that responsibility. What Studio 804 Inc. does is it makes the program a little bit more than a group of students who have gotten together to make something happen. Although becoming Studio 804 Inc. helped legitimize the studio, it really did not affect the operation within the studio.

CK: *How has Studio 804 handled liability issues, specifically injury and monetary liability?*

DR: All students enrolled in Studio 804 are required to have personal health insurance policies, which is easily obtained as most of them are already covered by an insurance policy. Studio 804 has to have commercial liability insurance, and on some of the state projects the requirements are very cumbersome and expensive. Also, depending on the project, Studio 804 occasionally carries a workers compensation policy; but this type of insurance is predicated on payroll, and we have no payroll. This makes the whole process a bit complicated.

CK: *What about errors and omissions insurance?*

DR: Good question. Rockhill and Associates carries that insurance, though it has not been required on the house projects since these do not require sealed architectural drawings. In those cases, we only need to have our engineers seal the engineering drawings. Rockhill and Associates does seal university projects, and in these instances I invoice Studio 804 for the direct expense of the policy as it applies to only that project.

CK: *In light of the supporting role Rockhill and Associates has played in the more complex projects of Studio 804, would you recommend an aspiring designbuild educator to establish a company in conjunction with the studio?*

DR: I think so. There are some logistical obstacles that, without this supporting entity, would be difficult, if not impossible. You may need to establish some form of business and have a clear business plan. I think it is also useful for the students to learn about business during their Studio 804 experience, so I see this as a benefit all the way around.

CK: *Yet many educators are drawn to designbuild for its pedagogical virtues and have no clear business plan or long-term strategy.*

DR: That is probably not a bad way to start, after all, these measures add up. It can be expensive and complicated. Until you are sure that you have got your legs under you, it is somewhat experimental for the first few years.

CK: *Designbuild is an emerging, some say emerged, pedagogy. Do you think it will endure, or is it a momentary reaction? What do you think it will look like in ten or fifteen years?*

DR: Designbuild education will be here to stay at least through our lifetimes. These programs require a lot of upfront investment. They take a considerable amount of mobilizing and can be difficult to establish. Having overcome significant resistance, it would be a great mistake to let go of it. The Yale Building Project, after nearly fifty years, is a good example of the staying power of designbuild programs.

Wrapping Up the Conversation

CK: *There are many variations on the designbuild experience, from the small-scale to the large-scale, from temporary to permanent, from low-tech to high-tech, from less than one semester long to multiple semesters spanning over several years. In the pursuit of larger, more complex projects, some designbuild programs have made the decision to divide the design phases from the building phases with different groups of students plugged in and out of the complex whole. Studio 804, on the other hand, has pursued larger-scale projects with a determination to complete the project within one year by one group of students. Why is the synthesis between design and build so important in Studio 804?*

DR: While designbuild education is not solely focused on design, it is equally not really about building. I doubt anyone involved in this considers designbuild education to be vocational training in any way. We are not intentionally training designbuilders either, although that does happen on occasion. I do this simply *to make better architects.* Honestly, I am often embarrassed by the building component. I do not care for the macho mentality that comes with it. I do it because I think it makes better designers. Students are most empowered by having experienced the intertwined relationship between designing and building, between the mind and the hand. Taking a project from an idea on paper all the way through to a tangible building can be exhilarating. The project is their baby, and I tell them as much. There are not many graduates that can boast of having already completed a building from start to finish.

CK: *It is inspiring to observe Studio 804 working at this scale, with a single group of students who have experienced the turmoil and the opportunities of the whole endeavor and who have synthesized the act of designing with the act of making.*

DR: When I stagger away from these projects, I think, "There has got to be an easier way." Ultimately I know the answer is no, there is not. In Kansas, our state motto is *ad astra per aspera,* which translates as *to the stars through difficulty.* In some ways, this aptly characterizes the philosophy of Studio 804. When I think about the hard work that my students dedicate to the project, when I see how far they have come, when I hear what Studio 804 has meant to them, I am encouraged. It is important that they endure the fullness of these works, that they discover the power of design all the way through the details. They see the impact on those who experience the work, those who intuit how we have agonized over the spacing of boards in the ceiling with countless mockups. They understand why everything has to be just right.

FIGURE 14.10 An exterior view of the Forum in the evening, *The Forum at Marvin Hall*, Lawrence, Kansas, 2014

Source: James Ewing/OTTO

CK: *I feel fortunate to teach a designbuild program at the same school where you have taught Studio 804 for more than two decades. Studio 804, as a pioneering and globally significant force in designbuild education, has artfully paved a path through the sometimes-thorny thicket of administrative obstacles, has shone a light on the value of this hands-on way of learning to our fellow architectural educators, and has graciously invited others to traverse this path of tremendous resistance, all in the name of a better architectural discipline.*

DR: Thank you, Chad!

BIBLIOGRAPHY

Abendroth, Lisa M. and Bryan Bell. *Public Interest Design Practice Guidebook*. New York: Routledge, 2016.

Alberti, Leon Battista. *On the Art of Building in Ten Books*. Translated by Joseph Rykwert, Neil Leach, and Robert Tavernor. Cambridge, MA: MIT Press, 1991.

Allen, Stan. *Practice: Architecture, Technique, and Representation*. New York: Routledge, 2009.

Anderson, Jane and Colin Priest. "Developing an Inclusive Definition, Typological Analysis and Online Resource for Live Projects." In *Architecture Live Projects*, edited by Harriet Harriss and Lynette Widder, 9–17. New York: Routledge, 2014.

Andre, Christophe. *Looking at Mindfulness: Twenty-five Ways to Live in the Moment Through Art*. New York: Penguin, Blue Rider Press, 2014.

Arieff, Allison and Bryan Burkhart. *Prefab*. Salt Lake City: Gibbs Smith, 2002.

Awan, Nishat, Tatjana Schneider, and Jeremy Till. *Spatial Agency: Other Ways of Doing Architecture*. New York: Routledge, 2013.

Bass, Rick. *Fiber*. Athens: University of Georgia Press, 1998.

Borges, Jorge Luis. *Selected Poems 1923–1967*. New York: Delacorte, 1972.

Boyer, Ernest L. and Lee D. Mitgang. *Building Community: A New Future for Architecture Education and Practice*. Stanford, CA: Carnegie Foundation for the Advancement of Teaching, 1996.

Breunlin, Rachel and Helen A. Regis. "Can There be a Critical Collaborative Ethnography?: Creativity and Activism in the Seventh Ward, New Orleans." *Collaborative Anthropologies* 2, no. 1 (2009): 115–146.

Burchard, Charles. "A Curriculum Geared to the Times." *AIA Journal* (May 1967): 101–105.

Cadwell, Michael. *Pamphlet 17, Small Buildings*. New York: Princeton Architectural Press, 1996.

Canizaro, Vincent B. "Regionalism, Place, Specificity, and Sustainable Design." In *Pragmatic Sustainability*, edited by Steven A. Moore, 150–168. New York: Routledge, 2010.

Carpenter, William J. *Learning by Building: Design and Construction in Architectural Education*. New York: Van Nostrand Reinhold, 1997.

232 Bibliography

Citizen Architect: Samuel Mockbee and the Spirit of the Rural Studio. Directed by Sam Wainwright Douglas. Austin, TX: Big Beard Films, 2010. DVD

Culvahouse, Tim, ed. *The Tennessee Valley Authority.* New York: Princeton Architectural Press, 2007.

Dean, Andrea Oppenheimer and Timothy Hursley. *Rural Studio.* New York: Princeton Architectural Press, 2002.

Dean, Andrea Oppenheimer and Timothy Hursley. *Proceed and Be Bold: Rural Studio after Samuel Mockbee.* New York: Princeton Architectural Press, 2005.

de Tocqueville, Alexis. *Democracy in America.* Translated by Arthur Goldhammer. New York: The Library of America, 2004.

Dewey, John. *Art as Experience.* New York: Capricorn, 1958.

Dewey, John. *My Pedagogical Creed.* Washington, D.C.: Progressive Education Association, 1929.

Dillard, Annie. *Teaching a Stone to Talk.* New York: HarperCollins, 1982.

Engle, Henrich. *Structure Systems.* New York: Van Nostrand Reinhold, 1981.

Erdman, Jori and Robert Weddle. "Designing / Building / Learning." *Journal of Architectural Education* 55, no. 3 (2002): 174–179.

Evans, Bill. "Improvisation in Jazz." Liner notes for "Kind of Blue" by Miles Davis, 1959.

Evans, Robin. *Translations from Drawing to Building and Other Essays.* Cambridge: MIT Press, 1997.

Ford, Edward. *Five Houses, Ten Details.* New York: Princeton Architectural Press, 2009.

Frampton, Kenneth. "Prospects for a Critical Regionalism." *Perspecta: The Yale Architectural Journal* 20 (1983): 147–162.

Frascari, Marco. "The Tell-the-Tale Detail," *Theorizing a New Agenda for Architecture,* ed. Kate Nesbitt (New York: Princeton Architectural Press, 1996).

Grandgent, Louis. *Houses at Norris, Tennessee.* A TVA report to Earl S. Draper, Director of Land Planning and Housing, 1936.

Greene, Joshua. *Moral Tribes.* New York: Penguin, 2013.

Gropius, Walter. "New Ideas on Architecture." In *Programmes and Manifestoes on 20th-century Architecture,* edited by Ulrich Conrads, 46–48. London: Lund Humphries, 1970.

Harrison, Jim. "Nesting in Air." In *Northern Lights: A Selection of New Writing from the American West,* edited by Deborah Clow and Donald Snow, 262–264. New York: Vintage Books, 1994.

Harriss, Harriet. "Co-Authoring a Live Project Manifesto." In *Architecture Live Projects: Pedagogy into Practice,* edited by Harriet Harriss and Lynnette Widder, 42–47. London: Routledge, 2014.

Hayes, Richard W. *The Yale Building Project.* New Haven, CT: Yale School of Architecture, 2007.

Hays, K. Michael. *Architecture's Desire: Reading the Late Avant-garde.* Cambridge, MA: MIT, 2010.

Heidegger, Martin. *Poetry, Language, Thought.* Translated by Albert Hofstadter. New York: Harper & Row, 1975.

Holden, Kimberly J. and Philip Nobel. *SHoP Architects: Out of Practice.* London: Thames & Hudson, 2012.

Holl, Steven. "Questions of Perception." In *Questions of Perception: Phenomenology of Architecture,* by Steven Holl, Juhani Pallasmaa, and Alberto Pérez Gómez, 40–42. San Francisco: William Stout, 2006.

Hospers, John, ed. *Introductory Readings in Aesthetics.* New York: The Free Press, 1969.

Husserl, Edmund. *Cartesian Meditations.* Translated by Dorian Cairns. The Hague: Martius Nijhoff, 1960.

Ihde, Don. *Postphenomenology and Technoscience*. Albany: SUNY Press, 2009.

Jackson, John Brinckerhoff. *Discovering the Vernacular Landscape*. New Haven: Yale University Press, 1984.

James, William. *A Pluralistic Universe*. Edited by Fredson Bowers, Ignas Skrupskelis, and Richard Bernstein. Cambridge, MA: Harvard University Press, 1977.

Kleon, Austin. *Steal Like an Artist*. New York: Workman Pub, 2012.

Kyle, John H. *The Building of TVA*. Baton Rouge: Louisiana State University Press, 1958.

Le Corbusier. *Le Poème de l'Angle Droit*. Translated by Kenneth Hylton. Paris: Fondation Le Corbusier, Editions Connivences, 1989.

Leopold, Aldo. *A Sand County Almanac: With Other Essays on Conservation from Round River*. New York: Balantine Books, 1966.

Levi, Albert. *Philosophy and the Modern World*. Bloomington, IN: Indiana University Press, 1958.

Louv, Richard. *Last Child In the Woods*. New York: Workman Publishing Co., 2005.

Mackay-Lyons, Brian. *Ghost: Building an Architectural Vision*. New York: Princeton Architectural Press, 2008.

MacKay-Lyons, Brian. *Local Architecture: Building Place, Craft, and Community*. Edited by Robert McCarter. New York: Princeton Architectural Press, 2015.

Mackun, Paul and Steven Wilson. *Population Distribution and Change: 2000 to 2010*. Washington, D.C.: U.S. Department of Commerce Economics and Statistics Administration U.S. Census Bureau, 2011.

Maki, Fumihiko. "The Art of Suki." *A+U* 10, *Carlo Scarpa* (1985): 206–207.

Marble, Scott, David Smiley, and Marwan Al-Sayed. *Architecture and Body, The Special Project from Precis, Columbia Architectural Journal*. New York: Rizzoli, 1989.

Maritain, Jacques. *Creative Intuition in Art and Poetry*. New York: Pantheon Books, 1953.

Marrey, Bernard. *Architecte: du maître de l'oeuvre au disagneur*. Paris: Editions Du Linteau, 2014.

McDonald, Michael J. and John Muldowny. *TVA and the Dispossessed*. Knoxville: The University of Tennessee Press, 1981.

Moe, Kiel. *Integrated Design in Contemporary Architecture*. New York: Princeton Architectural Press, 2008.

Moholy-Nagy, Sibly. *Native Genius in Anonymous Architecture*. New York: Horizon, 1957.

Morgan, Arthur. *Making of the TVA*. Buffalo, NY: Prometheus Books, 1974.

Mortimer, Samuel. "A New Norris House." *PLEA: Sustainable Architecture for a Renewable Future Conference* (2013): 51, 192.

Ng, Eddy S. W., Linda Schweitzer, and Sean T. Lyons. "New Generation, Great Expectations: A Field Study of the Millennial Generation." *Journal of Business and Psychology* 25, no. 2 (2010): 281–292.

Norberg-Schulz, Christian. "The Phenomenon of Place." *Architectural Association Quarterly* 8, no. 4 (1976): 3–10.

Norberg-Schulz, Christian. *Nightlands: Nordic Building*. Cambridge, MA: MIT Press, 1996.

Ockman, Joan. *The Pragmatist Imagination*. New York: Princeton Architectural Press, 2000.

Pallasmaa, Juhani. *Eyes of the Skin*. West Sussex: Wiley, 2005.

Pallasmaa, Juhani. *The Thinking Hand: Existential and Embodied Wisdom in Architecture*. West Sussex: Wiley, 2009.

Potié, Philippe. *Le Corbusier: Le Couvent Sainte Marie De La Tourette*. Boston: Birkhäuser, 2001.

Putnam, Robert D. *Bowling Alone: The Collapse and Revival of American Community*. New York: Simon & Schuster, 2000.

Pye, David. *The Nature and Aesthetics of Design*. New York: Van Nostrand Reinhold, 1978.

234 Bibliography

Pye, David. *The Nature and Art of Workmanship*. Cambridge: University Press, 1968.

Quale, John. *Sustainable, Affordable, Prefab: The ecoMOD Project*. Charlottesville: University of Virginia Press, 2012.

Quale, John, Matthew J. Eckelman, Kyle W. Williams, Greg Sloditskie, and Julie B. Zimmerman. "Construction Matters: Comparing Environmental Impacts of Building Modular and Conventional Homes in the United States." *Journal of Industrial Ecology* 16, no. 2 (April 2012): 243–253.

Quale, John, Matthew J. Eckelman, Kyle W. Williams, Greg Sloditskie, and Julie B. Zimmerman. "Two Recent Life Cycle Analysis (LCA) Studies for Buildings: On-Site versus Off-Site Construction and Building Material Reuse." *GreenBuild Thought Leadership Proceedings*, U.S. Green Building Council Annual Conference (2011).

Relph, Edward. "Modernity and the Reclamation of Place." In *Dwelling, Seeing, and Designing: Toward a Phenomenological Ecology*, edited by David Seamon, 25–40. Albany: State University of New York Press, 1993.

Rosenthal, Sandra B. and Patrick L. Bourgeois. *Pragmatism and Phenomenology: A Philosophic Encounter*. Amsterdam: Grüner, 1980.

Ryker, Lori. *Mockbee Coker: Thought and Process*. New York: Princeton Architectural, 1995.

Ryker, Lori. *The Creation of Second Nature: The Problem of Making for Students of Architecture*. Ann Arbor, MI: UMI Dissertation Services, 2000.

Sachs, Avigail and Tricia Stuth. "Innovation and Tradition: Eighty Years of Housing Construction in Southern Appalachia." *Construction History* 28, no. 1 (2013): 65–82.

Sass, Lawrence and Marcel Botha. "The Instant House." *International Journal of Architectural Computing* 4, no. 4 (2006): 109–123.

Sekler, Eduard F. "Structure, Construction, Tectonics." In *Structure in Art and in Science*, edited by Georgy Keppes, 89–95. New York: George Brazziler, 1965.

Sennett, Richard. *The Craftsman*. New Haven: Yale University Press, 2008.

Sennett, Richard. *The Uses of Disorder: Personal Identity and City Life*. New York: WW Norton & Company, 1992.

Shafer, Daniel. *Norris, TN 1933–1983*. Norris Historical Society, 1993.

Shepherd, Paul. *Nature and Madness*. San Francisco: Sierra Club, 1982.

Smith, Ryan E. *Prefab Architecture*. Hoboken: John Wiley & Sons, 2010.

Solnit, Rebecca. *A Paradise Built in Hell: The Extraordinary Communities that Arise in Disaster*. New York: Penguin Books, 2009.

Sorkin, Michael. "Sorkin Finds a Model in a Tennessee Small Town with a Genuine Sense of Purpose." *Architectural Record* 189, no. 7 (July 2001): 63–64.

Spector, Tom. "Pragmatism for Architects." *Contemporary Pragmatism* 1, no. 1 (2004): 133–149.

Spreckelmeyer, Kent and Bill Carswell. "Studio 804, Hands-On Thinking, and the Legacy of Harris Stone." Unpublished manuscript, 2014.

Stevens, James and Ralph Nelson. *Digital Vernacular: Architectural Principles, Tools, and Processes*. New York: Routledge, 2015.

Stromberg, Ronald N. *An Intellectual History of Modern Europe*. New York: Appleton-Century-Crofts, 1966.

Stuth, Tricia, Samuel Mortimer, Valerie Friedmann, and John Buchanan. "A New Norris House: Making Criteria for Sustainable Landscapes Visible." *The Visibility of Research: ARCC Spring Research Conference* (2013): 569–578.

Taylor, James S. *Poetic Knowledge: The Recovery of Education*. Albany, NY: SUNY Press, 1997.

Tehrani, Nader. "A Murder in the Court." In *Strange Details* by Michael Cadwell, vii–xii. Cambridge: MIT Press, 2007.

"Tennessee Valley Authority." *Architectural Forum*, no. 8 (August 1939): 73–114.

Tschumi, Bernard. *Architecture and Disjunction*. Cambridge, MA: MIT Press, 1994.

Van den Berg, J. H. *Things: Four Metabletic Reflections*. Pittsburgh, PA: Duquesne UP, 1970.

Van West, Carroll. *Tennessee's New Deal Landscape*. Knoxville: The University of Tennessee Press, 2001.

Vattimo, Gianni. *Dialogue with Nietzsche*. Translated by William McCuaig. New York: Columbia University Press, 2006.

Vico, Giambattista. *Vico: Selected Writings*. Edited by Leon Pompa. Cambridge: Cambridge University Press, 1982.

Weiner, Frank and Shelley Martin. "The Education of An Architect: 3 Points of View: Rowe, Hejduk and Ferrari." *Association of Collegiate Schools of Architecture 93rd Annual Meeting, The Art of Architecture/The Science of Architecture* (2005): 195–202.

Williams-Clay, LaTasha K., Cirecie A. West-Olatunji, and Susan R. Cooley. "Keeping the Story Alive: Narrative in the African-American Church and Community." *American Counseling Association Annual Meeting*, San Antonio, Texas (2001).

Weber, Eric. "After the Solar Decathlon: Creating a New Design-Build Program." In *Intersections and Adjacencies: Leadership in Architectural Technology Education*, Proceedings of the 2015 Building Technology Educators' Society Conference, edited by Jacob A. Gines, Erin Carraher, and Jose Galarza, 22–24. Salt Lake: Building Technology Educators' Society, 2015.

Zumthor, Peter. *Atmospheres: Architectural Environments, Surrounding Objects*. Basel: Birkhäuser, 2006.

Zumthor, Peter. *Peter Zumthor: Buildings and Projects, Volume 3 1998–2001*. Zurich: Scheidegger & Spiess, 2014.

INDEX

Abendroth, Lisa 2
academia 3, 14, 20–2, 29, 82; academic-
professional bridge 11–13, 129, 169
Adamson, Jim 3
administration teams 66, 71, 75–6, 131–2,
138, 178, 207–8
aesthetics 9–10, 12, 36, 41, 48
affordable housing 26–8, 36, 41, 172, 190
African American culture 52–4, 62
Alberti, Leon Battista 4
American Institute of Architects (AIA)
172
American Institute of Architecture Students
(AIAS) 74
American Society of Landscape Architects
(ASLA) 172
Anderson, Jane 2
apprenticeships 3–4, 129, 219
Architecture Live Projects 2
artisans 76, 129
assessment 39, 41, 43, 46
Association of Collegiate Schools of
Architecture (ACSA) 1, 174
Association for Community Design 35
associationalism 62, 74–8
Auburn University 1, 20, 48, 108

Badanes, Steve 3, 141
Ban, Shigeru 33
The Barn project 154–68
Bass, Rick 121
Bates, Randy 108
Bauhaus 3
Bell, Bryan 2

Berg project 71, 73
Berra, Yogi 154
Birch, Willie 53
Blackwell, Marlon 3
Boling, Terry 11, 140–53
Borges, Jorge Luis 9
Bourgeois, Patrick 10, 96
Bowne, Larry 9, 62–78
Boyer, Ernest 49
Boyer Report 49
Boys and Girls Club, Greensboro 22
Breunlin, Rachel 52
bridging 11–13, 70–4, 129, 169
Bruder Klaus Field Chapel 191
Bryant House, Mason's Bend 48
Building Information Modeling (BIM) 142

Cadwell, Michael 141–2
Callahan, Doug 224
Canizaro, Vincent 183
capitalism 6
Cardinal Homes 43
Carpenter, William J. 7
Cincinnati University 143
Clayton Homes 177–8
climate 26, 43, 155, 176, 184, 187, 189–90,
195, 208
codes of conduct 132, 182, 220
Coker, Coleman 10, 81–92, 108
Coleman Foundation 157
collaboration 38, 54, 60, 62, 71
Collie-Akers, Vickie 54
Colorado Building Workshop 187–8, 195,
198

Colorado Outward Bound School (COBS) 195

Colorado University (CU) Denver 187–8, 193

Columbia University 6

commodification 5

common good 8–9, 17

communication skills 131, 138, 177, 213

community designbuild 3, 48–61, 125–6, 129, 136–8

community engagement 8–9, 17, 19–33, 36–41, 46

Community Housing of Wyandotte County 55

complexity 132, 156, 165, 174, 177, 185, 200, 208, 215, 220, 224, 227

computer numerical control (CNC) 157–8, 161, 196

constraints 12, 66, 94, 105–6, 117, 161, 177, 191, 203–4, 213, 226

construction drawings 72, 164, 211, 221

context 86, 90–1, 116–17, 126–8, 131, 164–5, 176–7, 187, 189, 195, 221

Cooper Hewitt Design Museum 35

Le Corbusier 104

Corser, Rob 51–2

COTE Top Ten Green Award 172

Covington Farmers Market project 126

craft guilds 4

The Craftsman 192

craftsmanship 4, 12, 93, 104, 133, 138, 142–3, 146, 155, 161–2, 221, 225

Cranbrook Academy of Art 1

Crawford, Broderick 55, 57

Creole architecture 53

Criss, Shannon 8, 48–61

crowd source funding 6, 76

cultural stewardship 182–4, 216–17, 222

3-D printers 6

Da Vinci, Leonardo 105

Darwinism 189

Davis, Miles 150

De Carlo, Giancarlo 137

Decision Analysis Tool (DAT) 43

decision-making 27, 93, 131, 211

democracy 2, 8–9, 73–4, 97

DesertSol project 207

Design+Build Studio 12, 201–4, 207–13

Design Build Exchange 1

Design Futures 36

design studios 8, 10, 12–13, 32, 40–1, 93, 106, 135, 171, 174, 218, 220–1

design/buildLAB 11, 125–9, 131–2, 134, 136–8

DesignBuildBLUFF 188

Dewey, John 4, 8–9, 95, 106

dialogue 36–7, 41, 49–50, 52–3, 131

digital design 11, 41, 43, 93, 140, 142, 148, 154–68

"Digital Vernacular" 11, 154–68

Dillard, Annie 113

Dirt Works Studio 10, 94, 96–7, 106

disengagement 4–6, 9, 72, 109, 112–13

distributed authorship 188

Dotte Agency project 54–7

draughtsmanship 142

Durand, Jean N.-L. xiii

ecology 81, 84, 91, 182–3

ecoMOD 8, 36–7, 39–41, 43, 45–7

ecoREMOD 46

embedded knowledge 171–86

Enlightenment 4, 96, 109–10

Enterprise Foundation 36

environmental impact 33–4, 41, 43, 45, 82, 87, 109, 116, 189

Environmental Protection Agency (EPA) 174, 176

environmental stewardship 12, 24, 49, 65–6, 71

Etheridge, Dan 52

ethics 1, 8, 13, 22, 214–30

ethnicity 54

evaluation 41–6, 57, 133–4, 176, 183

Evans, Robin 141–2, 164

experience 9–10, 79, 96, 104, 106

experiential learning 2, 60, 128, 140, 143, 217

experts/expertise 38, 46, 58, 60, 62

failure 104–6, 136, 148, 150, 161–2, 221

feedback 1, 11, 21, 31, 46, 57, 94–5, 131–2, 140, 148, 155, 189

Fibonacci sequence 99

Five Points Alley project 144

food deserts 24

Ford, Edward 140

Frascari, Marco 104, 143, 146

Freear, Andrew 8, 19–32

Freedom by Design 74

full-scale prototyping 4, 11, 22, 57, 72, 140–53, 159, 200, 218, 221

funding 6, 12, 36, 43, 49

Gabbard, Todd 65

Gaia 87

Gallegos, Phillip 187–8

genius loci 90

gentrification 46, 53

238 Index

Gentry, Steve 20
geo-centricity 92
geoality 10, 86–7, 91
globalization 6, 21
Godard, Jean Luc 167
Goethe, Johann Wolfgang von 9
Gore, Nils 8, 48–61
Great Recession 35
Greene, Joshua 8
Greenhaus project 66
Greensburg Cubed project 64–9, 71, 75, 78
Gregory, Patsy 49–50
Gropius, Walter 3
Gulf Coast DesignLab 81–2, 84, 87, 92

Habitat for Humanity 36, 43, 46, 154, 163
Haddad, Natalie 11, 154–68
hands-on education 3, 8, 13, 94, 106, 164, 189, 215, 229
haptics 4, 93, 142, 164, 166
Harrison, Jim 113, 115
Hayes, Richard 7
Hays, K. Michael 95
health 23–31, 49, 54–7
Heidegger, Martin 10, 94
heritage 30, 62
Hoffman, Dan 1, 141
human condition 9–10, 19, 33–47, 79
Hurricane Katrina 51–2
Husserl, Edmund 96

Ice Cube project 66
imperialism 8, 19
improvisation 65, 150, 162
Industrial Revolution 4, 155
Information Age 155
infrastructure 52, 180, 182, 205, 207, 225
Ingels, Bjarke 96
innovation 3, 12, 66, 74, 187–200
insurance 40, 202, 204, 226–7
Integrated Design 176
Integrated Project Delivery (IPD) 12, 176–9, 187–91, 198–9
interdisciplinarity 12, 134, 174, 176–8, 182
intersubjectivity 10, 96

Jefferson, Thomas 37, 47
Jersey Devil 3, 141
Joy, Rick 3

20K Home 24–9
Kansas State University 64–6
Keats, John 103

Kleinmann, Matt 54
Kraus, Chad 1–16, 93–107, 214–30
Kundig, Tom 3

laissez faire 130
Lake Tahoe Shakespeare Festival box office project 209, 211–12
Lamar Station Classroom (LSC) project 198
landscapes 10, 31, 36, 55, 81
Latino Health for All Coalition 54–5
Lean Project Delivery (LPD) 198
LEED for Homes 45, 172, 179, 223
LEED Platinum 45–6, 172
Lewerentz, Sigurd 104
Lions Park project 31
Little Berg project 71, 73
Live Projects Network 2–3
Louder Than a Bomb project 144
Louis, Hank 188
Louisana State University 52

MacKay-Lyons, Brian 3, 137
Mac Namara, Sinéad 70
maintenance 22, 136, 138, 208
maker movement 6, 9–11, 13–14, 31–2, 78, 143, 146, 149, 152, 155, 217
Maki, Fumihiko 95
Manufactured Housing Division 202, 211
Manufacturers of Record 202
Maritain, Jacques 118
Masonic Amphitheater project 126
MASS Design Group 33
Massachusetts Institute of Technology (MIT) 158
master builders 4, 32, 142, 155
materiality 5, 10, 86, 89–91, 104
mindfulness 113–15, 117
Mississippi State University (MSU) 48–9
Mitgang, Lee 49
Mobile Collaboratory (moCOLAB) 60
Mockbee, Samuel 8, 19, 48–9, 108
modernism 4–5, 8, 83
Moe, Kiel 176
Moholy-Nagy, Sibly 166
Moore, Charles 7
Mori, Toshiko 33
morphologies 87, 155, 189
multidisciplinarity 182
Museum of Modern Art 35

National Architectural Accrediting Board (NAAB) 74
National Council of Architectural Registration Boards (NCARB) 174

National Renewable Energy Lab (NREL) 190
Navajo Nation 188, 190, 193
Neighborhood Story Project 52
Nelson, Ralph 11, 154–68
neo-colonialism 37
Nevada Division of State Parks 208–9, 211
Nevada Revised Statutes 202
New Deal 172, 175, 177
New Mexico University 36, 40, 188
The New Norris House (NNH) project 12, 171–85
Newbern, Alabama 20, 24–6
Newbern Library 29–31
Nobel, Philip 5
Norberg-Schulz, Christian 96
Norman, Marc 71

Occupational Safety and Health Administration (OSHA) 204
Occupy movement 35
Ockman, Joan 6, 8
Office of Metropolitan Architecture 189
offsite construction 43, 126, 172, 176, 178–9, 202, 207–9
Okolona Chamber of Commerce 49
Okolona Corner Park project 49–51
on-site construction 66, 76, 94, 165, 174, 176, 178–81, 191, 193, 195–6, 209
OnSite 128–9
open-source methods 6, 46
Oxford Brookes University 2

Paddock, Andy 199
Pallasmaa, Juhani 133, 146
parametric modeling 195
Park Studio project 70–4, 78
participatory design 137
passive design 12, 174, 190, 215
Passive House Standard 43, 46, 223
permits 182, 185, 198, 202, 224–6
Pew Research Center 35
phenomenology 6, 93–8
philosophy 4–7, 21, 94–8, 104, 109, 113, 142, 149, 174, 189, 222, 228
phronesis 7
Picasso, Pablo 4
Pine Creek Pavilion 119
place-based design 21, 110, 131
placemaking 5
Planned Development Unit 198
Plato 4
Play Perch project 74–8

poetics/poetry 7, 9–10, 79, 81–92, 108–22, 138, 217
poiein 83
poiesis 10, 81–4, 86, 90–1
Porch Cultural Heritage Organization project 51–4
positivism 4, 96
post-occupancy evaluation 43, 183
postmodernism 5, 7
poststructuralism 5
pragmatism 6–10, 77, 94
Prairie Earth project 98–103
praxis 7–8, 81
pre-reflexivity 96, 106
prefabrication 8, 12, 36, 126–7, 138, 161, 177, 187, 195–7
presence/presencing 93–107, 222
Priest, Colin 2
Project Solar House 65–6
prototyping 11, 55–7, 72, 95, 140, 142–4, 157–9, 163, 172, 176, 202
Public Interest Design Institute 35
public interest design (PID) 2–3, 5, 9, 33, 35, 41, 62
Putnam, Robert D. 70–3, 78
Pyatt, Rob 188
Pye, David 154, 161

Quale, John 8, 33–47

racism 49–50
Raine House project 190
rationalism 4–5, 182
reclaimed materials 30, 65, 95, 98, 101, 106, 117, 146, 192–5, 222
recycling 55, 65–6, 69, 177, 222
Recycling Bin project 66, 69
reflection 81–4, 86, 92, 113, 115–17, 126, 144, 150, 177, 200
regionalism 3, 6, 183–4, 190, 208
Regis, Helen 52
Relph, Edward 5, 95
Remote Studio 10, 108, 110–13, 116–17, 122
Residential Architect Design Award 172
reuse *see* reclaimed materials; recycling
Ringel, John 3
Rockhill and Associates 223–4, 227
Rockhill, Dan 13, 51, 214–30
Rocky Mountains 10
romanticism 83
Rose Architectural Fellowship 36
Rosenthal, Sandra 10, 96
Ross, Stephen 5

240 Index

Rural Studio 1, 8, 19–24, 29–32, 48, 108
Rural Studio Farm 24
Ruth, D.K. 19
Ryker, Lori 10, 108–22

Sain, David 224
salutary failure 104–6
Sass, Larry 158
Scarpa, Carlo 141–2
Sennett, Richard 104, 192
Sharon Baseball Fields project 126, 137
Sharon Fieldhouse project 126, 135, 137
Shop Architects 5
Skow Residence project 193
Small Town Center 49
Smith Creek Park project 126
Smith Creek Pedestrian Bridge project 126, 132
social capital 62, 70–1, 74
Social Economic Environmental Design (SEED) Evaluator 46
social justice 6, 8
Socrates 11
Solar Decathlon 12, 44, 65–6, 68, 202–8, 211–12
Solnit, Rebecca 63, 65, 69, 78
Sommerfeld, Erik 12, 187–200
Sorkin, Michael 182
Southern Utah University 190
Spector, Tom 9
stakeholders 8–9, 37–9, 71, 78, 131
State Public Works Board 211
Stevens, James 11, 154–68
Stone, Harris 218
structural insulated panels (SIPs) 212
structuralism 5
Structures for Inclusion 35
Studio 804 1, 51, 94, 214–29
Stuth, Tricia 12, 171–86
sustainability 6, 11–13, 24, 33–4, 49, 71, 116, 174–7, 183–4, 193, 207–13, 222–3
Syracuse University 70–1, 74

Tahoe Regional Planning Authority 211
team building 62–3, 131–3, 174, 177–9, 182, 205, 207
technology 6, 11, 21, 65, 68, 87–8, 93, 142, 155–6, 172, 174–5, 183–5
tectonics 4–5, 7, 10–13, 57, 62–3
Tehrani, Nader 142

temporality 86, 91, 141
Tennessee Valley Authority Act 175
Tennessee Valley Authority (TVA) 172, 175–6, 179–80, 182
Texas University 81
Tocqueville, Alexis de 74–5, 77
tolerance 32, 62, 66, 104, 141, 148–9, 156, 162–3, 165, 177, 220
trans-disciplinarity 54–5
Tulane City Center 52

United States (US) 1–2, 6–7, 12, 22, 204; Army Corps of Engineers 55; Centers for Disease Control 54, 56; Department of Energy 12, 202, 205; Forest Service 119; National Register of Historic Places 172
University of Kansas 1, 49, 51, 94, 98
University of Nevada, Las Vegas (UNLV) 12, 201–5, 207–8
University of Tennessee (UT) 171, 174–5, 185
University of Utah 188
University of Virginia 36, 40
UPSTATE Center 71

Van den Berg, J.H. 96
Vattimo, Gianni 96–7
ventilation 21, 172, 174, 179, 222
vernacular architecture 11, 39, 49, 51, 154–68
Vico, Giambattista 104, 149
Virginia Tech 125–6
volunteers 22, 35, 38–9, 46, 55, 58, 69, 71–2, 74, 128–9, 174

Washington University 1
waste 146, 174, 180, 182, 192, 198–9, 213
Watering Can project 66–7
Weber, Eric 12, 201–13
Whitehead, Alfred 113
Work Group for Community Health 54
Working Out: Thinking While Building 1–2

Yale Building Project 3, 7, 216, 227
Yestermorrow Design/Build School 1
YourHouse project 158

Zawistowski, Keith 11, 125–39
Zawistowski, Marie 11, 125–39
Zumthor, Peter 5, 12, 191